The Cooking of Spain and Portugal

TIME
LIFE
BOOKS ®

Foods of the World

The Cooking of Spain and Portugal

by

Peter S. Feibleman

and the Editors of

TIME-LIFE BOOKS

photographed by

Dmitri Kessel and Brian Seed

TIME-LIFE BOOKS, NEW YORK

The text for this book was written by Peter Feibleman, the picture essays by the staff. The recipe instructions were written under the supervision of the late Michael Field. Valuable aid was provided by the following individuals and departments of Time Inc.: Editorial Production, Norman Airey; Library, Benjamin Lightman; Picture Collection, Doris O'Neil; Photographic Laboratory, George Karas; TIME-LIFE News Service, Murray J. Gart; Correspondents Jean Bratton (Madrid) and Marvine Howe (Lisbon).

THE AUTHOR: Peter S. Feibleman *(above)* is a novelist, playwright, film and television writer from New Orleans. His books include *A Place without Twilight* and *The Daughters of Necessity*. His play *Tiger Tiger Burning Bright* was produced on Broadway in 1962. He lived in Spain for eight years, and traveled through the entire Iberian Peninsula while preparing this book. He is also the author of *American Cooking: Creole and Acadian* in this series and *The Bayous* in The American Wilderness series.

THE PHOTOGRAPHERS: The photography for this book on Spain and Portugal was done by Dmitri Kessel *(above, left)* and Brian Seed *(above, right)*. Kessel is a freelance photographer based in Paris, whose long career has included many distinguished photographic assignments for LIFE magazine. Seed is a freelance photographer based in London, whose pictures have appeared in TIME, LIFE and SPORTS ILLUSTRATED, as well as many British publications. The studio photography for the book was done in the FOODS OF THE WORLD test kitchen by Fred Eng and Arie deZanger.

THE CONSULTING EDITOR: The late Michael Field *(above, left)* relinquished a career as a concert pianist to become one of America's first-rank food experts and teachers of cooking. He conducted a school in Manhattan and wrote many articles on the culinary arts for various magazines. His books include *Michael Field's Cooking School* and *Michael Field's Culinary Classics and Improvisations*.
THE CONSULTANTS: Shirley Sarvis *(above, right)*, who served as the consultant for the Portuguese recipes, is the author of the cookbook entitled *A Taste of Portugal*. The Spanish recipes for this book were contributed and tested by Mr. and Mrs. Alberto Heras of the Spanish Pavilion in New York, Mrs. Anita Perez Heras of the Casa Felix Restaurant in Madrid, Paul Betancourt of the Chateau Madrid Restaurant in New York, and Josefina Yanguas of the Café Pamplona and the Iruña Restaurant in Cambridge, Massachusetts.

THE COVER: *Paella*, Spain's most famous dish *(Recipe Index)*, is a rich blend of chicken, lobster, shrimp, clams and mussels with peas and saffron-flavored rice.

Contents

The Recipe Booklet that accompanies this volume has been designed for use in the kitchen. It contains all of the 66 recipes printed here plus 39 more. It also has a wipe clean cover and a spiral binding so that it can either stand up or lie flat when open.

A Long-Standing Love Affair With the Food of Iberia

When I first went to Spain in 1950 I knew very little about it, and sensed not much more, beyond a certain curious and ignorant craving for flamenco dancing and singing, a hatred for the Spanish Fascist regime, a liking for the language, and some uncertain interest in the country. I was 20 years old: young enough to think living in a foreign place for even a short time would change what I thought of as the shape of my life, and old enough to know better. I had decided to visit Spain to find out for myself "what it was like." I went for a month's trip. I stayed eight years.

The southern coast of Spain in the early 1950s was a lazy, slow place of small fishing villages and no real hotels. I stayed for several months, living in two then-unknown coastal towns and in Seville; then I moved to Madrid because, by a sort of fluke, I had landed a job as an actor in a Spanish movie.

The actual finding of the job in Madrid had not been difficult. Many Spanish Catholic actors of the '50s dyed their hair blond and played Americans, so it was easy for an American Jew to play Spanish, or rather to find Spanish roles, if he could act at all. I couldn't, but nobody knew it. Most Spanish movies then were shot without sound and dubbed in later. I *looked* right for a particular kind of sad-but-strong juvenile—that is to say I looked asleep most of the time—and, until I was sure I could speak Spanish without an accent, I feigned chronic laryngitis (it was only for a few months), and had to be dubbed in by another actor. This meant that no one in the audience ever heard my real voice, which, as it happened, was a good thing. I made my living at acting, if you could call it that, and the only discomforting hitch was that I couldn't let myself be heard speaking English anywhere, because I would have lost my job: foreign nationals, at that time, were not permitted to play Spanish roles. I needed the money. I wasn't really worried about acting per se, because I wasn't really an actor. I was a writer, or thought I was, or anyway wanted to be, but I figured I'd be on the far side of 80 before I finished a novel that even pleased me, let alone a publisher. I was, as it turned out, 26 when that happened, but for the six years between 20 and that age, I "acted," spoke no English, had only Spanish friends, most of whom hated the government as I did and many of whom were actively trying to fight it. I lived as a Spaniard with a Spanish family, wrote secretly in English at night, and kept the result locked safely in a drawer. I traveled outside of Madrid or went to Portugal when I was required to go for location work, and sometimes on weekends and vacations, but otherwise I was based in that city as a resident. Though the whole setup had happened more or less by accident, it was the best possible way to learn about Spain and things Spanish from the inside. The country has been a kind of home to me ever since.

I remember very well my first meal with the Spanish family who boarded me. I was prepared to eat whatever they ate without comments and without requests for any substitutions, being constantly afraid that someone might discover how unfamiliar my surroundings really were to me. About 3 o'clock of the first day, I sat down with the family in a white-tiled kitchen that held a black coal stove, a long, white table, and a parrot in a cage who spoke Spanish better than I did. The woman of the house put a soup plate in front of me full of a thin, steaming liquid that smelled richly of olive oil and foods of the sea. In its center was a fish—a whole fish—floured and fried, its tail clamped firmly in its jaws. As the woman put the dish down, she gave it a swirl so that the fish appeared to be swimming slow circles in the broth. She sat opposite and watched me, and I had no time to think of an excuse not to begin. I tasted a spoonful of the soup. It was pungent and strong in an odd, delicate way, and extraordinarily good. I tried not to stare at the boned, swimming fish more than I could help, and anyhow about the tenth time around he began to look like a friend. I finished the soup, and to my own total surprise, asked for some more. Then came a rice dish with chicken and green peppers; it was tangy and garlicky and I had some more of that too. There was a good, dry red wine and for dessert there were peeled, sliced, juicy Valencian oranges with a sprinkling of sugar and a splash of sweet Triple Sec. There was fresh, white goat's cheese as well, tinged with a deep, damp taste like hidden mildew, spread with a thin layer of thick mountain honey, and afterward there was coffee. I knew by the time the meal was over that I was not going to have any problem enjoying Spanish food.

What I didn't know was that by the end of that first year, I would grow to like Spanish and Portuguese food to such a degree that I would not want to be very long away from them for the rest of my life. Once you grow used to the herb-fresh richness and variety of country food simmered, served and eaten in small, brown earthenware casseroles and taste the full range of Iberian seafoods, you begin to find the routine diets of other countries strangely pallid, a bit artificial and faintly dull by comparison. For those who love Spanish and Portuguese cooking, there is something here that is more solid, sturdier and at the same time brighter and more wholly satisfying than the cooking of any other people. We who have learned to love it never seem to want to forget it; we come from all classes, from all places, with all tastes. Shuffling, shy, "meat and potato" American cowboys and effete French gourmets become aficionados of Iberian food side by side.

In fact, we seem to have in common only that we are unable to give any valid reasons for our preference in terms that really mean anything to anybody else. Ask a New Yorker who is one of us why he likes the foods of Iberia so much, and he will stammer something about casserole-cooking and change the subject. Ask a Parisian, and he will only shrug, blush and turn away. There will be a guilty glow in both pairs of eyes. Lovers of Iberian cooking for some reason behave as if their love were at least illicit, possibly illegal and certainly immoral. We cannot tell you exactly why we have fallen in love with it—we would simply rather not eat anything else as a steady diet. We do not go into our reasons for liking it any more than a bachelor would talk about his lifelong mistress; it is too private a subject, and nobody who did not share the love would understand anyway. So we will not usually say why we love it; we just do. This book is an attempt to say why.

—*Peter S. Feibleman*

I

Cuisines from the People

Off the Atlantic coast of Spain near the town of Bayona, a few miles north of the Portuguese border, lies a rich lode of Iberian seafood. Fresh-from-the-sea crabs, lobsters, scallops, sardines, crayfish, octopus, clams and mussels like those in the basket and on the net opposite are among the attractions of the region's fine hotels, such as the luxurious Parador Nacional Conde de Gondomar (*background*).

Somewhere in the peninsula of land called Iberia that protrudes into the Mediterranean, the Bay of Biscay and Atlantic waters, a train is leaving a railway station. In a compartment of the dusty third-class carriage, a peasant woman in a plain black dress and black stockings sits on one of two hard wooden benches each bearing four other people. She holds a big black satchel, and inside it she carries a thick, golden, cold potato omelet (*Recipe Index*); three or four *bocadillos*, or hard-roll sandwiches of thin, cooked veal; several small loaves of crusty bread; a yellow chunk of pungent sheep or goat's cheese; some juicy, ripe oranges and apples, and a bottle of light, dry red wine. As the train pulls out into open country and the day wears on, the woman opens the swollen satchel and begins to take out food for her husband and two hungry children. But before she serves them, she turns to the other people sharing the compartment and asks each one individually whether he or she will share the meal. Each person will answer formally by saying no, and then by expressing a wish that the food may benefit both the woman and her family. Undiscouraged, the peasant woman continues to offer a small veal *bocadillo*, perhaps a wedge of the rich, country omelet, or some wine and cheese to each of them—until she herself is convinced that the strangers have enough to eat or are honestly not hungry. Only then will she hand some food to her own family and slowly eat with them as the carriage bounces and rattles through the rocky land.

At the other end of the same train, sitting in an upholstered chair in the plush, white-doilied dining car, an elegant young duchess who is traveling first-class makes certain that her companions and employees have been at-

8

tended to by the waiter. Then she orders for herself a meal of broiled Mediterranean sole followed by crisp roast partridge with small browned onions, sliced carrots and new potatoes, and finally coffee. While she eats, the duchess keeps an eye on her companions to make sure no one is lacking anything. Like the peasant woman, she eats slowly, watchfully, with a certain pride in the knowledge of her own individuality combined with a deep-grained sense of responsibility for others. Neither woman, noble or peasant, would think of eating without first seeing that those around her were already fed. These two women would respect each other if they met, for each would recognize in the other certain traits and characteristics—just as both would look down rather critically on women of the newly burgeoning middle classes of Spain and Portugal who may eat without regard for anyone else, and whose lack of formal manners may leave a great deal to be desired.

But there is something else that these two women share: the nature of the food they eat and the way in which it is cooked. Vastly different as their two meals may sound, both have the same culinary root. Iberian food, whether Spanish or Portuguese, whether it graces the poor man's kitchen or the rich man's dining table, is by nature *del pueblo* (food of the people). It is never classical cooking in the sense of *grande cuisine,* and it belongs to all of the people in a very personal way. In certain of its qualities it is unmistakably related to them and to the land called Iberia in which they live.

Like the people of the Iberian Peninsula, the cooking of this region is a blend of many ingredients. The blend is complex at times, but the ingredients are not disguised and never spiced to alter basically simple tastes. The strength of Iberian cooking is natural, and its subtlety is derived from the combination of ingredients, the fundamental mixture itself. It is strong and fine though often stark, as in certain foods of Spain, but it can also be gay and even flamboyant, as in some of the foods of Portugal. Yet it is always purely Iberian, and once you have come to know it, you will not be likely to mistake it for anything else.

Iberian food is easily recognizable. It is usually plain-looking and attractively appetizing in the simplest possible way. It is rarely overdecorated (the most famous Spanish dish, the elaborate *paella (Recipe Index),* is the exception, not the rule in Iberia); it is fresh and it is more concerned with good ingredients well combined than with additives that might alter their tastes or appearances. One of the false accusations made about Spanish cooking is that it is "hot" and highly spiced. The truth is more nearly the opposite. Spaniards tend to shy away from spicy foods; Mexican chili is anathema to the Spanish palate. It is one of Spain's paradoxes that a country largely responsible, along with Portugal, for providing pepper and other spices to the western world should have produced a cuisine that uses so *little* spice. This is not nearly so true of Portuguese cooking, which can at times employ a myriad of spiced tastes, and that fact accounts for the essential difference between the two cuisines—both integral parts of the Iberian whole.

Portugal is the land of explorers and of the explorer's kitchen. The elegant "pure Portuguese" gentleman you meet at a formal, "pure Portuguese" dinner will probably have a few Indian or South African or South American ancestors, and so will the dinner. It should be remembered that America was discovered by accident; what Columbus—as well as Magellan and Vasco da

Gama—was really after was a trade route to the east for spices. These spices were of tremendous monetary value a few centuries ago, when they were used as food preservatives as well as seasonings.

Portuguese cooking today is not only spicier than Spanish cooking—the use of cream and butter makes it richer. And local food prejudices have not inhibited the use of sudden new flavors brought back from Angola, Mozambique, India, Brazil or elsewhere. In short, Portuguese cooking is a florid, at times exotic art that has used the conquests its country made in far-off places to import and experiment with many unknown tastes—some results of which have enriched her native dishes to a degree that would seem to a Spaniard almost gaudy.

Until relatively recently, Portugal, like the two Castiles, Aragon and León, was one of the medieval kingdoms of Spain. From the beginning, the inhabitants of the Peninsula have shared ancestors as they have shared invaders. The original Iberians, believed to have come from Africa, were superseded through the centuries by waves of other tribes and cultures: Celts, Phoenicians, Greeks, Carthaginians, Romans, Visigoths, Muslims. In our day the French, Germans, English and finally Americans have all been attracted to this land of wonderful seacoasts, the body of which is scarred and divided by more mountain ranges than any other country in Europe and whose average altitude is second only to that of Switzerland. Communication has always been difficult here. Travel in Spain and Portugal is still often a problem, including travel from one pueblo to a neighboring pueblo not more than five or ten miles distant. The geography, topography and erratic climate have had a strong influence on all things Iberian including foodstuffs and cooking. In this land, a land split apart in as many directions by foreign invasions as by mountain ranges, it has been the individual who survived. He survived by means of a kind of fanatic pride. He learned by and large not to do things collectively; it was safer to do things alone. This is one of the important reasons why pride in individuality is at the heart of Iberian life.

Today each region of the Peninsula adheres vehemently to its own manner of cooking, even to the extent of choosing a different name for the same basic dish. In Cervantes' great novel *Don Quixote,* there is a delicious boiled dinner called *olla podrida,* literally "rotten pot." This dish is mother of the *cocido madrileño* (from Madrid, *Recipe Index),* the *cocido andaluz* (from Andalusia), the *escudella i carn d'olla* (from Catalonia), the *pote gallego* (from Galicia) and the *pote canario* (from the Canary Islands)—not to mention the *cozido portuguêsa* in the sister country, and, just to confuse matters more, the *puchero* (stew) in much of the rest of Spain. Ingredients vary slightly in each region, usually according to what is or once was available in the local market. Yet each version of the mother dish is ignored and often ridiculed in "alien" regions cooking the same food in their own way. The Catalans, for example, laugh at the idea of making a *cocido* as the Andalusians do, while to certain Andalusians the idea of serving the component parts of the dish separately, as they are served by *other* Andalusians, is a kind of desecration. Tribal differences within the Peninsula have come down through the ages and are visible today more than ever in the distinct ways of preparing food, as any foreigner will know after even a brief visit to this part of the world.

To understand this and to appreciate Spanish and Portuguese food, a visit of some kind is necessary. When a foreigner imagines what Spain is like, he is generally thinking only of Andalusia—of a rich, red soil sprinkled with wild flowers, herbs and spices, a sunny place where flamenco is danced and sung, and where the Spanish themselves say that a single carnation has an odor exceeding that of roses in other regions. Is Spain really like that? Or is it more like Castile, Don Quixote's flat and arid plain of land-locked living, hard purple sunsets and dust-dry dreams? Is Spain Valencia, on the Levantine coast, a place of orange blossoms, region of rice growers, land of the famous *paella?* Or is it Catalonia, cool, businesslike and rather European, with its own folk dance called the *sardana,* its own Romance language, literature and way of cooking? When we say Spain do we mean Aragon, whose light-footed folk dance, the *jota,* is as different from the *sardana* as it is from flamenco? Or do we mean the Basque country, home of a people who are truly great cooks and who do not know their own origin or that of the language they speak or even the warlike dances they perform? But then, too, what about Galicia—wet and lush and green, first land of seafood, mother kingdom to Portugal? And for that matter, what about Portugal itself, gay, pastel, lyric and carefree—how is this country related to Spain today? Can all these different peoples and all these different regions have anything in common?

In their kitchens, some answers to this last question are fairly simple. These people share the uses of ingredients such as olive oil, garlic and parsley. Almonds appear frequently, both raw and in cooking; egg and egg-yolk sweets are often seen. The range of fresh fish and shellfish from the waters of two seas and one ocean is more inclusive, more spectacular throughout Iberia than anywhere else in the world. And cooking methods, such as the slow simmering of foods in earthenware dishes that are moved back and forth over a flame rather than stirred, are shared by all.

But the differences between the culinary regions of Iberia are as important as the similarities for anyone who wishes to cook Iberian food. We can discover these differences easily by traveling, because Iberia divides itself helpfully into several zones of cooking *(see map)*. The central region of Spain is the zone of roasting and the hunt. Andalusia is the zone of frying and has also produced the excellent cold soup called *gazpacho (Recipe Index)*. The central eastern seaboard is the zone of rice; above it, the zone of sauces begins and leads west through the great kitchens of the Basques to the Bay of Biscay and its seafood, then down through the light, spangled, colorful kitchens of Portugal, land of surprising mixtures and glittering combinations.

The shape of this book is that of a gastronomic tour through the galaxy of Iberian cuisines. We will see what each zone provides, what its best dishes are, how and when they are cooked and served and how some are linked to religion, folk dancing, fiestas and other aspects of living. We will begin in the center of Spain, in Madrid and the surrounding provinces, and travel out in one long, unbroken spiral that will take us in a counterclockwise direction, south through the region of Extremadura to Andalusia; then east to the Levante, north all the way to the Pyrenees and then northwest until Galicia turns us south and into Portugal. Region by region, place by place, city by city and sometimes town by town we will visit Iberian homes, restaurants, inns and taverns, learning as we go that Iberian cooking is indeed simply a sum of all its parts.

The Regions and Provinces of Iberia

Continental Spain is divided into 13 regions (large type on the map above) whose boundaries are roughly those of its ancient kingdoms and ethnic regions. Many of these regions—such as the Castiles, Aragon and Navarre—retain their ancient names. The regions are divided into 47 provinces, most of them bearing the same names as their capitals (small type on the map). The exceptions are Navarre, whose capital is Pamplona and the three Basque provinces—Álava, Guipúzcoa, and Vizcaya. Portugal is divided regionally by geography into the mountainous, sometimes humid north and the more gentle, drier south. These two regions are organized into 11 provinces (small italics on the map). In preparing this book, author Peter Feibleman began his tour in Madrid. From there he traveled southwest through Extremadura, into Andalusia, and then counterclockwise through the Levante, Catalonia, the Basque Provinces, Asturias and Galicia, winding up with a generally north to south trip through Portugal.

The recipes in this chapter were chosen to illustrate some of the basic similarities and differences between Spanish and Portuguese cooking. Both the "ervilhas guisadas à portuguêsa" (below) and Spain's "huevos a la flamenca" (following pages) are made with eggs and fresh vegetables. Yet, characteristically, the Portuguese dish relies on an herb—fresh coriander—for its distinctive flavor, while the Spanish dish uses a typical, subtly seasoned base sauce known as a "sofrito."

Ervilhas Guisadas à Portuguêsa
PEAS PORTUGUESE

To serve 2 to 4

2 tablespoons butter
½ cup finely chopped onions
¾ cup chicken stock, fresh or canned
3 cups cooked fresh green peas (about 3 pounds), or substitute 3 ten-ounce packages frozen peas, thoroughly defrosted but not cooked
¼ cup finely chopped parsley
¼ cup finely chopped fresh coriander leaves (cilantro)
½ teaspoon sugar
Salt
Freshly ground black pepper
4 ounces *linguiça* or substitute *chorizo* or other garlic-seasoned smoked pork sausage, cut into ¼ inch slices
4 eggs

In a heavy 10-inch skillet or shallow flameproof casserole, melt the butter over moderate heat. When the foam has almost subsided, add the onions and, stirring frequently, cook for 8 to 10 minutes, or until they are lightly colored. Stir in the stock, freshly cooked or frozen peas, parsley, coriander, sugar, ¼ teaspoon of salt and a few grindings of pepper and overlap the sausage slices around the edge of the skillet. Bring to a boil over high heat, then reduce the heat to low, cover and simmer for 5 minutes.

Break 1 egg into a saucer and, holding the dish close to the pan, slide the egg on top of the peas. One at a time, slide the other eggs into the pan, keeping them well apart. Sprinkle them lightly with salt and pepper. Cover the skillet and cook for 3 or 4 minutes until the egg yolks are covered with an opaque film and the whites are set. Serve at once, directly from the skillet.

Broa
PORTUGUESE CORNBREAD

To make one 9-inch round loaf

1½ cups yellow cornmeal, pulverized in a blender until fine
1½ teaspoons salt
1 cup boiling water
1 tablespoon plus 1 teaspoon olive oil
1 package or cake of active dry or compressed yeast
1 teaspoon sugar
¼ cup lukewarm water (110° to 115°)
1¾ to 2 cups all-purpose flour

In a large mixing bowl combine 1 cup of the cornmeal, the salt and boiling water and stir vigorously until smooth. Stir in 1 tablespoon of the olive oil, then cool to lukewarm. In a small bowl, sprinkle the yeast and sugar over the lukewarm water. Let it stand for 2 or 3 minutes, then stir to dissolve the yeast completely. Set the bowl in a warm draft-free place, such as an unlighted oven, for 8 to 10 minutes, or until the yeast doubles in volume.

Stir the yeast into the cornmeal mixture. Stirring constantly, gradually add the remaining ½ cup of cornmeal and 1 cup of the flour. Gather the dough into a ball, place it in a bowl and drape a towel over it. Set it aside in the draft-free place for about 30 minutes, or until it doubles in bulk.

With a pastry brush, coat the bottom and sides of a 9-inch pie pan with the remaining 1 teaspoon of olive oil. Turn the dough out on a lightly floured surface and punch it down. Then knead it by pressing it down with the heel of your hand, pushing it forward and folding it back on itself repeatedly for about 5 minutes, meanwhile adding up to 1 cup more flour to make a firm but not stiff dough. Pat and shape it into a round flat loaf and place it in the greased pan. Drape a towel over it and set it aside in the draft-free place for about 30 minutes, or until it doubles in bulk again.

Preheat the oven to 350°. Bake the bread in the middle of the oven for 40 minutes, or until the top is golden. Transfer it to a rack to cool. *Broa* is served with *ervilhas guisadas à portuguêsa (above)* and *caldo verde (Recipe Index)*.

In Portugal's *Ervilhas Guisadas à Portuguêsa*, peas, eggs, and sausage are seasoned with fresh coriander *(lower right)*.

The *sofrito* that flavors *huevos a la flamenca* (right, recipe below) is one version of a favorite cooking base. Vegetables, meat and herbs are cooked to a saucelike blend (*far left*); then the *sofrito* is spread into a baking dish. The eggs are broken over it and peas, asparagus and pimiento are added.

To serve 6

SOFRITO

2 medium-sized tomatoes, or
    substitute ¾ cup chopped,
    drained, canned tomatoes
¼ cup olive oil
½ cup finely chopped onions
1 tablespoon finely chopped garlic
1 small sweet red or green pepper,
    peeled, seeded, deribbed and finely
    chopped
½ cup finely diced *serrano* ham, or
    substitute 2 ounces of prosciutto
    or other lean smoked ham
1 *chorizo* sliced into ¼-inch-thick
    rounds, or substitute 3 ounces
    other garlic-seasoned smoked
    pork sausage
1 tablespoon finely chopped parsley
1 small bay leaf
1 teaspoon salt
¼ teaspoon freshly ground black
    pepper
⅓ cup water

EGGS

2 teaspoons olive oil
6 eggs
½ cup hot cooked fresh or frozen
    peas
6 hot cooked fresh or frozen
    asparagus tips, 3 to 4 inches long
6 to 8 strips of drained, canned
    pimiento, each about 3 inches long
    and ¼ inch wide
3 tablespoons pale dry sherry
Parsley sprigs (optional)

Huevos a la Flamenca
BAKED EGGS WITH VEGETABLES AND MEAT

NOTE: *Sofrito* (which means "lightly fried") is a basic preparation widely used in Spanish cooking. One version is the base for *huevos a la flamenca*, but a *sofrito* has many variations and is used in numerous dishes. Every *sofrito* is made with onions or garlic or both; many also include tomatoes, red or green peppers, parsley and meats such as ham or sausage; some are thickened with ground almonds, sieved hard-cooked egg yolks or even bread crumbs. Whatever the ingredients, they are generally chopped and usually cooked in olive oil.

SOFRITO: Drop the fresh tomatoes into a pan of boiling water and let them boil briskly for about 10 seconds. Run cold water over them, and with a small, sharp knife peel them. Cut out the stems, then slice the tomatoes in half crosswise. Squeeze the halves gently to remove the seeds and juices, and chop the tomatoes as fine as possible. (Canned tomatoes need only be thoroughly drained and chopped.)

In a heavy 10- to 12-inch skillet, heat the oil over moderate heat until a light haze forms above it. Add the onions, garlic and chopped pepper, and, stirring frequently, cook for 5 minutes, or until the vegetables are soft but not brown. Stir in the ham and sausage, then add the tomatoes, chopped parsley, bay leaf, salt, pepper and water, and bring to a boil. Cook briskly, uncovered, until most of the liquid in the pan has evaporated and the mixture is thick enough to hold its shape lightly in a spoon. Set aside.

EGGS: Preheat the oven to 400°. Using a pastry brush, coat the bottom and sides of a 9-by-9-by-2-inch baking dish with the 2 teaspoons of oil. Discard the bay leaf and spread the *sofrito* evenly in the dish. One at a time, break the eggs into the dish, arranging them in a circle on top of the *sofrito*. Or break the eggs into a saucer and slide them gently into the dish.

Heap the peas in three or four mounds on the *sofrito* and arrange the asparagus in parallel rows, draping the pimiento strips decoratively over them. Sprinkle the eggs and vegetables with sherry, cover the dish, and bake in the middle of the oven for 20 minutes, or until an opaque film has formed over the egg yolks and the whites are firm. Serve at once, garnished if you like with parsley sprigs.

HOW TO PEEL PEPPERS: Impale the pepper on the tines of a long-handled fork and turn it over a gas flame until the skin blisters and darkens. Or place it on a baking sheet and broil it 3 inches from the heat for about 5 minutes, turning it so all sides color evenly. Wrap the pepper in a damp towel, let it rest for a few minutes, then rub it with the towel until the skin slips off. Cut out the stem and white membranes or ribs, and discard the seeds.

In Spain's *huevos a la flamenca*, peas, eggs, asparagus and pimiento strips are baked over a layer of the base sauce, *sofrito*.

II

The Land of
Don Quixote

In a village of La Mancha, the name of which I have no desire to call to mind, there lived not long since one of those gentlemen that keep a lance in the lance-rack, an old buckler, a lean hack, and a greyhound for coursing. His diet consisted of an *olla* of more beef than mutton, a salad most nights, boiled bones on Saturdays, lentils on Fridays, and a young pigeon as a Sunday treat; and on this he spent three-quarters of his income."

Here stands the opening of a great novel about a man who lived in the center of Spain, Don Quixote of La Mancha. It describes both him and his successors accurately. His two anchors of living, the lance and the *olla*, or pot, in which his food is cooked—his Dream and his Diet—have not changed very much since the 16th Century. Today's gentleman from central Spain remains the same in many ways, and his weekly diet, if larger, might be remarkably similar to the above menu, even after 400 years. Fashions may flicker around the man from La Mancha drastically and often: he has never been one for current vogue. He eats today for strength to dream of yesterday. Food for the stomach is only another way of feeding the fantasy, and if tomorrow comes at all, it will be an accident, only look out. Accidents like that happen every day.

Today and tomorrow and the day after, there remains a peculiar logic to all Spanish cooking; if Don Quixote didn't always keep it in mind, his wily companion, Sancho Panza, knew it well. The main function of food in the center of Spain is to nourish a man and warm him, to protect him from cold weather and from the arid harshness of the land where he abides so that he may be free to live, to dream—or to act out his dreams—as he likes. Life is

A windmill reminiscent of those with which the knight-errant Don Quixote tilted, stands lonely sentinel over a harsh and treeless landscape in La Mancha, in central Spain. Once used for grinding wheat—the major produce of the region—La Mancha's windmills are now honored relics, preserved to delight the eyes of tourists.

not easy here: "nine months of winter and three months of hell," say the inhabitants of Old and New Castile, well-known regions in the heart of Spain (*map, page 13*). The Castiles get their name from the many castles built within their borders for protection against the Moors, but the land here is also protected naturally by mountain ranges, among them the Sierra Morena, the Sierra de Gredos and the Sierra de Guadalupe. Most of the land between the mountains is cracked and forbidding, there are few trees and many glacial boulders in these valleys.

Visitors to the center of Spain do not often realize how hard life can be in this part of the world, particularly if they come directly to Madrid. The city is both the geographic and the culinary center of Spain. Country roads and byways go out from it like the spokes of a wheel. In through these roads come foods from all other regions of Spain—delicious fresh seafoods, vegetables, breads and wines—and restaurants of the other provinces are to be found in the capital, to the tourist's delight. Insofar as Spain has a national cuisine, it is here, for Madrid is the melting pot of the country.

During the 1950s I lived in Madrid for five years. I spent the first six months there without any accurate idea which regional food I was eating, what part of the region it came from or why. But when I finally left, I was so accustomed to the richness of Spanish central-plateau food that I found any other kind of cooking a little pallid by comparison. In those days Madrid was still a relatively small city, though growing slowly. I had an apartment with a view I still remember when I think of the city: looking down on the buildings as though from a skyscraper (although only on the ninth floor), the sherry colors of the walls shaved by shadows as the day moved; a city of amber, seeming always in the color of sunset until the sudden flush of thousands of sparrows from under the eaves announced the real end of the sunlight. Reluctantly, I gave up the apartment before I left because it was too far on the outskirts of town.

Last fall I went back to Madrid. Driving toward the city, I thought at first I had taken a wrong turn and arrived at some other place. The bustling hum of motors, of milling people and swarming traffic reached out between the new high buildings and threatened to engulf the approaching highway. My old apartment in the "outskirts" was nowhere to be seen; it is now considered in the "center of town."

I stopped a while and went into a bar for a glass of wine and a dish of anchovy-stuffed olives, a Madrid favorite, to remind myself that I was truly in the Spanish capital. The unmistakable smell of black tobacco, olives and old wine rose up from the glittering new pavements like a foretaste of the strong cooking that gave the people of Madrid strength to build this city and to keep on building it. I drank two glasses of dry red wine with the sharp, juicy olives and ate a whole dish of fresh dry toasted almonds, a staple appetizer that goes well with olives. Then I got back in the car, rolled the windows down and drove through the heavily charged air to a hotel.

The first day back I visited an old friend, a Castilian gourmet who lives with his large family in a building that is typical of the old quarter of Madrid. It is dark and cool here; there are shadows within shadows and a bottomless gray light fading into stone. You think the buildings have been torn out of the earth and forgotten. I had come to lunch at 2 o'clock, and at that time of afternoon in some parts of Madrid, when you go into a building, you need to wait for a few moments for your eyes to adjust to the sudden lack of light. Now in the darkness waiting for a rattling elevator that I could hear but could not see, there was a layer of familiar smells. From the *portería*, the janitor's quarters, came the mordant thin steam of a *sopa de ajo*, the garlic soup of Madrid, mixed with the smell of clear hot olive oil and parsley frying, and from somewhere else came the odor of a simmering *sofrito*, a base sauce made of olive oil, onions, garlic, parsley and chopped tomatoes. When the elevator came I got in, and the iron cage shook and clanked loudly up through the darkness and the deepening smells of Castilian cooking.

Like most apartments in old Madrid, my host's flat consisted of many small rooms strung along the main hall, which led directly from the front door to the kitchen. As the front door opened, I could tell that lunch was to be a *cocido*, a savory dish cooked with vegetables, pork, beef, ham bone and *chorizo* (a popular Spanish sausage), and traditionally served in three separate courses. *Cocido madrileño (Recipe Index)* is one of the best examples of the richness and strength of central Spanish cooking. People in Madrid say its smell gets into the walls of the house and keeps the family warm and in good temper all day. It is easy to believe this when you walk into a home where a substantial *cocido* is being made. The sudden odor that greets you is that of all the simple foods in the world fused in one steaming caldron, a smell that seems at the core of all cooking.

As we sat in the living room waiting for the *cocido*, my host's wife came in carrying a tray with a bottle of fine dry red wine, a plate of sliced *chorizo* and another plate of tiny Moorish shish kabobs on spears the length of a pencil. The cold *chorizo* slices had a sharp powerful flavor and, when tasted with the wine, they left a nutty hardness in the mouth. The shish kabobs were sizzling and had to be eaten carefully; the small bits of veal had been marinated in white wine with salt and garlic, parsley, paprika and a touch of cayenne before grilling over hot coals.

Finally our hostess announced that the *cocido* was ready. Her husband herded their four children and me into the dining room, where we sat around an ornate dark table in the center of which was a large, nearly empty space, soon to be filled by casseroles served in a definite order. One by one, the hostess proudly brought in the three different courses of the *cocido*. First in a large white tureen she presented the strained broth, to which she had added very fine noodles. It was as thin as consommé but as nourishing as stew. When that was consumed and the bowls removed, she came back with a steaming casserole full of chick-peas, boiled potatoes, carrots and fragrant cabbage that had been added to the *cocido* during the final minutes of its cooking. All the vegetables held the full flavor of the juices of the meats; the cabbage was a good textural contrast to the heavy potatoes and beans. In Castile you notice quickly that textural combinations are as important in the presentation of food as the blending of tastes. After we had finished the vegetables, the third course was brought in. This casserole contained small chunks of beef, *chorizo*, salt pork, shoulder of pork, chicken and meatballs. While we were eating the meat course, my host reminded me that the three courses of the *cocido madrileño* are referred to in New Castile as *sota*, *caballo* and *rey* (the jack, queen, king of our playing cards), for the *cocido* is supposed to grow in no-

The simplicity of garlic soup *(sopa de ajo)* epitomizes the cooking of central Spain. The base of this dish is nothing but garlic cloves and bread, browned together in olive oil. These ingredients are then cooked in water and the egg is dropped in last. The one shown here was poached on top of the soup, but in some versions it is stirred uncooked into the soup instead *(Recipe Index)*.

As prepared at the celebrated Valentín restaurant in Madrid, the *cocido madrileño* features a broad variety of meats. Displayed above, they are: chicken, beef, veal, bone marrow, *chorizo* sausage, a ham joint, blood sausage, fresh pork fat and salt pork fat. Chick-peas *(center)*, which are always included in the *cocido madrileño*, must be soaked overnight before they can be used.

bility as you go along. The steaming broth is intended to warm the stomach and prepare the appetite and the palate for things to come. The second course partly satisfies but also continues to open the way. The third course fulfills the promise of the first two.

Midway through the last course my host frowned, tilted his head, smiled slowly and curtly nodded his acceptance to his wife, much in the manner of a medieval king accepting a gift from one of his vassals. "A completely good *cocido*," he said, slicing the beef, "is as difficult to find as three good *toreros* in one afternoon's bullfight." Gratified, the wife walked back into the kitchen to replenish the last casserole for further helpings.

Like most Spanish dishes, the *cocido* should not be eaten without the accompaniment of fresh crusty bread. Bread is held in an almost mystical, as well as practical, esteem in most of Spain. When fresh bread is not available, Spaniards can become annoyed to the point of losing their tempers and their appetites. With each course my hostess had brought in a fresh section of a crisp warm oven-fresh loaf. When one of the children dropped a piece of it on the floor, his mother slapped his hand, picked up the crust and kissed it quickly before she unwillingly threw it away. "Bread was the food of Jesus," she said. She did not add that the hungry years after the Civil War had taught everyone in Spain the true value of bread. The Castilian bread we were served has a particularly hard crust and is ideal for eating with a nutritious rich food like *cocido*. "Dunking is permissible, mashing is advisable,

scooping is living," my host recited as he dipped into the casserole for a final helping of meat at the end of the meal. He proceeded to mash a piece of fatty meat with a hunk of dry bread until the fat was no longer visible and only the outside crust of the bread was dry.

The *cocido madrileño* we had eaten is the embodiment of Madrid's melting pot, a synthesis of all the *cocidos* from other regions of Spain. All of these dishes are descendants of Quixote's *olla podrida*, the original "rotten pot," or heavy stew, that itself was a descendant of an ancient Jewish dish called *adafina*, a kind of long-cooking boiled meal. The *adafina* was based on chicken or beef, vegetables and hard-boiled eggs. (It is still eaten in Algiers, Tangier and other North African cities.) In Spain, at the time of the Inquisition, when the central provinces became the stronghold of Christianity and it was necessary for the consumer to demonstrate his religious beliefs, the eggs in the *adafina* were replaced by large quantities of pork and pork fat. While the Moors and the Jews could eat no pork for religious reasons, a "pure" Christian, converted or otherwise, was a man who not only could, but did, eat pork once a day, preferably in public. Even at home he could never be caught off guard, for anyone who came unexpectedly to share his *cocido* could see clearly from the pork in it that this was not the house of an infidel but of a "pure believer in the True Faith." If the hams and sausages hanging heavily from the ceiling over the guest's head did not convince him, the cooking of the *cocido* did. Ironically, this new *cocido*, which was adapted from the

Traditionally, the *cocido madrileño* is served in three courses: soup, vegetables, then meats. The Valentín offers three different kinds of sauces —tomato, cumin seed and mint *(left to right, in small bowls at center)* with the vegetable and meat courses. The restaurant serves a white wine *(in the brown flask, upper right)* with the soup and a red wine *(in the glass)* with the vegetables and meats.

cooking of the Jews, became *the* dish in Madrid by which a man could quickly prove that he was a Christian.

Today the *cocido madrileño* is adaptable to the economy of any household. It is the rich man's food and the poor man's food. It can be simply a plain pot of chick-peas cooked with a chunk of meat of any kind, or just a piece of fat, potatoes and a vegetable. It can also be so much more inclusive that it seems an entirely different dish.

Another reason that the *cocido* has retained its popularity in Madrid is that it requires little attention while cooking. The woman of the house can put most of the ingredients together in the pot at the beginning of the morning and turn to other things. More ingredients may be added as they are needed, but the *cocido* is not a dish that requires nursing, as a Madrileña will tell you. When it is done, she pushes the pot to the back of the stove where it is kept warm until people are ready to eat.

The only real disadvantage of a *cocido,* my hostess assured me, is that it must be planned a day ahead to allow time for the chick-peas to soak so they will be tender. The chick-pea, which was introduced into Spain by the Carthaginians through Cádiz or Málaga, is important in a great deal of Iberian cookery. But it always needs soaking, which is a trial to many women whose husbands cannot learn to ask for a *cocido* the night before. "Men," my hostess explained sadly after lunch, "are a race of people who do not know what they want to eat until they want to eat it."

There are enough regional variations of the *cocido* to fill a book. Outside of the central plateau, many local ingredients have been added to achieve this variety. After the *cocido madrileño,* three versions seem representative. The Catalonian *cocido* (called *escudella i carn d'olla* in Catalan, the language of that region) makes use of its own beans and its own sausages; among the latter is the Catalonian *botifarra* (blood sausage), which is somewhat sweeter here than in other regions. Ox meat is sometimes used, rice may be added, and here the three courses of the *cocido* are usually served as one. In Andalusia, the Moors decoratively added saffron to the *cocido* as well as paprika, green beans, a different sort of cabbage and sometimes mint. Many Andalusians leave out the pork, thanks again to their Moorish heritage. The Andalusian *cocido* is therefore brightly flavored and light. The hot weather in this part of Spain does not encourage heavy eating. At the opposite end of the Peninsula, in Galicia facing the Atlantic, the *cocido* is called the *pote gallego* (Galician pot). Here pork definitely goes in, as well as turnips or turnip greens, various kinds of beans and often pork lard, but olive oil—an essential ingredient of most Spanish dishes—is sometimes left out. No part of Galicia touches the Mediterranean; her people are quite distinct in temperament and her cooks can afford to ignore Mediterranean necessities like olive oil when they choose.

But of all the *cocidos,* the central-plateau version is still the best. It is so rich and filling that one would think it might appease the Madrileño's appetite for a good 24 hours. Such is not the case. In Madrid there is a saying that the Spanish people "eat all day and some of the night." This is most spectacularly true of all peoples living in the central plateau and the north. Castilian appetites take second place only to those of the Basques, as we shall see. In Madrid there are five official meals, but these are only formal requirements, traditional and convenient acts in the play called living. The player is expected to ad lib a little too.

The first proper meal, the *desayuno*, or breakfast, is not impressive; like a great professional actor, the Castilian cook likes to make a simple entrance and begin in a humble way so that he may go on to bigger things. *Desayuno* is usually coffee, or sometimes chocolate, with a roll and jam or a thin hot pastry called a *churro (Recipe Index)*.

For early-rising working people in Madrid and the surrounding area, the second meal is *las onces* (elevenses) or *almuerzo* (lunch), eaten around 11 a.m. By now the stomach is awake; it demands more attention and gets it—anything from grilled sausage or tomato and bread to fried squid or an omelet, depending on what province you are in and on your individual taste.

In Spain midday is from 2 to 3 p.m., and by 2:30 in the afternoon it is time for the *comida*, the most important meal of the day. The need for an afternoon siesta becomes evident when we consider the courses of a well-to-do Castilian's midday *comida*.

He might begin with a salad, which in Spain is served before the main course rather than after. The Spanish theory is that salad is a *pre*-fresher, not a *re*-fresher. In the Castiles, salad may include fresh vegetables such as onions, beans, peas, young artichoke hearts and a spear or two of white asparagus. Because salad is considered an *entremés*, or hors d'oeuvre, a great many slices of sausage, meat, canned fish and olives may be added. Each component is then served in a separate oval dish, all of the dishes at once. This is what the Madrileño will get if he asks for *entremeses* as a first course in a restaurant. If he simply asks for a plain salad, he will be served lettuce and tomato. Oil and vinegar are brought to the table in glass cruets with thin spouts; they are poured directly onto the salad just before it is eaten, and a little salt is added. Many Castilians prefer their salad with just salt and oil, no vinegar at all; when vinegar is used it is always used sparingly. A Castilian saying has it that a good salad dressing needs only "a spendthrift for the oil, a miser for the vinegar and a madman to mix them together."

Instead of the *entremés* the Madrileño might, if the weather is not too warm, choose a *sopa de ajo (Recipe Index)*, hot garlic soup, another national dish with at least as many variations as there are regions in Spain. Like the city's *cocido*, Madrid's *sopa de ajo* is the classic version; it is the simplest and the one I like best. It is made from garlic, slices of bread and paprika sautéed in olive oil. Water is added, and then eggs or egg yolks are simmered in the brew until they become semifirm. The eggs may later be stirred in. The taste is not at all harsh and is very satisfying. As usual, outside of Madrid changes creep into this dish: in the north, cumin or parsley may be added; in coastal provinces, fish or shellfish are included and sometimes crushed almonds. But the essential thing is that *sopa de ajo* tastes like what it is—garlic soup. This may be the reason most people prefer the simple undisguised form made in the center of Spain. It serves as a fine bridge between a chilled, crisp salad and the main part of the meal.

After his soup or *entremés*, a Madrileño proceeding calmly through his midday *comida* will go on to the next course, which may be fish, perhaps crisply grilled, steaming hot trout or salmon from one of the mountain streams surrounding Madrid. To answer this need there is a salmon bank in the capital

Continued on page 28

At the El Gran Corrillo, a popular bar in Madrid, early evening patrons pick and choose among the selection of *tapas*.

Appetizers in Array for an Evening of Nibbling

In the evenings, Madrileños like to stop in at bars and cafés to enjoy a drink, usually sherry, and a choice of the tempting snacks known as *tapas*. The word *tapa* literally means lid, and the first *tapas* were pieces of bread used to cover wineglasses to keep out the flies. Today *tapas* are appetizers, but of a variety that is unknown in other countries. One café displays 32 kinds—not an exceptional number—ranging from eels to omelets. These snacks are so popular that at *tapa* time the bars and cafés in Madrid—and in other cities to which the convivial custom has spread—are filled with patrons, and some of them spend the whole evening nibbling, skipping the nighttime meal altogether.

The variety of *tapas* served nightly at the Corrillo de Ayala, another popular bar in Madrid, is pictured in the 32-dish display at left below; it includes:

1 Ham chunks garnished with red peppers
2 Pork with a sauce of olive oil, garlic, vinegar and spices
3 Kidney beans in vinegar sauce with parsley, onion and red pepper
4 Boiled potatoes garnished with parsley, mayonnaise and garlic
5 Broad beans with ham and sausage
6 Potato omelet
7 Mushrooms garnished with garlic and parsley
8 Fish in cognac sauce with crabmeat, carrots and seasoning
9 Kidneys sautéed in white wine sauce with onions, peas and red peppers
10 Shrimp in hot olive oil with garlic, parsley and red pepper
11 Chicken livers in meat sauce with egg slices
12 Salt cod with a Basque sauce, topped with slices of red pepper
13 Salmagundi of shellfish with hard-cooked egg
14 Small meatballs in gravy with peas
15 Red peppers sprinkled with garlic
16 Black olives marinated with onions and oregano
17 Fried bread crumbs
18 Salt cod stewed with garlic and cayenne
19 Tuna fish pies
20 Fried green peppers with red sausage
21 Pickled cauliflower
22 Stewed quail
23 Tripe stew
24 Snails in hot sauce
25 Pickled beets
26 Pigs' feet in tomato, olive oil, onion and garlic sauce
27 Green peppers stuffed with chopped veal in meat sauce
28 Baby eels boiled in oil, garnished with a cayenne pod
29 Clams *a la marinera* with parsley
30 Small squid "in their ink"
31 Stewed chicken with boiled potatoes and mushrooms
32 Stewed partridge

city where sports fishermen may deposit their river catch. The bank will clean the salmon and freeze or smoke it, as the owner likes, and if he wants to withdraw a pound for lunch, the teller marks down his account. The midday fish course might also be a thick slice of oven-cooked hake, prepared and served in a small individual casserole, the juices mixed with white wine and presented around the fish in a sizzling aromatic gravy. If it is Christmastime in Madrid, the fish will be *besugo*, sea bream, which is especially plentiful and popular at that time of year. The *besugo* is often accompanied by red cabbage with a rich sauce of almond cream, served with a dry white wine or champagne. The red cabbage dish is called *lombarda de San Isidro* after St. Isidore, the patron saint of Madrid.

In place of the fish course, the Madrileño may choose meat or possibly game if he or his friends have been hunting recently. Anything from oven-roasted veal to pork or lamb would suffice here, or perhaps a pigeon or partridge casserole or a stuffed pheasant, depending on what game is in season. Wild boar and venison are other possibilities. Game is popular in all of New Castile, as we shall see later on leaving Madrid for the surrounding countryside. It is cooked in a thick dark gravy in this central region of strong cold-weather foods.

When the hungry Madrileño has finished his meat course, he goes on to dessert: possibly a *flan*, or caramel custard, a thick slice of pungent Burgos cheese or perhaps rice pudding with a burnt cinnamon topping. If he is too full for any of these desserts, he may just ask for *fruta del tiempo*, fruit of the season. The best of these are the *fresones*, large cultivated strawberries, or *fresas*, the smaller and sharper wild variety. Both may be served with *nata*, whipped cream, or, better yet, they may be covered with freshly squeezed orange juice from Valencia oranges.

The *comida* ends with coffee, which is served after dessert, never with it. The meal is accompanied by wine—often white followed by red—and coffee may be accompanied by brandy.

The working class in Madrid must make substitutions in the daily *comida;* most of these people are far poorer than the government admits. They may eat *sopa de ajo,* because it is made without meat, but a thick lentil soup is more substantial, and the meat in this dish can be replaced by ham hock and veal bones which provide a meat flavor and a good consistency: Don Quixote's Friday meal of lentils can still keep people from starving in central Spain. If fresh salad is not available, and often it is not available to the poor, a thick slice of raw onion may be eaten with the lentils. This is a remarkably good combination, one that I have asked for in upper-class restaurants to the horror of many headwaiters. Another substitute for meat or fish in poorer households is a mixed dish of green beans, baby artichokes, cabbage or whatever vegetables are in season. The vegetables are first boiled and then tossed briefly in a little hot oil with garlic. Among poorer families, fresh fish gives way to dried codfish, which may be cooked in many ways, the most popular being a kind of stew with sliced potatoes.

But where there is plenty of money and plenty of food, the midday *comida* invariably is rich and vast. In Madrid, as in all of Spain, everything closes for three hours in the afternoon to give people a chance to consume this meal and recuperate by sleeping, which prepares the body for the second half of the day. At this point we have completed only three of the official meals. There are still two to go.

At 3 or 4 o'clock in the afternoon life is resumed, and nobody thinks about eating again until 6 p.m. Even then it is still considered early to mid afternoon. This is the time of the *merienda*, the penultimate meal, which usually is just coffee and pastries—cookies, fruit tarts, cream pastries or leafy layered honeyed desserts inherited from the Moors. But in Spain if company is coming, any meal becomes a serious meal whatever the hour. The *merienda* will then include meat pies, fowl or even fish.

In Madrid most people finish work around 7:30 p.m. and the evening meal, the *cena*, is eaten between 10 p.m. and midnight. It is usually referred to as the light meal, which is entirely believable, unless you happen to be in a restaurant watching people attack a series of courses only slightly less imposing than those of the *comida*. Again, the explanation is that people who go out to restaurants at night are often hosts or guests, so that the lightest meal takes on a heavy company glow. Eaten alone at home, the *cena* might consist simply of soup and an omelet; or asparagus with mayonnaise, vinaigrette sauce or melted butter, and a fish dish such as hake baked with béchamel sauce and a grated cheese topping. A popular dessert to top this meal is sliced oranges mixed with bananas.

The final proof of the Madrileño's capacity lies not in any of the formal meals he eats but in the snacks he consumes between meals. He may well give up a course here or there in the *comida* or *cena* if he thinks he can do better by going out on the town before either or both of these meals. Snacks are particularly popular in the center of Spain. When the icy winter winds come whining down from the Guadarrama Mountains trailing snows and freezing temperatures after them, a man does not wait until it is time to eat or drink; it is always time. To satisfy this need, there is a popular custom in Madrid called the *chateo*, a kind of ritualized snacking with wine. *Chato* means snub-nosed, and a *chateo* is a tour of the city's old bars where wine is drunk out of snub-nosed glasses, and *tapas*—a kind of hors d'oeuvre—are eaten with the wine. There is an enormous variety of *tapas* to be found in Spain, and most of them can be found in Madrid. You stand up to eat them at one of the city's bars during the hour before the midday meal or before dinner. If you ask for a glass of wine at a bar you will also be given a small oval dish of cold boiled seafood, almonds, olives or anchovies. But the best way to enjoy these snacks is to go out on a serious hunt for good *tapas* with a group of friends—to go on a *chateo*.

I have a favorite bar for *tapas* in Madrid, a small dark room off a narrow street near the square called Puerta del Sol (Gate of the Sun), which is considered by the government to be the exact geographic center of Spain. This bar has about 50 staple *tapas*, five of which change from week to week. It is tiled dark blue and white inside, and sawdust lines the floor against the bar to catch the peelings of shrimp and other shellfish. Lists of the *tapas* are printed in thick white paint on the outside window and the inside mirrors. A cook stands near the doorway at a permanently hot griddle ready to throw almost anything on it, or to scoop out a portion from a huge steaming casserole. As you walk in, the smells of stale wine and beef in the sawdust, of garlic, parsley, heated sauces, sizzling meats and seafoods on the griddle, heaping

Continued on page 32

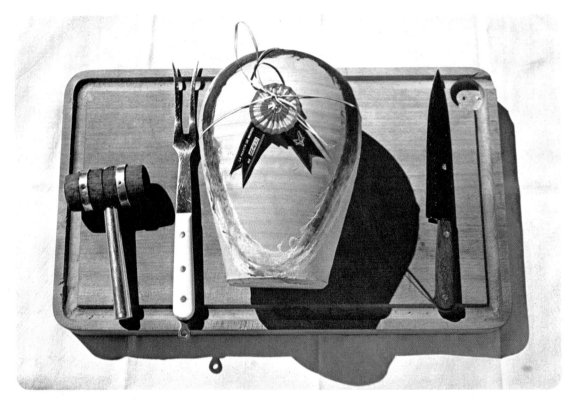

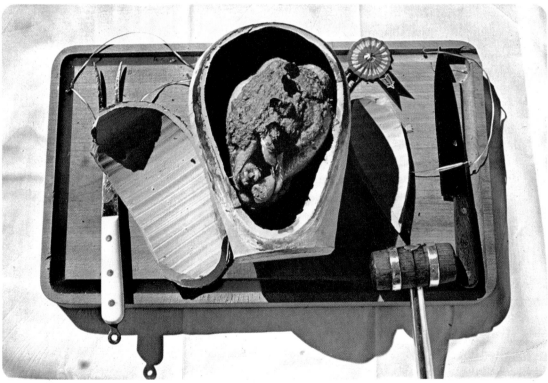

When you order *Pollo Puerta de Moros* at Madrid's fashionable La Puerta de Moros restaurant, the waiter brings a sealed sarcophaguslike clay pot decorated with a medallion in the Spanish national colors *(top)*. Besides the knife and fork at your place, he hands you a mallet. It is used—as demonstrated on the opposite page by the Duchess of Medina Sidonia for author Peter Feibleman—to crack the pot open. Inside is an elegant surprise: a baked chicken *(bottom)* seasoned with thyme, basted with cognac, and topped with foie gras and truffles.

platters of cooked shellfish, and bowls of marinating seafoods rise out of the little bar like an engulfing wave; five minutes later you cannot smell anything except what you are eating. I am fond of grilled veal kidneys with fresh chopped parsley and chopped garlic, a little oil, lemon juice and salt. Shrimp are good just grilled on the hot plate or griddle with coarse salt sprinkled over them. Only a little salt gets into the shell, and when the shrimp are cool enough to peel, they are still steaming and the meat is tender and sweet. Mushrooms make fine *tapas*, especially when skewered with alternating chunks of *jamón serrano* (mountain-cured ham), grilled over coals or on a griddle, dabbed with thick translucent *ali-oli* sauce *(Recipe Index)* and sprinkled with chopped parsley and celery salt. And *callos a la madrileña (Recipe Index)*, are wonderful: tripe simmered for hours in a rich tomato sauce with *chorizo*, ham, *morcilla* (blood sausage), onions, carrots, garlic, pepper and salt, paprika, oil, white wine and leeks and, perhaps, cloves and lard. There are many other *tapas* to choose from, made from every kind of meat, fish, shellfish and vegetable obtainable in the Iberian Peninsula.

For those who have stayed up especially late in Madrid, the *churro*, mentioned earlier as a breakfast food, serves as an after-supper snack. Vendors cook *churros* on the streets in pots of hot oil. They squeeze dough into the oil from a pastry tube that makes a thin fluted nut-brown loop. Five or six of these loops are tied together on a slick green reed, and you take them to a café where you eat them with thick hot chocolate.

Olive trees in neatly ordered rows cover a hillside in the high plateau region of central Spain near Toledo. Equipped by nature to withstand extremes of drought and heat, the trees in this region produce much of Spain's olive oil, an essential ingredient of the national cuisine.

The traveler who journeys outside of Madrid in rural parts of central Spain will find the abundance and variety of wild game one of the most impressive features of the cooking. Southeast of the capital, for example, the plains of Ciudad Real in New Castile teem with quail and partridge, silver rabbit, hare, wild turkey and pheasant as well as waterfowl. In the mountainous parts of this region wild boar are abundant, as are wild deer and mountain goat. The rivers offer trout, perch, carp, barbel, pike and other kinds of fish. All of these dishes are cooked in the typically rich manner of the central plateau, but first the game or fish must be killed or caught; and the hunter's job is no less formal, and no less valued, than that of the greatest of Castilian chefs. This is especially true if the quarry is wild boar.

The hunting of the wild boar is a ritual that must be performed properly if it is going to be done at all; it is not the kind of thing you should do by accident. The boar, which looks as if it were built only for sitting and snarling, moves with incredible agility and speed. It is large and black, and its body looks disproportionately small compared to its huge head. The animal attacks the attacker, and its long curved tusks are lethal. A seemingly gentle nuzzling movement of the big head to the right or left—almost the way a swan moves its neck—can slice through a man's heavy hunting boots like a razor. A man can lose an arm or leg and a hunting dog can be eviscerated by a wild boar. Today these animals are hunted in some parts of Spain, as they were in the Middle Ages, on horseback and with a lance rather than a gun.

This sounds safe for the hunter, but it is not. A single lance thrust almost never kills a wild boar and often does not even wound it badly. After one thrust the hunter must dismount and finish the job on foot with a knife. He may not stay on his horse and he may not use a rifle. Both of these tactics are considered unsporting; he would be called a coward at least, and a Castilian cares very much about his appearance in the eyes of his friends.

Dismounting to kill a wounded boar is dangerous; the hunter is aided only by his dogs, which are permitted to locate and surround the boar, though they must not touch it. That is the man's job. The boar may have only a minor flesh wound, which does not impair its movements at all but can enrage it to fury. Once on a hunt I dismounted behind a hunter who had wounded a boar; I walked the other way. It was a chilly morning and I stood in high grass and lit a cigarette and lifted a wineskin, squeezing it at the base so that the warming red wine spurted in a long arc that thinned in the wind into a spray too wide to drink from. One of the other hunters laughed and rode up to show me how it was done, drinking into the wind and holding the wineskin low and close to his face when the heavy gusts came, splashing it into his mouth and against his teeth. While he was showing me, there was a sound like distant thunder and the tall grass in front of me parted as if a scythe had cut it, and I could hear a soft deep grunting. I don't know how many Americans have been treed by boars, but I am one of the club. Minus wineskin, but with boots and gun, a chunk of Manchego

Most of these piglets undergoing inspection in the open market in Madrid will end up as a favorite delicacy of Spain's central plateau—*cochinillo asado* (roast suckling pig). Butchered when they are about three weeks old, the piglets will be roasted in wood-burning ovens. Each weighs about six pounds, enough to serve four.

cheese, a fresh loaf of bread, tobacco and matches, I rose with ease into the branches. When I explained afterward that I had never seen anything move as fast as that wild boar, my friends reminded me that I had not seen myself.

After the boar was killed, we sat on the hillside and lit a fire of wood and thyme branches and put a frying pan over it. Boar meat is very good to eat, solid and not too gamy, and not fat; the dark ham made from boar has a special taste, as has boar's head, pickled or stewed; but these require time, and the hams and meat must hang until they season. Fortunately, one of the hunters had bought some small perch from a fisherman we passed by a stream; another had a sack of coarse salt and a piece of ham fat. He heated the pan and swabbed it with a little of the fat and let that burn off almost completely and then we threw the perch in with some salt on top and grilled them on both sides and peeled them. We ate them whole, holding the head and tail between two hands and picking off the steaming white meat of the outside of the fish with our teeth. In the cold morning air, the smell of thyme from the fire was so strong you seemed to taste it, though no thyme had been added to the fish in cooking. Castilian hunters know that a fresh herb smell burning while food is being cooked and eaten gives another dimension to taste. In all of Spain, the sense of smell is a vital part of cookery.

Although we did not eat boar meat that day, when properly seasoned and prepared, it is so highly prized in central Spain that crossbreeding with tame pigs is sometimes practiced. Such crossbreeding has, however, to be permitted rather than arranged. At night certain Don Juan wild boars for reasons of their own sometimes take their big heads and little bodies to visit farms and give their affections to pink domesticated plump lady cousins who have big bodies and little heads. The offspring usually has a little body, big head, useless tusks and black and pink or black and white stripes. The adult of the crossbred species makes extremely good eating. To this end, barn doors are occasionally left open at night, and amorous squeals and grunts in the dark are politely ignored by the neighbors. The stew that will be produced a few months later is considered worth one night's loss of sleep.

The rural kitchens of New Castile are notable not only for wild game but also for the many fresh vegetable dishes to which a little ham and sometimes fresh eggs are added to enrich or strengthen fairly simple food. La Mancha in particular has provided the central Spanish melting pot with many fine examples of life-sustaining cooking. Among these vegetable dishes *pisto manchego (Recipe Index)* is superb. It can be made with many ingredients, but the *pisto* I prefer contains finely chopped sautéed onions, eggplant, young pumpkin, green peppers and tomatoes with bits of ham and eggs beaten into the vegetables. As an accompaniment to plain roast meat it is delicious.

In the northern half of Spain's central plateau, the regions of Old Castile and neighboring León provide still another source of nourishment to fortify men against the brutal elements of land and sky. The nutrition that New Castile derives from stews and dishes like the *cocido* is supplied in Old Castile both in that form and yet another—roasted meats. Like stewing or boiling, roasting is aimed at one result: sustenance, to provide enough strength to live through the bitterness of winter and the ability simply to exist on an earth that is dry and cracked either by ice or by heat all year around.

The best places in Spain to enjoy such delicacies as roast suckling pig

Wild boars, like the one a Stone Age artist depicted 12,000 to 17,000 years ago on a ceiling of the Altamira caves in northern Spain, still roam many wooded areas of Old and New Castile, and other regions of Iberia as well. Closely related to succulent domestic pigs (*opposite*), the ferocious boars yield meat that is lean and flavorful, yet not too gamy in taste.

In the town of Consuegra smiling señoras display freshly plucked cauliflower plants.

or roast baby lamb are the little towns of Segovia and Arévalo. Both animals are killed much younger than they would be in most other Western countries (as is veal, which is why there is little beef in Spain). The suckling pig, bred on farms and in villages of Old Castile, brings with it the taste of barley and a tinge of thyme and other wild herbs that its sow mother has been feeding on. The piglet itself has not tasted anything but milk; it has been killed two to three weeks after birth. The oven used for roasting is a baker's oven, which is deep and quite wide, and the fire is started long before it is going to be used. Chopped parsley, sometimes a few sprigs of thyme, and chopped garlic and onions are scattered under and over the split pig; occasionally a bay leaf is added and the pig is laid on an earthenware dish that is fed into the oven on a long baker's shovel, the kind used for heavy round loaves of bread. The piglet is turned as it browns and is basted frequently—often with a bird's feather. The skin is pricked to allow the fat to flow out, and the fat is removed as it renders. The result is so crisp and tender that most bacon would seem tough by comparison. At Casa Cándido inn in Segovia under the old Roman aqueduct that dominates the town, the roast suckling pig is brought to the table *en su punto*—cooked to just the right point and sputtering hot. If you appear doubtful about its crispness or tenderness, the waiter will discard his knife and cut the pig with a plate. It will be dry on the outside, but the meat will be juicy and light in color and texture; the taste is sweet to tangy and there is no oil slick left on the roof of your mouth. Baby lamb is roasted in much the same way, and if you are from a part of the world where lamb is so old it would be considered mutton by the Spanish, you may not immediately recognize the taste. It is more delicate than American lamb, more of it can be eaten, and there is no acrid smell.

The cooking of central Spain cannot be judged properly without a visit to Extremadura, the region that touches Portugal and leads down to western Andalusia. Among its other foods, Extremadura produces the best *chorizo* in Spain. The countryside and scattered villages of this region are picturesquely inhabited by men and animals who live in close association. Every farmer and villager has at least one pig. Most of them have several. Acorns grow abundantly in Extremadura, and in the country villages pigs are free to wander wherever they want. They forage for acorns during the day and come back by themselves at sunset, all at approximately the same time and of their own accord. Many Extremaduran pigs are dedicated to St. Anthony, and on his name day in January the piglets are showered with holy water to fatten them while their previously blessed and already fattened fathers are slaughtered. Shortly after the slaughtering the *chorizos* are prepared, and during this process a dish called *la prueba* is served. It is perhaps the best of all Extremaduran dishes, certainly the richest, and one that unfortunately is almost never served in restaurants. *La prueba* is a family affair. The name means "the test." The ingredients that will soon become *chorizo*—pork bits, brilliant red paprika, garlic and spices, herbs and other seasonings that have been cooking together for a long time—must first be tested before being inserted into the tripe skin and hung up for smoking. Family and friends gather in the kitchen for this occasion, where they are warmed by a wood fire from the stove; the bright red bits of pork that make the mixture to be tested are put sizzling in a pot in the center of the table. Everyone is given a tall glass of red wine and a long wooden spoon, and then everyone digs in and comments. *La prueba* is one of those dishes that looks so good you think you can finish the pot alone. You can, but as I know from experience, you should not. The taste is zesty and pungent; it is better than when the ingredients become *chorizo*, and like all central Spanish dishes it is full of nourishment. But even the Extremadurans themselves go at it carefully. Discomfort from overeating *la prueba*, they say, lasts until next year's *prueba*.

Driving south through Extremadura toward Seville in spring, you will notice young boys and girls by the side of the road selling great double handfuls of slim wild asparagus. It is a deep green, much thinner than the meaty white asparagus grown in gardens, and it has a daintiness of taste that makes it worth stopping for. If you happen to be the kind of person who travels with butter, you can cook your asparagus by the side of the road and dip it in. There is no better way to leave the forbidding central provinces for the warm, flowered air of southern Spain. As you drive along, the groves of knotty twisted olive trees that seemed in the Castiles to clutch at the arid land for life, appear now to straighten up and open their silver-backed leaves sparkling in the first warm wind.

On a roadside near Seville an enterprising boy offers wild asparagus for 50 pesetas (70 cents) a bunch. The slender green shoots are sometimes cooked and eaten with butter or a sauce, but Spaniards more frequently use them in omelets.

Come spring these sheep outside the walls of Ávila, in Old Castile, will produce their share of baby lambs, a favorite delicacy of the area. The heathlands of Spain's north central plateau are too arid for field crops but maintain large flocks of sheep, which can survive on rugged mountain pastures and scant summer forage. The lambs, butchered at a much younger age (about two weeks) than in most countries, provide an exceptionally delicate meat that has contributed to the fame of central Spain as "the land of roasting." The turreted wall in the background is famous in its own right. Surmounted by 88 towers dating from the 11th Century, it surrounds the city of Ávila and is among the best preserved medieval walls on the European continent.

CHAPTER **II** RECIPES

Sopa de Ajo
SPICY GARLIC SOUP

To serve 6 to 8

½ cup olive oil
2 tablespoons finely chopped garlic
3 cups coarsely crumbled French or
    Italian bread, trimmed of all crusts
1 teaspoon paprika
6 cups water
¼ teaspoon cayenne pepper
1 teaspoon salt
2 eggs, lightly beaten
1 tablespoon finely chopped parsley
    (optional)

In a heavy 3- to 4-quart saucepan, warm the olive oil over low heat. Add the garlic. Stirring frequently, cook for 2 or 3 minutes, or until the garlic is soft but not brown. Stir in the crumbled bread, raise the heat to moderate and cook until the bread is golden. Be careful not to let it burn. Stir in the paprika, then add the water, cayenne pepper and salt and bring to a boil. Reduce the heat to low and simmer uncovered for 30 minutes.

With a large wooden spoon beat the soup until the bread is thoroughly pulverized. Then slowly pour in the beaten eggs, stirring constantly. Simmer a moment or two (do not let the soup come anywhere near a boil or it will curdle) and taste. The soup should be highly seasoned; add more salt and cayenne pepper if it seems to be too bland. Pour the soup into a heated tureen or individual soup plates and serve it at once, garnished if you like with finely chopped parsley.

Cocido Madrileño
BOILED CHICKEN, MEATS AND VEGETABLES

To serve 6 to 8

1 cup (½ pound) dried chick-peas
    (garbanzos)
5½ quarts water
A 5- to 6-pound stewing fowl
2 pounds lean fresh beef brisket
1 pound boneless serrano ham, or
    substitute prosciutto or other lean
    smoked ham
½ pound salt pork, rind removed
1 large onion, peeled
2 medium-sized carrots, scraped
2 medium-sized leeks, including 2
    inches of the green stems
1 tablespoon finely chopped garlic
1 small bay leaf
4 parsley sprigs
½ teaspoon freshly ground black
    pepper
6 chorizos, or substitute 1 pound
    other garlic-seasoned smoked pork
    sausages
A 2-pound white cabbage, trimmed,
    cut lengthwise into 6 wedges and
    cored
6 small potatoes, peeled

Starting a day ahead, wash the chick-peas thoroughly in a sieve or colander under cold running water, then combine them with 2 quarts of cold water in a heavy 10- to 12-quart casserole. The water should cover them by about an inch; add more water if necessary. Soak the chick-peas at room temperature for at least 12 hours.

Drain the peas in a sieve or colander and return them to the casserole. Add 5½ quarts of fresh cold water, the stewing fowl and beef brisket to the casserole, and bring to a boil over high heat, meanwhile skimming off the foam and scum as they rise to the surface. Reduce the heat to low and simmer partially covered for 1½ hours. Then add the ham, salt pork, onion, carrots, leeks, garlic, bay leaf, parsley and black pepper, and cook partially covered for 30 minutes longer.

Meanwhile, place the sausages in a 10- to 12-inch skillet and prick them in two or three places with the point of a small, sharp knife. Add enough water to cover them completely and bring to a boil over moderate heat. Reduce the heat to low and simmer uncovered for 5 minutes, then discard the cooking liquid and transfer the sausages to the casserole. Add the cabbage and potatoes as well, and simmer partially covered for about 30 minutes, or until all the meat and vegetables and chick-peas are tender.

To serve, transfer the bird and meats to a carving board. Remove the vegetables from the broth with a slotted spoon, arrange them attractively on a large platter and mound the chick-peas in the center. Carve the chicken into suitable portions, and cut the brisket, ham and salt pork into ¼-inch slices. Arrange the chicken and meat on another heated platter and place the whole chorizos around them.

Traditionally, the broth is served alone as a first course, often with previously cooked fine noodles (called cabello de ángel or "angel's hair"). The platters of vegetables and meats then follow separately.

Perdices Estofadas

PARTRIDGES BRAISED WITH VEGETABLES AND GARLIC IN WHITE WINE

Wash the partridges under cold running water and pat them completely dry with paper towels. Sprinkle them inside and out liberally with salt and a few grindings of pepper, then dip each bird in flour and shake it vigorously to remove any excess.

In a heavy 1½- to 2-quart casserole, cook the bacon in the olive oil over moderate heat, stirring occasionally, until crisp and golden. With a slotted spoon, transfer the pieces to paper towels to drain.

Heat the fat remaining in the casserole over high heat until it splutters. Add the partridges and brown them well on all sides, turning them with tongs and regulating the heat so they color quickly and evenly without burning. Transfer the birds to a plate. Pour off and discard the fat from the casserole and in its place add the wine and water. Bring to a boil over high heat, meanwhile scraping in any brown particles clinging to the bottom and sides of the casserole.

Return the partridges and bacon to the casserole and add the garlic, cloves and bay leaf. Cover tightly, reduce the heat to low and simmer undisturbed for 30 minutes. Add the onions, potatoes and carrots, cover again, and cook for 15 minutes longer. Then add the green peas and simmer covered for about 5 minutes more, or until the partridges and all of the vegetables are tender. Garnish with the parsley and serve at once, directly from the casserole, or if you prefer, transfer the partridges and vegetables to a heated platter.

Pollo en Pepitoria

CHICKEN BRAISED IN WHITE WINE WITH ALMONDS AND GARLIC

Pat the chicken thoroughly dry with paper towels. Sprinkle it liberally with salt and a little white pepper, dip the pieces in flour and shake them vigorously to remove the excess. In a heavy 10- to 12-inch skillet, heat the olive oil over high heat until a light haze forms above it. Starting them skin side down, brown 3 or 4 pieces of chicken at a time, turning them with tongs and regulating the heat so that the pieces color quickly and evenly without burning. Transfer them to a heavy 4- to 6-quart casserole.

Pour off all but 2 tablespoons of fat from the skillet and add the onions. Stirring frequently, cook them over moderate heat for about 5 minutes, or until they are soft and transparent but not brown. Spread the onions over the chicken in the casserole and add the parsley and bay leaf. Pour in the wine and water, and bring to a boil over high heat. Reduce the heat to low, cover tightly, and simmer, undisturbed, for 20 minutes.

With a mortar and pestle or a wooden spoon, mash the pulverized almonds, egg yolks, garlic and saffron to a smooth paste. Thin it with ¼ cup of the casserole liquid and stir the mixture gradually into the simmering casserole. Cover again, and cook for 10 minutes longer, or until the chicken is tender. With tongs, transfer the pieces to a deep, heated platter and drape it loosely with foil to keep warm.

Bring the cooking liquids to a boil over high heat and boil briskly uncovered until the sauce has reduced to about half or enough to intensify its flavor. Taste for seasoning and pour it over the chicken. Serve at once, accompanied if you like by hot boiled rice.

To serve 2

2 one-pound oven-ready partridges
1½ teaspoons salt
¼ teaspoon freshly ground black pepper
½ cup flour
2 slices lean bacon, coarsely chopped
2 tablespoons olive oil
½ cup dry white wine
1 cup water
1 small whole head of garlic, trimmed of root fibers and dry outer casing, but not peeled or separated into individual cloves
2 whole cloves
1 small bay leaf
6 to 8 peeled white onions, each about 1 inch in diameter
2 medium-sized potatoes, peeled and cut into 1-inch cubes
3 medium-sized carrots, scraped and cut into 1-inch lengths
¼ cup fresh peas (¼ pound) or thoroughly defrosted frozen peas
1 tablespoon finely chopped parsley

To serve 4 to 6

A 4- to 5-pound roasting chicken, cut into 6 to 8 serving pieces
Salt
White pepper
1 cup flour
½ cup olive oil
2 cups finely chopped onions
1 tablespoon finely chopped parsley
1 large bay leaf
1 cup dry white wine
2 cups water
¼ cup blanched almonds, pulverized in a blender or with a nut grinder or mortar and pestle
2 hard-cooked egg yolks
1 tablespoon finely chopped garlic
⅛ teaspoon ground saffron or saffron threads crushed with a mortar and pestle or with the back of a spoon

In La Mancha, fresh vegetables and olive oil are cooked almost to a purée for the classic vegetable dish called *pisto manchego (recipe opposite)*. All *pistos* are made with tomatoes and green peppers; the more elaborate version shown at right incorporates zucchini squash and onions, and is garnished with hard-cooked egg.

To make 12 to 15

2 cups water
1 teaspoon salt
2 cups all-purpose flour
Vegetable oil or shortening for deep-fat frying
Sugar

Churros Madrileños
CRISP-FRIED CRULLERS

In a heavy 2- to 3-quart saucepan, bring the water and salt to a boil over high heat. Immediately remove the pan from the heat and pour in the flour all at once. Beat vigorously with a wooden spoon until the mixture forms a thick coarse paste that pulls away from the sides of the pan in a mass. Cool to room temperature.

Heat 2 to 3 inches of oil or shortening in a deep-fat fryer or large, heavy skillet until it is very hot but not smoking, or until it reaches a temperature of 400° on a deep-frying thermometer.

Spoon about half of the dough into a large metal cookie press fitted with a star disc, and press three or four 6-inch-long ribbons of dough directly into the hot fat, cutting the ribbons off at the tip with a small knife as you proceed. Turning the crullers occasionally, fry them for 5 to 8 minutes, or until they are a rich golden brown on all sides. Using kitchen tongs, transfer the browned crullers to a double thickness of paper towels to drain while you fry the rest.

Serve the crullers while they are still warm. Just before serving, sprinkle them liberally with sugar.

NOTE: Do not try to force the *churro* paste through a pastry bag—the mixture is so stiff it must be shaped with a cookie press or, if you can find it, one of the special *churro* makers used in Spain.

Pisto Manchego

STEWED PEPPERS, TOMATOES, SQUASH AND ONIONS

In a heavy 12-inch skillet, heat the olive oil over high heat until a light haze forms above it. Add the onions, squash, peppers and salt, stir together, then cover the pan, and reduce the heat to its lowest possible point. Cook for about 40 minutes, or until the vegetables are tender, stirring occasionally.

Meanwhile, place the tomatoes in a 1- to 1½-quart saucepan and bring to a boil over moderate heat. Stirring and mashing them against the sides of the pan, cook briskly uncovered until most of the liquid in the pan evaporates and the tomatoes become a thick, fairly smooth purée.

Stir them into the vegetables, then pour in the beaten egg, stirring constantly. Simmer about 10 seconds but do not let the mixture boil. Taste for seasoning and serve at once. Garnish the top, if you like, with the hard-cooked egg. *Pisto* is usually served as an accompaniment to roasted meat.

To serve 4

⅓ cup olive oil
3 cups coarsely chopped onions
2 medium-sized zucchini, scrubbed
    and cut into ¼-inch cubes
2 large green peppers, deribbed,
    seeded and coarsely chopped
2 teaspoons salt
4 medium-sized tomatoes, peeled,
    seeded and coarsely chopped (*see
    huevos a la flamenca, page 16*)
1 egg, lightly beaten
1 hard-cooked egg, the white cut
lengthwise into ¼-inch strips and
the yolk crumbled (optional)

Judías Verdes con Salsa de Tomate

GREEN BEANS IN TOMATO SAUCE

In a heavy 3- to 4-quart saucepan, bring the salt and 2 quarts of water to a boil over high heat. Drop in the beans, a handful at a time. Bring to a boil again, reduce the heat to moderate and boil uncovered for 10 to 15 minutes, or until the beans are barely tender. Drain in a colander or sieve and set the beans aside.

Heat the olive oil in a heavy 10- to 12-inch skillet until a light haze forms above it. Add the onions and garlic and, stirring frequently, cook over moderate heat for 5 minutes, or until the onions are soft and transparent but not brown. Stir in the tomatoes, parsley, sugar and a few grindings of pepper, bring to a boil, and cook, uncovered, until most of the liquid evaporates and the mixture is thick enough to hold its shape lightly in a spoon.

Stir in the beans and simmer for a minute or two until they are heated through. Taste for seasoning and serve at once from a heated bowl.

To serve 4

1 teaspoon salt
1 pound fresh green string beans,
    trimmed and cut into 2-inch
    lengths
2 tablespoons olive oil
¼ cup finely chopped onions
1 teaspoon finely chopped garlic
4 medium-sized tomatoes, peeled,
    seeded and finely chopped (*see
    huevos a la flamenca, page 16*), or
    substitute 1½ cups chopped,
    drained, canned tomatoes
1 tablespoon finely chopped parsley
2 teaspoons sugar
Freshly ground black pepper

Leche Frita

FRIED CUSTARD SQUARES

In a 1½- to 2-quart saucepan, combine the cornstarch and 1 cup of the milk and stir until the cornstarch dissolves completely. Stir in the remaining 2 cups of milk and ½ cup of the sugar. Bring to a boil over high heat, stirring constantly, and cook briskly until the custard mixture comes to a boil and thickens heavily. Pour the custard into a shallow 8- to 9-inch square baking dish, spread it out evenly with a spatula and refrigerate for at least 4 hours, or until it is firm.

With a knife dipped in hot water, cut the custard into 1¼- to 1½-inch squares. Dip the squares into the beaten eggs and then into the crumbs and place them on a sheet of wax paper. In a heavy 10- to 12-inch skillet, melt the butter in the oil over moderate heat. When the foam begins to subside, add 6 or 8 custard squares and brown them for about 2 minutes on each side, turning them over carefully with a large metal spatula. Transfer them to a heated serving platter and sprinkle with a mixture of the remaining 2 tablespoons of sugar and the cinnamon. Serve hot.

To serve 6 to 8

½ cup cornstarch
3 cups milk
½ cup plus 2 tablespoons sugar
2 eggs, lightly beaten
1 cup fine fresh crumbs made
    from French or Italian bread,
    trimmed of crusts and
    pulverized in a blender or torn
    apart with a fork
4 tablespoons butter
2 tablespoons olive or vegetable
    oil
1 teaspoon ground cinnamon

III

The Light Touch
of Andalusia's Cooks

Andalusia, the eight provinces that make up the Spanish land of the Muslims on the southern apron of the Iberian Peninsula, takes its visitors by a storm that might best be described as a sensual onslaught. The slash of colors and odors comes like a seizure; it clouds the eyes and dizzies the mind. When I went to Seville in the early 1950s I expected a soft southern version of central Spain. At first I was blinded. I walked into a street and stopped in the wheeling brightness. The light was harsh and shattered. There is no way to define or wholly describe the sun-swollen air laden with the smells of olives, violent flowers, fish frying in oil, tomatoes, bitter orange and bitter lemon groves, tobacco, cinnamon, cloves, rotting river odors and the sharp, tangy smells of sea animals mixed with the tar of boats and the open, burned smell of earth itself.

I sat at a dusty outdoor bar in the shade near the river under a trellis of bougainvillea topped with jasmine like a surf of flowers and ate a plate of big shrimp the color of pink that is associated with very slow sunsets. It was June and the heat shone in the city. It was hard to breathe and Seville was like a huge balloon of dust with the sun in it. Seville is a river port on the Guadalquivir, not a seaport, and the iced, boiled shrimp had been brought up by boat from the Mediterranean. They were not mealy or tough as large shrimp sometimes are and they tasted sharply and sweetly of the sea. In Andalusia something acts like a chemical in the air to sharpen the senses. That something seduced the Muslim peoples from the deserts of North Africa to inhabit "Al Andalus," a place where they could live a life of "sensuality and repose." In Seville you sense quickly the lure that brought them to Spain and held them there for eight centuries; you feel the ripening of your own body. I remember sitting under the froth of blinding flowers, and hearing in the heat bubble the muted sound of a child's castanets that floated out of a distant courtyard like the spilling of shells under the sea.

A week later I rented a house that was built around a central patio in which there was a white well that was no longer used and a loud trickle of water from a broken faucet that echoed hard in the galleries above. The walls had been whitewashed and you could not look at anything for very long. Andalusian houses are built to be cool in the center in summer and warm in winter. I was shown inside and up a narrow staircase to a room on the second floor. On a terrace off the main living room next to my bedroom was a large clay bowl full of liquid, half in sun and half in shade, like a miniature bull ring. The maid who had shown me in stopped long enough to push the bowl completely into the shadow on the far side of the terrace. "It's 3 o'clock," she said, looking at the bowl and the shade across the terrace as if she were examining a sundial. She meant that it was mealtime. I was not at all hungry but I was very thirsty and I said so. She closed the doors to the terrace to keep the heat out. While I unpacked she brought some slivers of ice up from the kitchen and put them in the bowl outside; then she brought a jug of white wine and carried the bowl in from the terrace and ladled out a portion into a soup cup. I sat down to try the soup. The thin dust-colored liquid in front of me was one I had heard about, but never tasted. There were pieces of chopped cucumber, tomato and green pepper floating on it, and the soup smelled like a fresh summer salad with garlic. It is called *gazpacho (Recipe Index)* and it is to Andalusia what *cocido* is to the center of Spain.

I dipped my spoon in and took some; the liquid was only cool, not ice-cold, but satisfying to the thirst. It tasted of chilled vegetables, of wine vinegar, oil and water, with garlic and a tinge of bread, and it had the faint aftertaste of earth-cool clay from the bowl. (The name *gazpacho* derives from the Arabic for "soaked bread.") I asked the maid to leave it and I finished about one fifth of it. The chopped cucumber on top was fresh in taste and texture, and the bits of green pepper were still brittle and bright green. It was a light meal in itself, all that you could think of eating in the heat, and with the crisp, dry white wine it was all you could want to drink. Lightness was the order of the day.

If there is a single key to the quality of the Andalusian kitchen, it is that, lightness. The Spanish are a weather-conscious people. In the blistering, sun-steeped cities of Andalusia food must be so lacking in heaviness and so easily digestible as hardly to appear to be food. Liquid should be thirst-quenching, and it should contain salt to replace the salt lost through the pores of the skin. *Gazpacho* meets all these requirements; it is typical of the Andalusian's ability to serve food that is more a product of the cook's *gracia,* his graceful cleverness or wit, than of the ingredients he uses. Like his light humor, the Andalusian's food must somehow exist under the ponderous southern sun without wilting. It seems a conglomeration of nothing—"a little of this, a little of that" will be the answer if you ask what it contains for Andalusian dishes like Andalusian jokes do not bear heavy scrutiny. You are meant to enjoy the results without knowing why. "What else would you eat?" the cook asks. Heavy, hot sauces of any kind would not be agreeable in this climate most of the year, nor would roasts or rich stews. Strong central-plateau food is generally shunned here. Roast suckling pig is anathema both to the Andalusian's heat-conscious body and his Islam-oriented mind; not many southern dishes contain large quantities of pork. The rich somberness of the Castilian kitchen is replaced here by an airy grace. In their simplicity and quantity the ingredients of Andalusian cooking appear almost childlike; but they are prepared in ways that lend freshness and a certain weightless magic to each dish.

The best example of this magic is *gazpacho,* the making of which is worth watching in Seville if only because it is so simple you wonder why other hot-weather countries have not adopted it as a national food. To prepare *gazpacho,* seeded tomatoes, garlic, oil, salt and some crustless pieces from the center of fresh bread are ground together in a mortar and pestle. The mixture is emptied into the clay bowl, and a few more tomatoes and maybe a bit of sweet pepper are ground in the mortar and added, sometimes with pimientos as well. Water and a little wine vinegar are added and the soup is garnished with chopped vegetables—cucumbers, green peppers and occasionally hard-boiled eggs. The *gazpacho* is allowed to settle for a while in the bowl to mix its own tastes with the odor and the deep earth flavor of the cool clay; it is placed in shadow and moved as the shadow moves through the day. Some people add their own ingredients to the floating layer, from croutons to fresh pitted cherries. Those who like to dip into the cold soup at all hours add bits of ice. As is the rule in Spain, different towns make different versions of this dish—ranging from Jerez de la Frontera, where chopped raw onions are added, to Sanlúcar de Barrameda where mayonnaise is sometimes included and all the ingredients are crushed and put through a sieve, to Málaga where *gazpacho* is called *ajo blanco con uvas* (white garlic with grapes) and has a base of almonds. There is even a hot, winter *gazpacho* from the province of Cádiz, called simply *ajo* (garlic), which is a kind of dried-bread soup. But it is the city of Seville that has made the plain, summer version of *gazpacho* famous throughout the world by keeping the simplest and lightest formula and by adopting modern cooking methods as they appear.

Seville has a special talent for taking an ancient, forgotten custom, first making it her own in grace and lightness, and then popularizing it while keeping it modern all the while. A second, summer *gazpacho* has resulted from this talent for combining the very old with the very new. (*Gazpacho* is not by any means a new dish; it is mentioned in Greek and Roman literature as a "drinkable food," and references to it appear in both testaments of the Bible.) It was during my first summer in Seville that the city was struck by the Plague of the Electric Blender. The first omen, a cylindrical brown package, arrived late in the afternoon and was looked at suspiciously through the geraniums lining the balconies as the postman carried it up the street to one of the new hotels. For a time then it was ignored. But the seductive sound that came out of the hotel kitchen in the evenings was hard not to listen to. The mechanical siren sang softly and by mid-August everybody had to have one. While Europeans and Americans living in Seville collected Andalusian antique furniture, the Andalusians installed American refrigerators in their living rooms and enshrined new blenders on red velvet in glass cases

A tureen of *gazpacho*, southern Spain's deservedly renowned cold vegetable soup, sits on a terrace table at the Rio Grande restaurant in Seville. Around it are bowls of garnishes made from some of the ingredients included in the soup. Clockwise, starting above the ladle, are: bread cubes, chopped egg, onions, tomatoes, cucumber and red and green peppers. Diners add these garnishes to the *gazpacho* to suit their tastes.

that were locked at night. The maid in the house where I lived prayed for a blender, and the cook went to church and promised the Virgin of the Macarena five candles if she could provide her with one by October. In the hot, humming streets the September sounds of singing and castanet playing were joined by the new, happy noises of atonal buzzing. Many of the houses of Seville, the home of Don Juan, did not have guitars; but they all had blenders. With their new blenders, the people invented a fine and very thick *gazpacho*, leaving behind them an excellent new recipe before they got bored with the whole idea and went back to their original dish. The thick *gazpacho*, which because of its consistency is better refrigerated, is often served today in Seville side by side with the older version. Despite its thickness it remains a light, summer dish, for the Andalusians have an incredible ability to do anything with food without making it heavy or strong.

Another outstanding example of the light touch of Andalusian cooks is also to be found in Seville, as well as Cádiz and Málaga. It is the frying of fish. In other countries fried foods are considered heavy and are the first to be eliminated from a diet that requires lightness in any form. Not so in Andalusia, which has been referred to in the rest of Spain as the zone of frying. What the Andalusians do to make their fried foods so light is again a kind of culinary magic. Only the best olive oil is used, but there are no mysterious ingredients, and it is said that you can watch an Andaluz fry fish all day and still not know how he does it. Try it. Walk along the Calle Sierpes, a wide, trafficless street in Seville that is shaded by an awning to keep off the sun—the awning is dampened from time to time to freshen the bloated, summer air. Sierpes is a sort of shopping bazaar and meeting place for the citizens of the city. Along the side streets you will see stands where fish is fried and sold. Under the summer sun the thought of eating hot, fried food is strange to those who are not used to it. But go and watch the man in the first stand you pass. Behind him is a deep vat of hot oil, beside him the prepared flour, in front of him a wide variety of raw fish. Ask him for a mixed order, and he will dip the bright pink mullets, sole, fresh sardines and other fish into the flour and then gently slide them into the glittering oil. If you are a man, he will tell you jokes, if a woman he will pay you compliments in the Andalusian accent of thick sibilants and shortened words, and he will know when the fish is done behind him and scoop it out, allowing it to drain while he prepares a cone of brown paper to hold it. He will watch you carry the fish back to the Calle Sierpes, wait as you wait until it is cool enough to touch and keep his eyes on the back of your head while you taste it. The fish, no matter what kind, will be so crisp that you must hold a hand under your mouth to catch the splintered slivers as you bite. It will be more delicate in texture and flavor and much lighter than any fried food you have eaten. You may take it to the nearest bar or cafe and sit and order a glass or two of *fino*, dry white wine, and no matter how steaming the day you will manage to finish the paper coneful of fish because by now you will think of it as perfect hot-weather food.

In summer an Andalusian does not often sit down to a proper meal. Things are eaten almost unnoticeably as the day moves slowly in the heat, and life is touched lightly as it goes. The hot hours are many and a man prefers to sit with his friends, lazily chatting and eating a bit of this or that. He may well choose fish or shellfish, for once outside the center of Spain, seafood is the best fare, the freshest, most abundant and most remarkable in its variety. A few spiny lobsters will do nicely, or some *langostinos,* a species of shrimp-like shellfish, then perhaps even some raw oysters or clams with freshly squeezed lemon juice, or a saucer of broiled river crabs. A man may prefer a small casserole of *huevos a la flamenca (Recipe Index)*, a Sevillian invention of eggs baked with "just a few vegetables" such as fresh garden peas, asparagus tips, tomatoes, pimientos, sweet peppers and a few green beans with a slice or two of *chorizo* and ham and perhaps a drop or two of sherry. By early afternoon enough food and white wine have been consumed to send the Sevillano into one of the cafés along the Calle Sierpes. The long rows of shop windows here are lined with armchairs where he may drink a cup of sweetened coffee, smoke a cigar in the cool shade of a building and watch the hot, wandering tourists who in turn are watching him. In the hottest part of the day he will go home to sleep behind closed, dampened green shutters overlooking the now noiseless streets of Seville, which will be empty during the afternoon hours. On a working day he will return to the office around 4 p.m. At 6 o'clock he will have a snack, maybe a single pastry or a sweet and after that a little wine. He will go home around 8 o'clock, and later he may want some sherry and a dish of squid *a la andaluza,* a term which generally means that the food is simmered in a light flavorful sauce of tomatoes and pimientos. He will not want anything heavy, not really any dinner that he will admit to, for serious meals are limited to the short winter months, unless a man is a host entertaining friends. Here in the south, life is a series of light *tapas* while a man stores up his energy for the many feast days and festivals when he must do things in one long siege, whether he likes it or not.

Among the most elaborate of all Spanish festivals is Holy Week, celebrated throughout the country, but nowhere as it is in the south and nowhere in the south quite the way it is in Seville. This is a time of Catholic processions, Moorish sweets, Andalusian foods, coffee, chocolate, *anís* and other liquors, a period in which the Sevillano literally stays up all night eating, drinking and watching the floats pass by. If he is lucky enough to live in an apartment with a balcony, on a street where a procession will pass, he will invite his friends in to watch—or they will come uninvited—and his wife must prepare food, wines and liquors to last around the clock, for guests will come before the passing show and will stay after it is done. There will be sausages and there will be cooked dishes such as *menudos a la gitanilla* (sweetbreads gypsy style) simmered slowly in a sauce of onions and chickpeas—a dish invented in Triana, the gypsy quarter of Seville separated from the main part of the city by the Guadalquivir River. There may be a casserole of hare, not laden with heavy pork and other meats as are stews of the central plateau, but freshened with vegetables and a light wine-flavored gravy. And there might also be a dish of sliced, tender veal kidneys cooked in dry sherry *(Recipe Index)* with the quick, almost volatile taste of that wine. Platters of cold, boiled shellfish will stand next to a bowl of *ensalada sevillana,* the Seville salad whose bright taste is made simply of escarole and pitted, small, green olives with a little fresh tarragon in the dressing. At one end of the table, next to the liquors and liqueurs, will be an array of Holy Week pastries and other everyday sweets whose recipes have been inherited from the Muslims and carefully protected for centuries by the nuns of Catholic convents. Andalusians have an almost oriental liking for sweets, and the Moorish, Arabic and Jewish desserts here are by far the best in Spain: *tortas de aceite (Recipe Index),* cakes made with olive oil, sesame seeds and *anís; cortados rellenos de cidra,* small rectangular tarts filled with puréed sweetened squash; *torteras,* large round cakes made with cinnamon and squash and decorated with powdered sugar are among the most typical. The recipes for these flaky pastries and wine-soaked cakes call for flour, sugar, butter, oil, cinnamon, cloves, honey or a tart-sweet syrup made from apples, squash, wine, and the juices and pulps of lemons and bitter oranges. They do not seem to fill the stomach, and their taste, the quintessence of sweetness, avoids cloying richness. They may be surrounded decoratively by a line of *yemas de San Leandro,* egg-yolk sweets made by the nuns of the nearby convent of San Leandro whose recipes are secured with them inside the convent walls. The egg yolks are poured through needlelike holes onto boiling syrup, and the threads collected into strands of "angel hair" that are twisted to cool; the result is fine and so sweet it makes your teeth hurt. In the center of all the *yemas* and pastries there may be a pie-shaped marzipan, cobwebbed with geometric designs, a reminder that the Koran prohibits the representation of human figures.

Holy Week is a week of rivalry in Seville. Each hostess tries to outdo her neighbor in the quality of food she serves as well as the elegance of its presentation. On the streets of the city, the rich, jeweled Virgin of the Macarena with her wide gold-encrusted train vies with the poor gypsy Virgin of the Esperanza from the church across the Guadalquivir River, who has almost no jewels and whose train is embroidered not with gold, but with flowers. The *cofradías*, or brotherhoods, from each church carry the figures of Christ and the Virgin through the city, the two agonized faces almost invariably appearing the same age, more like husband and wife than mother and son. They are followed by barefoot penitents bearing crosses and dragging chains from their ankles, some of them barebacked and carrying whips. The men of each brotherhood walk ahead of and behind their floats, dressed in long, formal, hooded robes of the Inquisition, carrying candles and incense and sometimes strewing rosemary branches in the path of the Virgin. I once watched the brotherhoods of two rival Virgins arrive at the same square at the same time. The resulting argument—to decide which Virgin would cross first—sounded anything but reverent.

In the pagan fury of the Holy Week celebration, the heads of the brotherhoods tend to forget that each rival figure is meant to represent the same Lady, and they may call each other's Most Holy Virgin by names unrepeatable to their wives the next morning. From balconies and streets along the way spectators sing to the Virgins songs of torment and flattery called *saetas*, arrows, or songs shot to heaven. The men carrying the floats pause and rock the Ladies from side to side while a singer finishes the cry of praise. Then the bands in front take up the mournful tune of Holy Week and the processions move on. People in the balconies sit dewy-eyed drinking *anís* or brandy, eating the last of the light pastries, in the heavy night air that is thick with the odors of incense, crushed rosemary and candle smoke. On the streets below others sit at tables to watch the dawn, sipping cups of chocolate and eating *buñuelos de viento*, fritters "of air" that are weightless bubbles made of dough much like that of the Madrid *churro*. It has been said that the Sevillanos are so expert in the art of frying that they can even fry air.

Holy Week in Andalusia is followed by a week or more of rest to recuperate and clean up the streets for the week of the *Feria*, the fair that is celebrated in city, town and country village as a kind of antidote to the last grievous processions of the Crucifixion. In the south everything, food to festival, must end on a light, buoyant note. The famous *Feria* of Seville is worth seeing, but I prefer to travel down the river during the time of the fair to a town where late at night the *cante jondo*, or deep flamenco song, is sung. In Sanlúcar de Barrameda at the mouth of the Guadalquivir where the river meets the sea, flamenco singing, wines and foods of the town are all superb.

Visit Sanlúcar at 4:00 in the morning. A tavern filled with dust near the port. The moon dirty and strong on the water, and the tang of open bottles of dry *manzanilla* sherry, some spilled and evaporating on the sea-warped tables. Smells of wine and the soiled, emptying river and the acrid, fresh wind from the sea. A dozen people too poor to visit the Seville Fair, sitting at tables, drinking the *manzanilla* and sometimes dipping into a pot of cooked, tiny squid and broad beans tasting of the open sea and the warm land. A plate of fried squid rings and another of cold, juicy rolls of thin veal. The river water sounding on the sand outside and then the piercing, deep, guttural wail of the flamenco singer—almost a scream—starts, stops, starts again and slides into a harsh gut-bled song of lament. A guitar follows the singer, whose face and voice express hurt and then anguish, joy in agony, pain in ecstasy. That is *cante jondo,* the lament of a people enslaved, of lovers of Christ and Mohammed and the God of Wrath, of a lost land: of Spain.

There is more wine and a plate of raw, pickled fish fillets covered with finely chopped, fresh garlic and parsley, and there is a platter of wonderful small clams that were thrown live on a griddle to steam in their juices, and a deep saucer filled with bits of boiled white fish, pimientos, eggs and raw purple onions, all marinated in wine vinegar and oil. Then there is more food and wine and more singing until the *manzanilla* lightens the head of the singer and his music achieves an unearthly gaiety. Deep song changes to a light gypsy rhythm known as *bulerías.* An old woman stands up and lifts her arms, freezes, then breaks the freeze and jerks forward, twisting with the music, having fun with the singer, dancing with the controlled, infinite wit of the *bailadora,* the guitar dancer that only Andalusia can produce and that, like very great aged wine, does not travel well. Of all the folk arts of the earth, true flamenco is second to none. Like Andalusian food it has grace. It is deeper and it is lighter and more completely moving than seems possible, and there is no emotion it does not hold, for its range is that of the universe.

The singing and dancing end now in Sanlúcar as the day breaks over the white morning mouth of the river. People walk off not to sleep but to coffee, a sugar pastry, possibly a taste of *anís* and then to work. Summer days are long here and in a port town work starts early. The fishermen will have gone out before dawn, and some are coming in to sell their catch at auction on a pier at the river edge of town.

The fishermen's auction begins as each catch is separated and the fish are sorted in rows of dark wood boxes along the wet pier. There are boxes heaped with inch-long *chanquetes,* a kind of whitebait from Málaga waters, and others of *boquerones,* anchovies. There are sardines, live lobsters, brown clams and translucent squid of all sizes. And there are gnarled-looking green and rosy octopuses with a hundred more varieties of fish and shellfish that have been caught in the Atlantic waters of the Gulf of Cádiz down to Algeciras and through the Strait of Gibraltar into the warmer Mediterranean waters. Sharks too big for the boxes lie in rows between with flat eyes and bared teeth, and the now slithery pier reeks with the many live and dead odors of the seas—of scales and iodine, seaweed and sand. The auctioneer puts his foot on a box of pink medium-sized mullet and intones a list of prices from very high to low until someone raises a hand or grunts his acceptance. Those who buy are not housewives, for this is a wholesale auction. The buyers are market-stall owners or managers of fish markets and chefs from restaurants and hotels in this and the neighboring province. Once someone has bought a large box wholesale, a housewife may then approach him for what she needs, half or a quarter of a kilo from its contents. Many

In a gaily decorated cart, happy young travelers from Seville set out for the shrine of the Virgin of El Rocío. The pilgrimage, described in this chapter, attracts people from all over western Andalusia.

52

women come here to buy because the prices are lower than they will be even in the noon market of the town a short walk away. They watch the auction carefully and listen to the prices so they can later argue over the amount of profit. Some bring their children, little boys and girls who seem to wander about aimlessly, but who watch carefully as clams are poured into boxes and who pick up the few that spill over the side, one by one. A handful is worth taking over to the mother, who opens her market basket without looking as the child comes near to drop the clams inside. The mother seems hardly aware of what the child is doing. But five or six clams, three shrimp "found" outside a box, the heads of a few *langostinos,* the head or body of a fish that was sliced off accidentally as two boxes jostled together—and there will be a grand fish soup by afternoon.

The fish soup of the poor people in Sanlúcar is like a light essence of the sea, a kind of seafood consommé, in which the ingredients have been brewed until only shell or bone is left. Little seasoning is used, maybe just a bay leaf and a little salt. The broth is first reduced to a purified liquid about the consistency of good perfume and about as strong in its odor. Sometimes river fish and crabs are cooked in it too, thickening the soup and mingling the elements of river and ocean. The soup may be drunk on even the hottest days, because there is no heaviness to it no matter how much fish it contains. A bowl of it with half a bottle of cool dry *manzanilla* from one of the Sanlúcar cellars where it is bottled, and you will feel lighter for having eaten. This is perhaps the most important function of the Andalusian kitchen, and the wines of the region have been designed to suit this single purpose.

White wines, including sherries, are often preferred for food accompaniment in Andalusia, just as red wines usually take the precedence in central Spain. All of the whites—the *manzanilla* of Sanlúcar, the *finos olorosos* of nearby El Puerto de Santa María, the more famous sherries of Jerez de la Frontera and the *blancos de pasto* of Chiclana de la Frontera—can be enjoyed shortly before Pentecost, together with a collection of many of the best Andalusian peasant foods, near a small shrine called El Rocío in the province of Huelva, which is separated from the province of Cádiz by the Guadalquivir River. If you wish to know the quicksilver quality of country cooking in Andalusia, El Rocío is the place to go.

The yearly Pentecostal pilgrimage to the shrine of the Virgin of El Rocío is a shining event. Caravans start out from cities and villages in the neighboring provinces, converging on the little Huelva town. I left from Sanlúcar with a caravan that started early one Sunday morning in the first week of June from the courtyard of the long, elegant palace of the Duchess of Medina Sidonia high on top of the village. The palace has belonged to the family of Medina Sidonia since the 14th Century and now is the property of the young duchess. Luisa Isabel Alvarez de Toledo y Maura, Duquesa de Medina Sidonia, is known as the Democratic Duchess, and she is one of the country's most controversial figures. Bearing the oldest title in Spain, she is the only member of the Spanish nobility who has dared to criticize openly the Franco dictatorship—as a result of which she has lost everything from her passport to the custody of her three children. In 1969 she spent eight months in a prison for writing a novel called *The Strike* that is critical of the Franco regime. This gallant woman opposes Fascism and Communism equally, and is a favorite of Sanlúcar's working class, many of whom came to the palace on this day to escort her to El Rocío.

There were 28 of us on horseback as we started on the pilgrimage, the men dressed in the manner of the Andalusian rider, wearing tight, striped riding pants and boots, short high jackets and flat gray hats. Many carried women behind them on the saddles, each woman sitting crosswise, feet crossed at the ankles below the left rear haunch of the horse and right arm pressed tight around the waist of the rider. They were dressed in the bright pastels of the Andalusian fiesta costume of tight bodice and sensual wide scalloped skirt. The horses clattered in the white palace courtyard, and the duchess ran down to meet us, looking young and small and very slim, dressed to ride alone like the men. She gave us steaming coffee and *anís* and wine-cakes and then mounted and rode down with us, the horses' hooves resounding over cobblestones in the sleepy, early morning village as we headed out for the river near the port of Sanlúcar.

A covered wagon containing provisions was waiting for us, and another covered wagon decorated with silver and blue paper embroidered in white with an image of the Virgin was standing by. The morning was fresh and a stinging, salt-laden wind blew in from the sea. Horses reared at the water's edge, and the people of Sanlúcar came to wave goodbye as the caravans started across the river. Some brought bottles of wine and plates of shrimp to offer the riders; others danced frothy, light *sevillanas* on the sand while the horses and wagons were loaded onto barges. *Sevillanas* are danced by couples, a man and a woman or two women, and there are four determined *coplas*, or couplets, to dance. They are sung as well, accompanied by a guitar if there is one, or by loud clapping if there is not. We could still hear them behind us as the barge pushed out into the flowing winds of the river and started for the western bank. The rider next to me was a field hand, his face burned dark by the sun, brown and gleaming in the white dawn, and ahead of him was the duchess. There are no class distinctions in the Rocío pilgrimage; food and drink are shared by all equally, for the only superior rank is that of the Virgin waiting at the shrine.

There was a light, chill mist from the open ocean to our left, and a woman from one of the wagons handed back a chunk of *serrano* ham, a piece of bread and a wineskin of *manzanilla* that was full to bursting. The barge tossed and the wagons rattled as we came near the middle of the river. The wind from the ocean was strong now and sharp, and I ate a little of the ham with the bread and drank some of the wine. *Serrano* ham, which is similar to prosciutto, is cured in the snows of one of the mountain ranges in the Sierra Morena. It is cut thicker than prosciutto and is sweeter than any ham in the world. *Serrano* ham from Jabugo in Huelva, 50 miles from where we were going, is the best in Spain and is eaten throughout the Iberian Peninsula. The chunks are almost crunchy and the sweet-salt taste unbelievably good. But crossing the Guadalquivir in the fresh, running winds over the water, where the spraying ocean joins the river, even Jabugo's ham flavor is heightened. On the barge, ham, sausages and wine were passed to all the riders and to the bargemen. From where I sat I could see the empty beaches of Huelva ahead, and behind us the high, white town of Sanlúcar topped by the red Moorish castle and by the sleek Medina Sidonia palace. The tastes of the ham and the wine on the barge and the look of the houses and the castle and palace growing smaller behind it have probably not changed a great deal since the day Columbus set sail on his third voyage from this same port, the town of Sanlúcar de Barrameda.

Horses neighed before the tossing barge landed and a few riders in front began to clap and sing, a loud rhythm of their own against the rhythms of the river and the sea. Then the horses plowed into the low surf on the Huelva beach and cantered up the powdered sand to the edge of the grass. The wagons were drawn by mules, and as they were beached, a few women carried pots and casseroles of food onto the sand to keep them from spilling. Then they climbed back inside and the caravan started overland, skirting the soggy earth at first, then aiming straight across the marshes of Huelva known as Las Marismas.

There were five to six hours of hard riding ahead of us before we would come to a place dry enough to stop for lunch, and now a man on horseback rode up and down the caravan passing open wineskins, plates of fried fish and a pot of the tiny oysterlike bivalves called *ostiones*. These are found only in the province of Cádiz and are tough unless cooked but tender and sea-sharp when simmered in white wine with tomatoes, pimientos, onions and bay leaf. There were several spoons in the pot, and the riders dipped in, for foods that might spoil under the sun had to be eaten now. People drank long from the wineskins, holding them high so that the amber glitter of white wine turned to a hard gold under the light of the day. To the left of the caravan a tall, pink flamingo rose, flapping loudly. The rider with the food tossed me the last wineskin and told me not to dismount until we reached a dry place where the earth was safe.

Riding under the sun is thirst-making and much wine was consumed as we wove the wagons, carrying the embroidered image of the Virgin and the provisions, around flat patches of dark water and lighter quicksand and then into the Coto Doñana game preserve, one of the largest in Europe. Flights of wild duck winged over us and an eagle soared high, sitting on the wind and very still against the fierce, flat blue. I rode ahead for a while and watched the grass before us flow in the wind. A few riders galloped fast beyond me, laughing and singing, one of them chewing on a loaf of bread filled with raw, sweet peppers soaked in oil. We were all hungry by noon but we rode on farther into the marshes, a little dizzy from the sun and the wine and the sway of the horses in the deep earth.

By 3 o'clock we reached a place that had been a clearing, but water had seeped in and there was hardly room for half a dozen people to stand. Women from the provision wagon stepped down with bowls of brick-red and white almond *gazpacho*, a plate filled with hard-roll sandwiches of grilled, thin veal and breaded cutlets and a heaping platter of green peppers that had been grilled that morning over coals, peeled and salted. There were cold, crisp roasted chickens and a casserole of chicken that had been simmered in white wine. The peppers were warm from the heat inside the wagon, but the taste of the green was refreshing and the salt went well with more wine. Most people ate on horseback, passing the food around. Now it was not the dangers of the marsh, but the effect of the *manzanilla* in the glowing heat, that made standing a problem. I dipped a spoon into the delicate, thin wine gravy of the chicken casserole and scooped out a piece of dark meat onto a chunk of bread. The tastes of sherry and bay leaf had soaked through the meat; the quick, pungent smell was light and fine, we were hungry in the marsh air, but we did not wait long after eating to ride again.

Before the endless blue Andalusian twilight began to gather, we had passed herds of wild deer and tall, handsome stags with high-branched antlers, and late in the day we came to a blur on the horizon that turned quickly into a chain of wild horses. Some of the riders chased them, calling out as they rode, but the wild horses were faster than the tame ones and quickly blurred blue as smoke into the darkening marshland. The riders were hungry again but there was no safe place for us to stop before night. And so the caravan kept moving.

In the distance were three dark blots too big to be horses. I kept my eyes on them but they did not move. Then I heard a man shout, and I looked to my left in time to see a horse wheel and several riders follow as the young duchess rode off suddenly in the direction of the distant dark blots. Her horse floated over the marsh grass and I watched the blots move sharply ahead of her, running to the right. They were bulls. The eastern rim of the marsh is not a preserve but a *criadero*, a breeding place for brave bulls to be sent later to bull rings all over Spain. Running the bulls alone in the marsh is not safe. The horse can fall, or the bulls may turn viciously on the rider. The duchess was running three of them dangerously toward a far-off river with the low east wind behind her. Riders went after her, several forgetting that they carried women on the backs of their saddles, and there were screams and mud-spattered horses neighing and a burst of laughter for a few moments in the wet air. The running of bulls, outside the ring as well as in, is a national Spanish sport, pastime or art; seldom is it done as gracefully or wittily as in the south. A great horsewoman in Andalusia, like a great cook, has a natural lightness and a special ease and simplicity that are marvelous to watch. For half an hour the slight, young, boyish figure stayed far ahead of the other riders, turning the huge, black bulls evenly to the right or left as she chose, as if at the end of an invisible whip, once knifing quickly between them before she let them go and rode back alone and smiling to join the caravan. "Now we are all hungry," she called, laughing, as she passed and took her place in the line of riders. The air turned cool then and the twilight deepened as we rode out of the marsh.

Fires were lit near the Palace of Santa Ana in the Coto Doñana where we camped for the night, and the women in the second wagon hurriedly reheated the chicken casserole and cooked new food. Two large slabs of meat that had been marinating in wine were salted and turned on spits over the fire, allowed to burn fast so that the juices were seared in. People cut off thin slices that were black on the outside and purple within, and ate them with bread, tomatoes and paper-thin slices of raw, purple onion. The wine-soaked meat was alive with flavor, light and juicy on the slivers of onion and bread crusts warmed by the fire, and the tomatoes were sweet and bursting. The casserole was still simply flavored, but reheating it made the quick taste still sharper. Nothing had been kept that might spoil during the day. One of the women from the wagon had a few eggs in a bowl of water that was cooled with ice. She broke them into a dry bowl and then peeled and sliced a few po-

Continued on page 60

Gifts for the World from Andalusia

Andalusia's heel-stomping flamenco danced to the rhythm of handclaps and guitar, is enjoyed everywhere—Mariquilla *(below)*, from Granada, performs it in the Chateau Madrid in New York. Equally international today is the wine of Andalusia, the golden sherry *(following pages)* that is now savored the world over.

Beyond Spain's borders, sherry is sometimes regarded—or disregarded—as a drink for old ladies or retired gentlemen in overstuffed clubs. The wine was given its name by the Englishmen who could come no closer to pronouncing Jerez (the full name is Jerez de la Frontera), the town in Andalusia where the sherry is produced. In its home country, sherry is everyman's drink. At ordinary bars like the one shown below, it is served from the cask, while in more elegant places (*opposite*) it is accompanied by *tapas*, such as bowls of shrimp, potato chips and olives.

tatoes into a hot skillet with a little oil. She let the potatoes sizzle on the fire while she beat the eggs with a fork; then she salted and poured the eggs into the skillet and covered the mixture with a plate till it browned on one side. She turned the skillet deftly upside down over the fire, caught the half-done potato omelet, or *tortilla de patata (Recipe Index)* as it is called in Spain, in the plate, turned and slid it back onto the skillet. The potato omelet steamed in the cool of the night, its odor joining those of other foods, and when done, it was cut like a pie from the center, its wedges handed out to those who were hungriest. The women from the wagon quickly made another potato omelet, this one with slices of onion cooked in it. Eaten hot now, or cold later on, the omelets were as light and fresh as the evening. In case the night turned cold, there was a casserole of hot winter *gazpacho* and there were roasted sardines lying on a bed of sweet red peppers. There was a basket of pale pink apricots, ripe Japanese plums from the trees of Sanlúcar, oranges and sun-warmed apples. The evening meal was truly a light feast and people went about it slowly, savoring the foods with the wine, many of them falling asleep stretched out where they had eaten.

The sun was high the next morning when we reached El Rocío; I was thirstier than I could remember ever having been before. Hundreds of people were already walking and singing and dancing and riding around the little church with the shrine, until the dry earth rose in a dusty cloud over the moving bodies. I walked in the dust until I found a man who was pouring a bottle of light, red wine into a blue and green ceramic pitcher, and I waited while he washed some oranges, sliced them into the wine and then added slices of lemon, a bit of sugar, a long splash of brandy, and finally a small bottle of soda water and some ice. He mixed it hard with a wooden spoon, crushing some of the fruit, and then he gave me a glassful. The blood-red *sangría* *(Recipe Index)* is the exception in this land of white wine, but it is the most cooling summer drink I know and one of the most thirst-quenching. It is fruity and light and sparkling on the tongue. It need not be strong and can be made sweet or dry according to the amount of sugar used. Any fruits at all and many liqueurs may be added, among the latter Cointreau, Triple Sec or other fruit liqueurs. The simpler the better is the rule in Spain, and the plain *sangría* I drank at El Rocío is the best I have tasted. It was our staple liquid for the next six hot days.

Singing and dancing to guitars and reed pipes and drums lasted until the following Sunday, with people sleeping under the wagons or in the fields and villages nearby, and when the figure of the Virgin was finally carried out, the whole camped pilgrimage was fevered with wine, sun and fiesta. There was a moment's silence as she appeared in her gilded shrine, tall and white-faced, grim in sadness, and then a long shivering shout exploded out of the crowd while people climbed, reached, jumped and tore over each other to touch her skirts or the bottom of the float. Bowls of food and pitchers of wine were trampled and plates were broken in the dust and the pilgrimage reached its climax, with people dizzily screaming, *"Viva la Virgen del Rocío . . . Viva! . . ."* through the night till morning when spirits ebbed as the light grew and each wagon, sad and empty, started for home.

We took the long route, looping down around the Huelva beaches, and stopped to buy bottles of sherry and to roast wild ducks over an open fire in the sand. While the ducks were crisping, a horseman rode out to a fishing village for some fresh sardines. We cut long canes from a field and split the canes open halfway down. Then we slipped the sardines crosswise inside the split canes and stuck the canes deep into the sand, leaning at an angle over the fire until the sardines had cooked, sputtering their oil into the high, licking flames. We ate them with our fingers, two bites from each side of the fish. They were pungent and fresh and light in the open ocean air, and the dry sherry and crisp-skinned, steaming chunks of tender duck that followed made a meal that could not have been better for all the sauces, spices and herbs in the world. Some of the simplicity and magic of that meal is the essence of Andalusia.

On the return to Sanlúcar from the pilgrimage I drove east, through endless, small towns in the green and brown hillsides. I stopped for an afternoon in the city of Córdoba to see the building I like best in Andalusia, the Mezquita, an 8th Century Moorish mosque that is a magnificent thrust of high, delicate columns made of onyx, jasper, marble and granite, a rainbow of colors filtering through them under a tinted, cedar ceiling. The lightest and airiest structure imaginable. Behind the Mezquita to the left is a restaurant so small you pass it if you walk too quickly; it serves a special local dish of bulls' tails in a sharp thin sauce with an herb-wine flavor that tastes both meaty and green.

I drove east from there over snow-topped mountains to Granada, where the Alhambra palace, summer residence of the caliphs and the last stronghold of the Moors in this land, stands next to the white Generalife Garden, each detail of which is designed to enhance repose in a cool forest of carefully kept jasmine, cypress and yew trees. It is good to see, and you can drive from it down over the Sierra Nevada to the Mediterranean, thus avoiding the high-built, hotel-ridden, playground beaches of Málaga, and then follow the coast up toward the part of Spain known as the Levante.

On the way, I detoured one last time to see some friends in Almería, the easternmost province of Andalusia. On a Mediterranean beach we collected mussels from the rocks and cooked them over a small fire with garlic, parsley, lemon juice and white wine, with a bit of mustard thrown in. The mussels steamed open and the juices and the sauce simmered together. We ate them with bread dipped in the light sauce and drank a bottle of dry almost colorless wine from that region. The province of Murcia and those of the Levante lay above, along the coast, and below us was Africa and the warm southern winds of the desert across the sea. That too is Andalusia.

In the morning I drove north, taking the inland road at first and then going by the poorer, coast road through pine trees out of the south into fields spotted with red poppies like a sprinkle of blood on the earth. And from there I came into the first gentle, dark yellow land of the saffron growers that marks the next way of cooking in Spain.

The small Andalusian town of Jabugo is famous for its hams and spicy *chorizo*
sausages. The sausages are used in many dishes including some versions of *paella*
and *cocido madrileño (both in Recipe Index)*. They are stuffed and tied *(left)* by
women of the village, working in a cooperative plant. The tied sausages are then
hung on the rafters of a drying room, where they are exposed for about two
weeks to smoke from several small fires made of *encina*, an evergreen oak.

To serve 6

6 tablespoons olive oil
1 cup finely chopped onions
1 teaspoon finely chopped garlic
1 small bay leaf
2 tablespoons flour
½ cup beef or chicken stock, fresh or canned
2 tablespoons finely chopped parsley
2 pounds veal kidneys, split lengthwise in half, trimmed of all fat, and cut into 1-inch cubes
Salt
Freshly ground black pepper
½ cup pale dry sherry

Riñones al Jerez
SAUTÉED KIDNEYS WITH SHERRY SAUCE

In a heavy 8- to 10-inch skillet, heat 4 tablespoons of the olive oil over moderate heat until a light haze forms above it. Add the onions, garlic and bay leaf. Stirring frequently, cook for 5 minutes, or until the onions are soft and transparent but not brown. Add the flour and mix thoroughly. Pour in the stock and, stirring constantly, cook over high heat until the mixture thickens heavily and comes to a boil. Add the parsley, reduce the heat to low, and simmer for about 3 minutes. Set aside.

Heat the remaining 2 tablespoons of olive oil in a heavy 10- to 12-inch skillet. Sprinkle the kidneys liberally with salt and a few grindings of pepper. Then cook them in the hot oil for 4 or 5 minutes, turning them about with a large spoon and regulating the heat so that they brown quickly on all sides without burning.

Transfer the kidneys to a plate and pour the sherry into the pan. Bring to a boil over high heat, meanwhile scraping in any brown particles clinging to the bottom and sides of the pan. Return the kidneys to the pan, stir in the reserved onion sauce and bring to a boil. Reduce the heat to low, simmer a minute or two and taste for seasoning.

Serve the kidneys at once, accompanied if you like by saffron rice (*Recipe Index*) and garnished with strips of pimiento.

To serve 6 to 8

SOUP
2 medium-sized cucumbers, peeled and coarsely chopped
5 medium-sized tomatoes, peeled and coarsely chopped
1 large onion, coarsely chopped
1 medium-sized green pepper, deribbed, seeded and coarsely chopped
2 teaspoons finely chopped garlic
4 cups coarsely crumbled French or Italian bread, trimmed of crusts
4 cups cold water
¼ cup red wine vinegar
4 teaspoons salt
4 tablespoons olive oil
1 tablespoon tomato paste

GARNISH
1 cup ¼-inch bread cubes, trimmed of crusts
½ cup finely chopped onions
½ cup peeled and finely chopped cucumbers
½ cup finely chopped green peppers

Gazpacho
COLD FRESH VEGETABLE SOUP

In a deep bowl, combine the coarsely chopped cucumbers, tomatoes, onion and green pepper, garlic and crumbled bread, and mix together thoroughly. Then stir in the water, vinegar and salt. Ladle the mixture, about 2 cups at a time, into the jar of a blender and blend at high speed for 1 minute, or until reduced to a smooth purée. Pour the purée into a bowl and with a whisk beat in the olive oil and tomato paste.

(To make the soup by hand, purée the vegetable and bread mixture in a food mill or, with the back of a large spoon, rub it through a sieve set over a bowl. Discard any pulp left in the mill or sieve. Beat the olive oil and tomato paste into the purée.)

Cover the bowl tightly with foil or plastic wrap and refrigerate for at least 2 hours, or until thoroughly chilled. Just before serving, whisk or stir the soup lightly to recombine it. Then ladle it into a large chilled tureen or individual soup plates.

Accompany the *gazpacho* with the bread cubes and the vegetable garnishes presented in separate serving bowls to be added to the soup at the discretion of each diner.

NOTE: If you prefer crisp croutons for the garnish, fry the bread cubes. In a 6- to 8-inch skillet, heat ¼ cup of olive oil over moderate heat until a light haze forms above it. Drop in the bread cubes and, turning them frequently, cook them until they are crisp and golden brown on all sides. Drain on paper towels and cool.

Ternera a la Sevillana
SAUTÉED VEAL WITH SHERRY AND GREEN OLIVES

To serve 6

In a small glass, enameled, or stainless-steel saucepan, bring 2 cups of water to a boil over high heat. Drop in the olives, reduce the heat to low and simmer for 2 minutes. Drain the olives in a sieve or colander and run cold water over them to stop their cooking. Set aside.

For the *sofrito,* heat ½ cup of the olive oil in a heavy 10- to 12-inch skillet over moderate heat until a light haze forms above it. Add the onions, garlic and green pepper and stirring frequently, cook for 5 minutes, or until the vegetables are soft but not brown. Add the mushrooms, tomatoes, olives, ham and pulverized almonds, and bring to a boil, stirring constantly. Cook briskly until most of the liquid in the pan evaporates and the mixture is thick enough to hold its shape lightly in a spoon. Set aside.

Sprinkle the veal scallops liberally with salt and a few grindings of pepper. Dip them in the flour and shake them vigorously to remove all but a light dusting. Heat the remaining ½ cup of oil in another 10- to 12-inch skillet until a light haze forms above it. Cook the scallops (in two batches if necessary) for 3 or 4 minutes on each side, turning them with tongs and regulating the heat so that they brown quickly and evenly without burning.

As they brown, transfer the scallops to a plate. Discard the oil remaining in the pan and in its place pour in the sherry and water. Bring to a boil over high heat, meanwhile scraping in any brown particles clinging to the bottom and sides of the skillet. Then add the reserved *sofrito* and stir together thoroughly. Taste the sauce for seasoning.

Return the veal to the skillet, lower the heat, cover tightly and simmer for 4 or 5 minutes, or until the scallops are tender when pierced with the point of a small, sharp knife.

To serve, arrange the scallops attractively in a row down the center of a deep heated platter, overlapping them slightly, pour the sauce evenly over them and serve at once.

12 pitted green Spanish olives
1 cup olive oil
2 cups finely chopped onions
1 tablespoon finely chopped garlic
2 small green peppers, deribbed, seeded and finely chopped
¼ pound fresh mushrooms, sliced ⅛ inch thick (about 2 cups sliced)
4 medium-sized tomatoes peeled, seeded, and finely chopped (*see huevos a la flamenca, page 16*)
½ cup finely diced *serrano* ham, or substitute ⅛ pound prosciutto or other lean smoked ham
2 tablespoons blanched almonds, pulverized in a blender or with a nut grinder or mortar and pestle
Salt
Freshly ground black pepper
1 cup flour
6 veal scallops, cut about ⅜ inch thick and pounded ¼ inch thick
½ cup pale dry sherry
½ cup water

Veal kidneys are cooked in olive oil and tossed in sherry sauce for *riñones al Jerez,* which may be served with rice and pimientos.

To serve 4 to 6

½ lemon, cut into ¼-inch slices
½ orange, cut into ¼-inch slices
½ large apple, cut in half lengthwise,
   cored, and cut into thin wedges
¼ to ½ cup superfine sugar
1 bottle dry red wine, preferably
   imported Spanish wine
2 ounces (¼ cup) brandy
Club soda, chilled
Ice cubes (optional)

To make one 15-inch roll

2 tablespoons butter, softened
6 tablespoons flour
4 egg yolks
¼ cup sugar
⅛ teaspoon salt
4 egg whites
Rum cream filling *(below)*
Confectioners' sugar

To make about 2 cups

2 cups milk
2 two-inch pieces stick cinnamon
1 four-inch piece vanilla bean,
   broken into ½-inch lengths
2 egg yolks
¼ cup sugar
¼ cup flour
1 tablespoon dark rum

Sangría
RED WINE AND FRUIT PUNCH

Combine the lemon, orange, apple and ¼ cup sugar in a large pitcher. Pour in the wine and brandy and stir with a long-handled spoon until well mixed. Taste. If you prefer the *sangría* sweeter, add up to ¼ cup more sugar.

Refrigerate for at least 1 hour or until thoroughly chilled. Just before serving, pour in chilled club soda to taste, adding up to 24 ounces of the soda. Stir again, and serve at once in chilled wine glasses. Or the glasses may be filled with ice cubes before adding the *sangría*.

Brazo de Gitano
SPONGE CAKE ROLL WITH RUM CREAM FILLING

Preheat the oven to 400°. With a pastry brush, coat the bottom and sides of a 10½-by-15½-inch jelly-roll pan with 1 tablespoon of butter. Line the pan with a 20-inch-long strip of wax paper and let the extra paper extend over the ends. Brush the remaining butter over the paper and sprinkle it with 2 tablespoons of flour, tipping the pan from side to side to spread it evenly. Turn the pan over and rap it sharply to remove the excess. Set aside.

With a whisk or a rotary or electric beater, beat the egg whites until they are stiff enough to form unwavering peaks on the beater when it is lifted from the bowl. In another bowl and with the same beater, beat the egg yolks, sugar and salt together until thick and lemon colored. Then sprinkle the remaining 4 tablespoons of flour on top of the whites, pour the yolks over them and, with a rubber spatula, fold together lightly but thoroughly, using an over-under cutting motion rather than a stirring motion.

Pour the batter into the pan, spread it into the corners with a spatula, and smooth the top. Bake in the middle of the oven for 8 minutes, or until the cake begins to come away from the sides of the pan. Remove the cake from the oven and carefully turn it out on a fresh sheet of wax paper. Gently peel off the layer of paper on top of the cake and, starting at one long edge, roll the cake into a loose cylinder. Set aside to cool to room temperature.

To assemble the cake, unroll it and spread the top evenly with rum cream filling. Roll up the cake and place it on a serving plate. Just before serving, sprinkle the top and sides of the cake liberally with confectioners' sugar.

Crema Pastelera al Ron
RUM CREAM FILLING

In a heavy 1- to 1½-quart saucepan, bring the milk, cinnamon stick and vanilla bean to a boil over moderate heat. Cover and set aside off the heat.

In a large mixing bowl, beat the egg yolks and sugar with a whisk or a rotary or electric beater until thick and lemon-colored. Beat in the flour 1 tablespoon at a time. Discard the cinnamon stick and vanilla bean and slowly pour the milk into the egg yolk mixture, beating constantly. Return the mixture to the pan and cook over low heat, stirring constantly with a whisk, until the mixture comes to a boil and thickens heavily. Stir in the rum and set aside off the heat to cool to room temperature. Stir every now and then to prevent a crust from forming on the surface. The cream can be kept in the refrigerator for 2 or 3 days, before being used as a cake or tart filling.

Red wine, brandy, fresh fruit and soda water are stirred together in *Sangría* to make a refreshing drink for the cocktail hour or mealtime.

Almejas a la Marinera
CLAMS IN WHITE WINE WITH GARLIC, ONIONS AND TOMATOES

To make the *sofrito*, heat the oil over moderate heat in a heavy 8- to 10-inch skillet, until a light haze forms above it. Add the onions and garlic. Stirring frequently, cook for 5 minutes or until the onions are soft and transparent but not brown.

Stir in the bread, tomatoes and sieved egg yolk. Cook for about 5 minutes, mashing and stirring with a spoon until most of the liquid in the pan evaporates and the mixture becomes a thick, smooth purée. Set aside.

Place the clams hinged side down in a heavy 10- to 12-inch skillet, pour in the wine and bring to a boil over high heat. Cover tightly, reduce the heat to low, and steam for 8 to 10 minutes or until the clams open. With tongs or a slotted spoon, remove the clams from the skillet and place them on a deep heated platter. Discard any clams that remain closed.

Strain the liquid remaining in the skillet through a fine sieve directly into the *sofrito*. Bring to a boil, stirring constantly; taste and season with salt and a few grindings of pepper.

Pour the sauce over the clams, sprinkle the top with the egg white and parsley and garnish the platter with the lemon wedges. Serve at once.

To serve 2 as a main course, 4 as a first course

3 tablespoons olive oil
½ cup finely chopped onions
1 teaspoon finely chopped garlic
2 tablespoons coarsely crumbled white bread, trimmed of crusts
½ cup peeled, seeded and finely chopped tomatoes (*see huevos a la flamenca, page 16*)
1 hard-cooked egg, the yolk sieved and the white finely chopped
2 dozen small hard-shell clams, washed and thoroughly scrubbed
1 cup dry white wine
Salt
Freshly ground black pepper
2 tablespoons finely chopped parsley
1 lemon, cut into 6 or 8 wedges

67

IV

The Levante, Home of Paella

The east coast of Spain, starting in the south at Cabo de Gata and winding northward past warm Mediterranean waters, has many names. Traditionally it is known as the Levante; *levantar* in Spanish means to rise, and the sun rises in the east. Composed of four provinces—Murcia, Alicante, Valencia and Castellón de la Plana—it has been referred to as the Phoenician Coast because it was a trading place for the Phoenicians, one of the few peoples who did not care to invade the land beyond the mountains. The Spanish Ministry of Information and Tourism has named the southern half of the Levante the White Coast for its brilliant light, and on many maps the northern half is ornately labeled Coast of Orange Blossoms. But it is the kitchens of Spain that have given the Levante its plainest and most accurate title. They call it the Land of Rice.

You will not immediately know how the Levante has earned this name if you enter the region from the southern province of Murcia; the place will not produce its best dishes until it has first shown its wares. But the trip is worth taking to see the ordinary ingredients that will later become elegant and finely wrought, arabesque dishes under the spell of the Levantine cooks. Starting from the south in autumn you will see fields of hot red peppers laid out to dry in the sun, looking like misshapen Andalusian poppies. Sweet red peppers grow in the wide *huertas*, the intricately irrigated vegetable orchards developed by the Moors. There are acres of the dark green Spanish melons, of tomatoes, bitter lemons, white mulberry trees whose leaves are food for the Levantine silkworms, and soft purple beds of crocuses whose dried orange stigmas once provided a highly prized bright yellow dye and now are

A tile-roofed farmhouse and a domed parish church near Valencia stand beyond young rice shoots growing in mud-walled plots known as *planteles*. The shoots are started from seeds in these irrigated plots, then are transplanted to paddies, just as they are in the Oriental homeland of the grain that is so important a part of the Spanish cuisine.

utilized as the equally expensive pungent spice called saffron. You will see olive trees here leading from the Mediterranean to inland salt lagoons, the biggest of which is the Mar Menor, the Lesser Sea, inhabited by roe-laden mullets, eels, snails and *langostinos,* shrimplike creatures native to these waters.

The cooking of this area is a festive prelude to the infinite variety of rice dishes to be encountered farther north in the Levante—for the foods here seem to be produced and designed to be eaten before, with or after some form of rice. Breakfast in Murcia is often just a cup of chocolate, served so thick it has to be eaten rather than drunk, sweet enough to remind strangers that they are still in Muslim territory. As the morning progresses Murcian tables fill with sweet roasted peppers cooked with tomatoes, a combination even more important here than in Andalusia. These ingredients appear in everything from the Murcian omelet to the *pastel murciano,* a pastry whose flaky shell, filled to the brim with roasted peppers and tomatoes, can be further packed to include *chorizo,* veal bits, calf's brains, pieces of hard-boiled egg and other foods. Both of these serve as fine pre-lunch, or rather pre-rice dishes. Another good pre-rice specialty is a baked dish strongly influenced by the Arabs, whose liking for sweets was not limited to desserts, but extended to fish: *merluza,* or hake baked with cinnamon and slices of orange.

After these Murcian dishes have prepared and sweetened the palate for rice, the visitor driving northward in the Levante is ready to approach the midday *comida,* which might best be found in the neighboring province of Alicante. Here you will find a dish worthy of its reputation as the finest example of the way rice ought to be cooked. Look at a map as you drive along in the late morning. At about the midway point on the Levantine coast, there is a huge loop of land pointing out toward the Balearic Islands. Around this loop, where palm and olive trees edge the water, the semi-African scenery changes without warning to a panorama of gentle orange groves and endless, wet, rectangular patches of rice.

Stop at one of the small country restaurants along this part of the coast where the narrow beach slices inland to a very small salt lake. As you come near the restaurant you will see a kind of vast outdoor grill under the open sky, unprotected from the weather, backed only by a plain wall to stop the sandy sea winds. This is the kitchen. Stop and watch the cook make a rice dish for a family of four. He will enjoy your company, and he will not appear to need much concentration for his work. With the deceptive simplicity of a Levantine sorcerer, he will first make an ordinary open-air wood fire of sticks that point in like spokes toward a central point—the point at which the fire will be hottest. In front of the cook is an iron grill large enough to hold as many cooking pans as there are orders from the dining room. When the flames are at their peak, the cook reaches for a flat, round, black metal pan whose slightly sloped sides are about an inch and a half high. He grasps it by the handles on both sides and places it on the grill over the high fire. From a bottle to his right he pours a heavy soundless splash of olive oil into the pan. The oil looks like liquid gold in the glaring Levantine light. He waits until the oil is barely beginning to smoke, and then he throws in a few pieces of pork, some chicken parts, giblets and some slices of sausage. Behind him on a wooden table are peeled tomatoes and other vegetables, plates of cooked red shrimp, white fish, black mussels and very small clams next to *cigalas*, pinkish shellfish that are so big they look like baby lobsters. While the meat is browning, the cook talks willingly about the weather and his work; if you ask he will explain that rice dishes are always better cooked out-of-doors because the high flames must cover and constantly lick the entire bottom surface of the wide black pan, a requirement that would be difficult to manage indoors. He talks and works simultaneously, peeling cloves of garlic while keeping one eye fixed on the flames, for the most important consideration in preparing rice is the intensity of heat, which will determine the cooking time. When all the meats have browned he lifts them out of the pan with a long metal spatula and sets them on a plate, replacing them with three or four raw *langostinos*, which sizzle in their shells quickly on either side before they too are removed and set aside. The cook throws in a loose handful of opaque thin onion slices, fries them almost to the color of rust, and adds tomatoes, mashed garlic and coarse salt. For a few seconds he slides the pan off the fire and adds some paprika that is so dazzling red that it seems like red dye. Then he pushes the pan back over the flames.

The mixture in the pan, which is called a *sofrito*, bubbles in the oil until the ingredients have blended while the imperturbable cook crushes some strands of dried saffron in a mortar. He tosses the saffron into the *sofrito*, puts the meats and the *langostinos* back and gives the whole thing a stir. Then once again he checks the flames, which are a bit lower now; he heightens them simply by pushing the partly burned wood sticks further in toward the center. After that, with a casual air, almost as if it were an afterthought, he reaches down into a gunny sack and takes out a few fistfuls of short-grained rice. He casually throws them in the general direction of the middle of the pan, glances critically at the heap he has made in the steaming *sofrito*, adds another half fist of rice, and stirs it all into a flat layer that sinks into the thick, tomato-colored mixture. Of course he knows just how much rice has gone in, almost to the grain. While the rice is browning, the first mingled smell rises hard out of the pan—a pungent heady combination of foods from sea and land blended and sharpened with saffron.

Now the waitress from the restaurant comes with another order, so that the cook must set another black round pan on the grill and start the dish all over again while he finishes the first. Each pan is cooked over its own fire, so that the cook can control the heat. He seems oblivious to the timing problems involved and just goes on working; he can in fact stagger ten pans on the grill if he has to and effortlessly cook them all so that each one is ready at its proper time. Soon the rice in the first pan is browned. A long splash of boiling water is added, apparently unmeasured but precisely twice the amount of rice; the water is whitish, taken from a big pot in which the fish and shellfish have cooked. Squid rings, young tender artichokes and fresh garden peas are put in and the easygoing sorcerer gives a last stir with his spatula. Now he kills the flames by pulling the remainder of the wood sticks out of the spokelike formation and away from the pan, leaving only the hot embers while the rice finishes cooking.

Then he attends the second pan, peels a few more vegetables and goes on talking about the evils of timing rice with your watch rather than your brain. When something like 18 minutes and 12 seconds have passed, he glances at the rice, which is dark yellow by now and almost to the top of the sides

Continued on page 76

71

Spain's World-famous Paella: One Dish in Many Guises

The colorful *paella*, the Spanish culinary triumph best known outside the country, gets its name from the pan it is cooked in, like those at right in Valencia's Central Market. The dish draws upon a variety of possible ingredients: lobster, shrimp, clams, mussels, squid, *chorizo* sausage, chicken, rabbit, string beans, peas and red peppers. Only olive oil, rice and saffron (which provides the yellow glow) are always used, and *paella* may appear in any form from the elegant one below to the picnic fare on the following pages.

As his wife dices tomatoes and garlic, Señor Banacloy builds a pine-twig fire under a pan into which he has poured olive oil.

Tomatoes and garlic are added to the rabbit, chicken and beans.

Cooking a Paella Alfresco

The first *paellas* were cooked out-of-doors over open fires, and some *paella* buffs maintain that this is still the best way to cook them. Many Spanish picnickers plan a *paella* cookout as the main feature of their outings, taking along the ingredients and building their fire with whatever fuel is handy. When the family of Antonio Banacloy, a truck driver from Perellonet, held a picnic (*above*) in a park near Valencia, they brought with them rabbit, chicken, vegetables, saffron, olive oil and a *paella* pan. They set up the pan on a tripod, and after the four Banacloy children had collected pine twigs they built a fire and cooked the *paella* as shown in the sequence at the right.

74

Wielding their spoons with practiced proficiency, the Banacloys eat *paella* as tradition requires, directly from the pan.

The chicken set aside, the rice, peas and kidney beans are cooked.

As the final step, the chicken is replaced for reheating.

The "Lady of Elche," a Fourth Century B.C. sculpture of an early Iberian, was discovered in the village of Elche in the Levante's Alicante province. Her serene features closely resemble those of many modern dwellers in the south of Spain.

of the pan. The red *sofrito* has disappeared. Under the shimmering glare of the sky, each grain of rice is so separate and distinct from all the other grains that the dish appears to have achieved another dimension. The cook scrapes the last of the hot coals out from under the pan with a stick, inserts in the rice some of the cooked mussels, clams, shrimp and pieces of white fish, and lets the completed dish sit for three or four minutes before he garnishes it with some strips of sweet red pepper and four or five pieces of cooked *langosta*, the spiny Mediterranean lobster. The saffron-sharp smell is now a perfect balance of animals and vegetables, of sea and land, all delicately mingled, but piercing and magically whole. The finished concoction is named *paella (Recipe Index)* after the utensil in which it is cooked, and from which, ideally, it should be eaten. The black, round, metal pan with the handles on both sides is called a *paellera* and the rice feast named for it is by far the most internationally famous of all the dishes of Spain.

In order really to appreciate the *paella,* let us follow it to the table and join the family who will eat it. There is always enough for one more, and if you are alone, the Levantine country people will insist that you join them; otherwise you must eat something else, for a *paella* is too big an undertaking to cook for one person. They will pull up a chair for you to their square outside table on a terrace overlooking the reed-protected, flat, salt lagoon. Then they will give you a wooden spoon. The hot *paella* will be placed in the center of the wooden table and a small white plate then slapped, upside down, onto the center of the rice itself. On top of this plate, but right side up, is placed another plate of the same size, heaped with a crisp salad of lettuce and tomato and raw onions. When the *paella* is attacked, each person will begin from his side of the pan and eat toward the salad in the center, stopping now and then to pierce a piece of tomato or a thick wedge of fresh onion touched with a plain vinegar and oil dressing to blend with the flavor of the saffron. By the time the salad has been eaten the *paella* around it will also be gone, and the two plates will then be lifted to expose the final center portion, still warm, to be offered to those last hungry diners whose appetites have not been exhausted by the trip through the rice. Around the table there are several empty plates for shells and bones, as no one is likely to stop long enough to pass a plate while eating.

Now, with the table properly set, the feast begins. Each person grabs his wooden spoon, and from here on it's every man for himself. The first taste of a good *paella* is sharper than sweet, then sweeter than sharp, not rich, but aromatic—a high flavor that is almost indefinable. It is one of those rare dishes that get better and better as you eat, because what the Levantine sorcerer knows is that rice cooked *with* certain other foods absorbs and combines all their tastes until it has a special taste of its own that is different from—and better than—any of its ingredients.

Paella is the most important Levantine dish as well as the most famous, in that it embodies the basic cooking values and taste combinations found in all of the rice dishes of the Levante. If the culinary ability of the Levantines seems remarkable it is because they have taken rice, an ordinary plain food—relatively tasteless and simple in appearance—and transformed it to a visual and olfactory delight by adding a few simple ingredients easily found nearby. Like many great dishes, *paella* is a poor man's food that has become the rich man's treat. The original *paella* came into being near La Albufera, the freshwater lagoon close to the city of Valencia. The three ingredients cooked with the rice were local snails, green beans and eels, and the dish was eaten with whole small onions rather than with bread. Rice has been a staple food in many poor countries where it has been boiled for centuries, added to whatever else there is, and mixed in as a kind of filler and gravy-holder. The Levantines began to eat it quite recently in their history, and learned to mix it with many local products. But Levantine cooks accomplished something else besides. For rice here is not just an additive but an integral part of each dish in which it appears. And the number of such dishes is countless.

From a simple beginning there is now a rainbow of *paellas* in the Levante, reflected in all the rest of Spain, and culminating in the spangled, all-inclusive, baroque presentation we have just eaten, which is referred to on menus the world over as *paella valenciana*. The term is a misnomer. The authentic Valencian *paella* is only about a third of the way up the rainbow—a fairly simple dish whose main ingredients are rice, chicken, snails, green peas and beans, for the Valencians traditionally have strict inhibitions regarding the mixing of meat with fish, fish with certain shellfish, or even meat with certain other kinds of meat. The baroque polychrome *paella* at the country restaurant in Alicante is probably a collection of the finest *paellas* of this coast in one pan. It is said that if you ask 100 average male Spaniards what really goes into a *paella* you will get 100 different answers; but if you ask 100 Levantines, you will get 300 answers, each man giving one for himself, one for his grandmother and one for his wife. The proliferation of recipes has reached such proportions that there is actually one *paella* that substitutes tiny needlelike noodles for the rice. But the true answer to what really goes into a Levantine *paella* is usually rice, saffron and whatever happens to be fresh and cheap at the market. Far from being a complicated dish, *paella* is easy enough to make and could be the pride of the white-aproned chef at any outdoor barbecue; it requires no special equipment. The grill can be replaced by three large stones, and the pan may give way to a large, deep iron skillet.

The glowing province of Alicante provides many preludes and aftermaths to rice dishes, as well as a great number of these dishes themselves. The range is as great as the varied scenery of the province. The date palms of the elegant avenue in the city of Alicante known as the Explanada, shade a sweltering 90° in the summer. You can easily escape by driving only a very few miles to a cool pine wood 4,000 feet above and overlooking the sea. In either place you will be served by dreamy-seeming Levantine women whose strong, extravagantly beautiful faces are not particularly Moorish in appearance. They resemble early Iberians far more than they do the modern Spanish women of other regions, as can be seen from the features of the masterful 4th Century B.C. sculpture, the Lady of Elche, found in this province at the turn of this century. They seem impervious to the fever of summer as they move, cool as marble, down from the mountains through the breathless, hot, coastal cities and towns and onto the beaches, gathering food and cooking it outdoors under the intense sun as if they were working by moonlight. They do not concoct dishes with an eye to the heat, as do the Andalusians, but seem only to be concerned with the most decorative and delicious ways of presenting a broad variety of foods around the central theme of rice.

A balanced menu is vital to Levantine cooking, and the women who serve you, either in their homes or in restaurants, are as adept at combining different dishes as they and their husbands are at preparing them. If the first course of a *comida* in Alicante is a rice dish—perhaps rice simmered with sweet Mediterranean sole, or a wonderful dish called *arroz en caldero,* which is rice cooked with the blended juices of three different fish—then the second course will be a plain meat course. But if the first course is one of rice cooked with meat—lean pink pork liver or maybe wild rabbit—the second will be a simple, fish course such as crisp broiled mullets. The reversing of the usual order that dictates fish before meat is common here, for balance is what counts most when a meal revolves around rice. Dessert may then be any of a variety of fresh fruits, including sun-colored oranges, iced or sun-warm watermelon, ripe dates or deep red sweet pomegranates. Levantine fruit is generally excellent and is considered the proper finish to a meal whose main dish is rice, while Levantine pastries and sweets are often reserved for the afternoon *merienda* where they will counter but will not upset the balance of the main meal.

The best sweet to be found here is a candy known as *turrón,* a specialty of Alicante and another world-famous food. *Turrón* is a nougat paste made usually of toasted almonds, honey and egg whites. At Christmastime market stalls and stores of Alicante as well as the whole Levantine coast and most of Spain are filled with varieties of *turrón* containing many other ingredients such as powdered coriander, pine nuts, walnuts and cinnamon. *Turrón* is both chewy and crunchy, the sweetness of the honey offset by the nut flavor, and it is good the year round—anytime, the Alicantinos say, except after a visit to the dentist. Good *turrón* is quite hard; opening the mouth quickly after the first bite threatens to pull the teeth out of the skull, to say nothing of their fillings. It should be eaten slowly and carefully enough to allow it to dissolve in the mouth while being chewed, and it is well worth the time that it takes to consume this way.

Dinner in the province of Alicante is often a kind of afterthought. Its main dish may not contain rice but rather is meant to complement the filling midday *comida.* Soup with rice or a plate of fresh vegetables will be followed by an egg dish or one of rabbit or hare, for rabbit and hare tend to replace turkey and chicken. A fine example of these dishes is grilled, unspiced rabbit, served firm and steaming with *ali-oli (Recipe Index),* the cold sauce that has become an institution in this part of the world.

Ali-oli, which means garlic-oil, is a thick, opalescent, pale yellow sauce, with a tangy bite all its own that is a great taste accompaniment to plainly cooked foods. It has been referred to under a variety of names as the oldest culinary monument in the world. Vergil wrote of it 2,000 years ago—the Latin name was *moretum.* In ancient Spain it was called *ajolio,* and in France of the Middle Ages it was known as *aillouse.* In modern Spain the name varies from one region to another. It is called *ajiaceite* in Old and New Castile, and *ajoaceite* in Aragon. By any name, the basic sauce is simply raw garlic crushed in a mortar with olive oil, salt and possibly a few drops of lemon juice. It is properly served in the mortar in which it is made. There are variations including crushed almonds and other nuts, wild thyme, milk, cream cheese or eggs. Spanish gastronomic authorities claim that when Richelieu visited Mahón, the capital of the Balearic Island of Minorca in 1756, and tasted the egg version of *ali-oli,* he liked it so much that he took it back to France —where the garlic was eliminated, more lemon juice added, and the sauce called *Mahón-aise,* eventually changed to mayonnaise. Whether this story is apocryphal or true, the virtues of *ali-oli* are most apparent in its most basic version, whose smooth strength and sharpness go wonderfully with plain broiled meats, fresh-water fish, shellfish and all other simple foods.

After sampling the good and varied cooking of Alicante, the visitor should try that of Valencia, the best known province in all the Levante. Drive north in the lingering afternoon light past miles of rice fields, and as the day ends, you will be startled by one more unexpected example of Levantine magic, because evening is when the white orange blossom *azahar* opens.

It happens quite fast, when the sun bloats on the horizon, just as the light dies; the smell comes so suddenly it catches you like a summer storm. On my first night driving through Valencia I had not been warned about the smell of the *azahar* and it came unlike any other flower smell I knew—in a thick wave, heavy and dense and at first unrecognizable. I stopped the car and got out on a road between the groves. The smell was overpowering, the kind that is so strong it can make you dizzy, and standing there under the trees I could feel it exploding in my lungs.

Valencian orange juice serves as a good beginning or equally good ending for a Levantine rice meal. A tall cool glassful is good between meals too, and if you are driving up the coast, it is one of the things you stop for at any of the fishing villages. You may drink it there quietly while enjoying one of those unheralded town fiestas that seem to take place all year round in nearly all of the Iberian Peninsula.

Once in the province of Valencia I stopped for some orange juice in a pueblo called Cullera; hearing that there was to be an all-night fishermen's celebration, I decided to stay. On a high hill in Cullera where the smell of *azahar* rises, there is a church built as an addition to a Moorish castle that dominates the town. One night each spring the fishermen go up to the church and carry a small figure of their Lady, *La Virgen del Castillo,* down through the dark town to the water—not rambunctiously, as the Andalusians do their many religious figures, but with a staid and stately air that befits fishermen who wish to pray for luck in the coming year. I sat at an open-air bar-restaurant on the beach and waited with the people of the town for the float to arrive on the shoulders of the men. The restaurant had selected a special dish for the occasion, to be served all night. It was a fine simple one of rice and baby squid with tomatoes and onions. The delicate taste was hunger-making and at the same time satisfying when taken with a bottle of red wine at the sea's edge as the cool night winds came over the water. While I ate, fishing boats from the open sea and from the inland lagoons appeared before me gathering slowly near the beach to pay reverence to the Lady, their lights flickering like eyes in the darkness.

The float finally appeared at 6 o'clock in the morning while it was still dark, silently carried by fishermen straight down over the sand and into the sea. The townspeople stood on the land while the Lady was carried into the water, and then up and down parallel to the beach. The water reached the knees of the fishermen, and men farther out in the fishing boats surrounded the Lady with lighted candles to acknowledge her presence while the tossing boats themselves seemed to bow to her in the light flat surf. As the night started to pale she was carried back to a makeshift wooden altar low on the beach that was strewn thickly with branches of white orange blossoms. The fishermen lifted the Lady higher and gave her to the village priest, who set her on the altar, and as he did so the sky exploded white overhead. Fireworks blanched the sky, bursting loudly over the Virgin, the quiet waiting people and the sea. Then abruptly the dawn came, as if the rockets had called it up out of the night.

Early morning Mass was held on the beach for all the village before the Lady was carried back to her castle church. Then there was coffee and orange juice and a pastry called a *tostada*, made of rice flour with oranges, eggs and *anís*. The rice-flour base was filling and the *tostada* sweet enough with the sugar of the fresh oranges and *anís* to give energy for morning work. There was the faint last fragrance of *azahar* from the empty altar and the first harsh smell of the early sun on the tide.

Driving still farther north in the Levante you find a perfect contrast for the gentle fishermen's night in Cullera in the nonreligious *Fallas de San José* that takes place in the capital city of Valencia during rice-planting time. The festival occurs in March, when almost every popular rice dish is cooked and eaten, and it proves that all things in the Levante are not revered. The *fallas* features huge floats bearing monumental satirical figures of politicians and other personages of the times. The figures are often savage burlesques of the people they represent, and they move like giant clowns in a rollicking fiesta through the dusty city—to be heaped together at last and burned in a vast bonfire that seems to threaten the earth and sky. People flock into the streets, moving into restaurants to eat dishes of rice with chicken, rice with clams—rice with anything—but rarely with more than one sharp main flavor at a time. The one I like best contains soft white beans, fresh turnips, pork sausage and dark strong pork. The taste of the pork is enhanced by the slightly bitter turnips and sinks into the beans and rice so that no gravy is needed beyond the cooking juices. The dish is very good and afterward it is fine to watch the passing parade of the *fallas* for an hour or two before going into a pastry shop to enjoy one of the many local pastries that are as varied as the rice dishes of the Levante. Levantines say that there is no woman in Valencia who cannot make pastry.

North from Valencia in the last province of the Levante, Castellón de la Plana, there is a seafood-rice dish I like very much, *arroz a la marinera al estilo de Castellón*. It is made with the changing fare of the sea all year round—a good last meal to stop for on your way up the coast. In it shrimp are crushed and cooked with the rice and with any seasonal fish that is firm-fleshed, or even with crab or any large shellfish, sharpened with pimiento and slices of potato. After cooking, the fish and potatoes are served separately. The two-course meal of plain ingredients is a complete fish-flavored tribute to the culinary talents of the Levantines.

Beyond Castellón de la Plana the sea road begins to writhe, first in and out, then up and down. And now it approaches the rocky steep slopes of the almost melodramatically beautiful Costa Brava that protects the region of Catalonia and winds northward to France.

Arroz con Pollo

CHICKEN WITH SAFFRON RICE AND PEAS

Pat the chicken pieces completely dry with paper towels and sprinkle them liberally with salt and a few grindings of pepper. In a heavy 4-quart casserole, melt the lard over moderate heat. Add the salt pork dice and, stirring frequently, cook until they have rendered all their fat and become crisp and golden brown; then, with a slotted spoon, transfer them to paper towels to drain. Add the chicken to the fat in the casserole and brown it, turning the pieces with tongs and regulating the heat so that they color quickly and evenly without burning. Set the chicken aside on a platter.

Pour off all but a thin film of fat from the casserole. Stir in the onions and garlic and cook for about 5 minutes, or until the onions are soft and transparent but not brown. Stir in the paprika, then the tomatoes and bring to a boil, stirring frequently. Cook briskly, uncovered, for about 5 minutes, or until most of the liquid in the pan evaporates and the mixture is thick enough to hold its shape lightly in a spoon.

Return the chicken and pork dice to the casserole, and add the rice, peas, boiling water, saffron and 1 teaspoon of salt. Stir together gently but thoroughly. Bring to a boil over high heat, then reduce the heat to low, cover tightly and simmer for 20 to 30 minutes, or until the chicken is tender and the rice has absorbed all the liquid. Stir in the parsley, and taste for seasoning. Cover and let stand off the heat for 5 minutes before serving directly from the casserole.

To serve 4

A 2½- to 3-pound chicken, cut into
   6 to 8 serving pieces
Salt
Freshly ground black pepper
1 tablespoon lard
¼-pound salt pork, finely diced
1 cup finely chopped onions
1 teaspoon finely chopped garlic
1 tablespoon paprika
1 cup finely chopped tomatoes
1½ cups raw medium or long-grain
   regular-milled rice or imported
   short-grain rice
1 cup fresh or frozen peas
3 cups boiling water
⅛ teaspoon ground saffron or saffron
   threads crushed with a mortar and
   pestle or with the back of a spoon
2 tablespoons finely chopped parsley

Sopa al Cuarto de Hora

"QUARTER-HOUR" CLAM, SHRIMP, HAM AND RICE SOUP

In a heavy 3- to 4-quart saucepan, bring 1 quart of water to a boil. Drop in the clams, cover tightly and boil briskly for 5 to 10 minutes, or until the shells open. With a slotted spoon, transfer the clams to a plate, remove the clams and discard the shells. (Discard any clams that remain closed.) Set the clams aside and reserve the cooking liquid.

Meanwhile, prepare the *sofrito:* In a heavy 8- to 10-inch skillet, heat the oil over moderate heat until a light haze forms above it. Add the onions, garlic and bay leaf. Stirring occasionally, cook for 5 minutes, or until the onions are soft and transparent but not brown. Add the tomatoes, ham and parsley, raise the heat and cook briskly for about 5 minutes, or until most of the liquid in the pan evaporates and the mixture is thick enough to hold its shape lightly in a spoon. Set aside off the heat.

Strain the clam cooking liquid through a fine sieve, and return it to the saucepan. Add the *sofrito*, rice, wine, saffron and lemon juice, bring to a boil over high heat, and reduce the heat to low. Stir once or twice, partially cover the pan and simmer for about 15 minutes or until the rice is tender. (This cooking period is the quarter hour from which the soup gets its name.) Add the shrimp, egg and clams and simmer for 2 or 3 minutes longer until the shrimp turn pink. Taste and season with salt and pepper if desired. Serve at once from a heated tureen or individual soup plates.

To serve 4 to 6

1 quart water
8 small hard-shelled clams, washed
   and thoroughly scrubbed
2 tablespoons olive oil
½ cup finely chopped onions
1 teaspoon finely chopped garlic
1 small bay leaf
1 large tomato peeled, seeded and
   finely chopped (*see huevos a la
   flamenca, page 16*)
¼ cup finely chopped *serrano* ham,
   or substitute 1 ounce prosciutto
   or other lean smoked ham
2 tablespoons finely chopped parsley
¼ cup raw medium or long-grain
   regular-milled rice or imported
   short-grain rice
¼ cup dry white wine
⅛ teaspoon ground saffron or saffron
   threads crushed with a mortar and
   pestle or with the back of a spoon
½ teaspoon fresh lemon juice
8 medium-sized raw shelled shrimp,
   cut into ½-inch pieces
1 hard-cooked egg, finely chopped

To serve 6

A 1½- to 2-pound live lobster
6 medium-sized raw shrimps in their
    shells
6 small hard-shelled clams
6 mussels
3 *chorizos*, or substitute ½ pound
    other garlic-seasoned smoked
    pork sausage
A 1½- to 2-pound chicken, cut into
    12 serving pieces
2 teaspoons salt
Freshly ground black pepper
½ cup olive oil
2 ounces lean boneless pork, cut
    into ¼-inch cubes
½ cup finely chopped onions
1 teaspoon finely chopped garlic
1 medium-sized sweet red or green
    pepper, seeded, deribbed and cut
    into strips 1½ inches long and ¼
    inch wide
1 large tomato, peeled, seeded and
    finely chopped *(see huevos a la
    flamenca, page 16)*
3 cups raw medium or long-grain
    regular-milled rice or imported
    short-grain rice
¼ teaspoon ground saffron or saffron
    threads pulverized with a mortar
    and pestle or with the back of a
    spoon
6 cups boiling water
½ cup fresh peas (½ pound) or
    substitute ½ cup thoroughly
    defrosted frozen peas
2 lemons, each cut lengthwise into
    6 wedges

Paella
SAFFRON RICE WITH SEAFOOD AND CHICKEN

NOTE: In Spain, a *paella* may be simple or elaborate. Vary the combination of chicken, meats and shellfish, if you like, to suit your taste. For example, you may omit the lobster altogether or replace it with 6 or 8 additional shrimp. Clams and mussels may be used interchangeably. Add rabbit or let it replace the chicken. Cubed ham, veal, or beef might be used instead of the pork or the sausage. Squid—even snails—are appropriate. Cooked green string beans or artichoke hearts may be added, or substituted for the peas.

With a cleaver or large, heavy knife, chop off the tail section of the lobster at the point where it joins the body and twist or cut off the large claws. Remove and discard the gelatinous sac (stomach) in the head and the long intestinal vein attached to it. Without removing the shell, cut the tail crosswise into 1-inch-thick slices and split the body of the lobster in half lengthwise, then crosswise into quarters. Set aside.

Shell the shrimp, leaving the tails intact. With a small, sharp knife, devein the shrimp by making a shallow incision down their backs and lifting out the intestinal vein with the point of the knife. Scrub the clams and mussels thoroughly with a stiff brush or soapless steel-mesh scouring pad under cold running water and remove the black, ropelike tufts from the mussels. Set the shrimp, clams and mussels aside on separate plates.

Place the sausages in an 8- to 10-inch skillet and prick them in two or three places with the point of a small, sharp knife. Add enough cold water to cover them completely and bring to a boil over high heat. Then reduce the heat to low and simmer uncovered for 5 minutes. Drain on paper towels and slice them into ¼-inch rounds.

Pat the chicken dry with paper towels and season it with 1 teaspoon of the salt and a few grindings of pepper. In a heavy 10- to 12-inch skillet, heat ¼ cup of the olive oil over high heat until a light haze forms above it. Add the chicken, skin side down, and brown it well, turning the pieces with tongs and regulating the heat so they color evenly without burning. As the pieces become a rich golden brown, remove them to a plate.

Add the lobster to the oil remaining in the skillet. Turning the pieces frequently, cook over high heat for 2 or 3 minutes or until the shell begins to turn pink. Set the lobster aside on a separate plate and add the sausages to the pan. Brown the slices quickly on both sides, then spread them on paper towels to drain.

To make the *sofrito*, discard all the fat remaining in the skillet and in its place add the remaining ¼ cup of olive oil. Heat until a light haze forms above it, add the pork and brown it quickly on all sides over high heat. Add the onions, garlic, pepper strips and tomato. Stirring constantly, cook briskly until most of the liquid in the pan evaporates and the mixture is thick enough to hold its shape lightly in a spoon. Set the *sofrito* aside.

About a half hour before you plan to serve the *paella*, preheat the oven to 400°. In a 14-inch *paella* pan or a skillet or casserole at least 14 inches in diameter and 2- to 2½-inches deep, combine the *sofrito*, rice, the remaining 1 teaspoon of salt and the saffron. Pour in the boiling water and, stirring constantly, bring to a boil over high heat. Remove the pan from the heat immediately. (Taste the liquid for seasoning and add more salt if necessary.) Arrange the chicken, lobster, sausage, shrimp, clams and mussels on top of the rice and scatter the peas at random over the whole. Set the pan on the floor of the oven and bake uncovered for 25 to 30 minutes or until all the liquid has been absorbed by the rice and the grains are tender but not too soft. At no point should the *paella* be stirred after it goes in the oven.

When the *paella* is done, remove it from the oven and drape a kitchen towel loosely over the top. Let it rest for 5 to 8 minutes. Then garnish the *paella* with the lemons and serve at the table directly from the pan.

OUTDOOR COOKING: In Spain, *paella* is often made out-of-doors on wood fires, but a large charcoal grill serves as well. Following the recipe above, prepare the seafood, chicken, sausages and *sofrito* at the kitchen stove and have the other ingredients ready for the final assembly outside.

About an hour and a half before you plan to serve the *paella*, light a 2- to 3-inch-thick layer of coals in a charcoal broiler and let them burn until white ash appears on the surface. This may take as long as an hour. Adjust the grill to place it 2½- to 3-inches above the coals. If your grill is not absolutely flat on top or tends to tilt, remove it and use a rack from the oven large enough for its four corners to rest on the rim of the grill.

In a 14-inch *paella* pan, or a skillet or flameproof baking dish 14 inches in diameter and 2 to 2½ inches deep, combine the *sofrito*, rice, 1 teaspoon of salt and the saffron. Place the pan on the grill, pour in the boiling water, and stir the ingredients thoroughly, spreading the rice evenly over the surface of the pan. Quickly arrange the chicken, sausage and seafood on top, making sure that the clams and mussels are turned with their hinges downward. Scatter the peas over the top and let the *paella* cook briskly, uncovered and undisturbed, for 15 to 18 minutes, or until all the liquid has been absorbed by the rice. At no point after the *paella* has come to a boil should it be stirred.

When it is done, remove the *paella* from the grill and drape a kitchen towel or a large piece of aluminum foil over the top of the pan. Let the *paella* rest for 5 to 8 minutes, then remove the towel or foil, garnish with lemons and serve directly from the pan. Almost always, because of the intense heat generated by the charcoal, the rice will form a light brown crust on the bottom of the pan. The Spanish prefer it this way and generally serve the crust with the *paella;* however, should the crust char, it is best to leave it clinging to the pan and not serve it with the rest of the rice.

Arroz con Azafrán
SAFFRON RICE

In a heavy 10- to 12-inch skillet, heat the oil over moderate heat until a light haze forms above it. Add the onions and, stirring frequently, cook for 5 minutes, or until they are soft and transparent but not brown. Pour in the rice and stir for 2 or 3 minutes to coat the grains well with oil. Do not let the rice brown. Add the water, salt and saffron, and bring to a boil, still stirring. Cover the pan tightly and reduce the heat to its lowest point. Simmer undisturbed for 20 minutes, or until all the liquid has been absorbed by the rice and the grains are tender but not too soft.

Fluff the rice with a fork before serving and taste for seasoning. If the rice must wait, drape the pan with a towel and keep it warm in a preheated 200° oven. *Arroz con azafrán* may be served with *riñones al Jerez, zarzuela de mariscos* and *mariscos a la Costa Brava (all in Recipe Index).*

To serve 4 to 6

2 tablespoons olive oil
2 tablespoons finely chopped onions
1½ cups raw long-grain rice
3 cups boiling water
1½ teaspoons salt
⅛ teaspoon ground saffron, or saffron threads pulverized with a mortar and pestle or with the back of a spoon

V

Catalonia: All Things in Season

Bounded by France on the north, Valencia on the south, Aragon on the west and the Mediterranean on the east, the region called Catalonia is inhabited by a cosmopolitan, industrious people who seem on first contact more European than Spanish, and whose separatist tendencies in fact extend from politics to cooking. You don't often say, "I speak Spanish," in Catalonia—not and get away with it. It is better to say, "I speak Castilian." The Catalan tongue is not simply a dialect but a language in its own right, with its own grammar and syntax and its own literature—including, incidentally, the oldest printed cookbook in Spain and one of the oldest in the western world. The Catalans have fully documented their recipes since the Middle Ages to such a degree that Spanish gastronomes writing in the present century no longer make any effort to discover "new" dishes in Catalonia.

Although the teaching of Catalan has been outlawed by General Franco in an attempt to unify Spain under his personal dictatorship, the unique language continues to be used, and the region of Catalonia remains a distinct and self-sufficient entity. Perhaps the salient feature of the Catalonian character is a thrifty, piercing business sense, which has affected the region's modern kitchens as much as it once did her castles and palaces. Nothing is misused and nothing misplaced in a land where independence is all, wealth is independence, and plentiful good food symbolizes wealth.

Catalonian cooking is a seasonal rather than a geographic affair. There are very few local food prejudices, for most food that is edible is eaten. If a dish is prepared a certain way in one of the four administrative provinces of Catalonia—Barcelona, Tarragona, Gerona or Lérida—it is usually prepared about that way, give or take one or two ingredients, in the three others. Throughout the region the cooking is closely tied to seasonal produce from land, sea, farm, woods and air. All year round whatever there is to eat is of the best quality and is always well prepared: thrift in the kitchen sometimes leads to the use of ingredients or combinations of ingredients that require careful attention. Visitors have had their hair raised in excellent restaurants by menus that calmly announce a dish of fowl cooked with seafood, followed by one of chicken blood with liver. But in this land where "waste not, want not" is practically a religion, every visitor will almost literally find that anything he eats—during any season of the year—is sure to be worth eating. In short, in the hands of Catalonian cooks, all food is good.

Summer provides the best weather and some of the best food in this cool, northern Mediterranean climate. The most pleasant place to eat it is no longer a Catalonian secret. In the last 20 years the English, Americans and Europeans have come during the three summer months to the rocky slashing landscape of the Costa Brava (Rugged Coast), whose towns and fishing villages, dark blue water and beaches of white foam spread and collide in places where the earth appears to violate the sea. If you drive 90 miles from the Franco-Spanish town of Port-Bou south to the Spanish town of Blanes, avoiding the fishing villages and beaches spoiled by tourism, you find scenery ranging from savage beauty to stultifying prettiness, and eat food that makes you forget what you are looking at. Seafood is the first thing to order on a seacoast, and the *zarzuela de mariscos (Recipe Index)* is the best way to order it here; it is one of the finest achievements of Catalonian cooking.

The word *zarzuela* means a light operetta. I ordered the *zarzuela de mariscos*, a light operetta of seafood, one summer at a beach restaurant in a town on the Rugged Coast called Tossa. It was the house specialty, and the restaurant was not crowded, but the waiter explained that I would have to wait a short time. A *zarzuela* is a meal that cannot be prepared in advance but must be cooked when people are ready to eat because it has to be served immediately. Despite its many ingredients, it takes only 20 minutes to make. The waiter brought me a bottle of cool dry white Torres wine from Villafranca del Panadés, the Catalonian vineyard that lies south of Barcelona. I enjoyed it the way I like it best, with a salad that included lettuce, tomatoes, sweet peppers, green olives, celery, radishes, anchovies, canned tuna fish and sardines. The Catalans are rightly proud of their garden produce, and each vegetable was at a peak of ripeness. The pale lettuce was the sweetest in the world and the whole dish made a fine first course. The window by my table was open, and the cool, full winds from the sea met with the cooking air of the kitchen behind me that smelled of herbs and simmering fish. Then the waiter came back with a long earthenware platter that steamed up around him as he walked. He put it down to one side of me and let me serve myself a little at a time, leaving the rest of the *zarzuela* to stay warm in the earthenware container. The smell was gentle and the contents of the platter looked like a collection of all edible foods of the sea thinly covered by a rich brown sauce in which they had simmered and blended. The taste of each fish was separate under the bright sauce. The sauce itself was a blending of many tastes: shellfish such as mussels and the shrimplike crustaceans called *langostinos* with squid and many kinds of firm white fish, aided by oil, tomatoes, onions, crushed hazelnuts, garlic and parsley. A few drops of absinthe had been added at the last to give a final zest to the flavor.

Summer is the time of cold lobster salads, which efficiently supplant the salad and main course by combining them: thick chunks of lobster, brittle-crisp celery, tomatoes and sweet lettuce are mixed with a thin lemony-mayonnaise that has a taste of light oil. Another substitute for these two courses is achieved by cooking the ingredients of the salad—the result of which is a food called *xanfaina,* often used to garnish fowl or light meat dishes. It tastes of ripe garden vegetables tossed in a little blistering oil till just done, holding the freshness and flavor. *Xanfaina* may contain anything from the garden and it rounds out and freshens a good summer meal.

Summer also provides braised white fish cooked with fennel and lobster with chicken, a dish of seemingly contradictory tastes that are mingled into a smooth, sweet-herbed, double flavor by industrious Catalonian chefs. And during the height of this season, cold boiled *langostinos* are best served with two cold sauces, *ali-oli* and a Catalonian sauce of Tarragonese origin called *romescu (Recipe Index)* made from oil, hot peppers and sometimes tomatoes.

Romescu is a reddish brown mixture that tastes not unlike New Orleans Creole *rémoulade* sauce. It has a sharp quick flavor that makes the mouth water for any accompanying food. I like *romescu* with cold shellfish, but it is often eaten with rabbit and with other grilled meats. It is usually brought to the table with *ali-oli,* and the two sauces are mixed on the plate to suit the individual palate. Some people prefer a half-and-half mixture; some like the dominant base of *ali-oli* edged by the pungency of red *romescu.* I happen to like a version that is mostly *romescu,* with a dab of the white *ali-oli* mixed in to enrich and strengthen the sharpness.

With *romescu,* as with all foods in Catalonia, it is a good idea to taste before you eat. The spectrum of *romescu* is as wide as that of mustards. Recipes for it vary, as the "original" is held to be a great secret. Once years ago in a then-unknown seaside village on the Costa Brava I had a meal with the family of a fisherman whose wife made a *romescu* she had learned from her grandmother. It was the color of terra cotta with a deep shine. The fisherman's house was on a cliff high over the water, and the smell of the sea through the strings of garlic and dried vegetables hanging from the ceiling had given me an appetite. I ate a heaping spoonful of the sauce by itself while the family waited happily for a reaction. They got one. While I was waiting to breathe again, which took a full minute, I wiped the tears off my face and wondered whether my hostess's grandmother had enjoyed a genetic immunity to the more lethal effects of hot red pepper. "You are very brave," the fisherman said, nodding. "And a little stupid," his four-year-old son added, watching me in a puzzled way. It developed that nobody in the family for four generations had ever used more than a small dab of grandma's *romescu* in a whole cupful of *ali-oli.* When mixed that way it was delicious and the fierce sharpness dwindled to a high tang. My hostess gave me a piece of dry bread soaked in milk and olive oil to suck, which, incidentally, is a good antidote to any spice burn. My mistake had been in thinking I knew *romescu* well enough to handle it as I chose in any quantity. This *romescu* was at one extreme of the taste spectrum, and the sauce is not often made that hot. Alone or mixed, *romescu* will normally flatter many foods, from shellfish to rabbit.

Continued on page 90

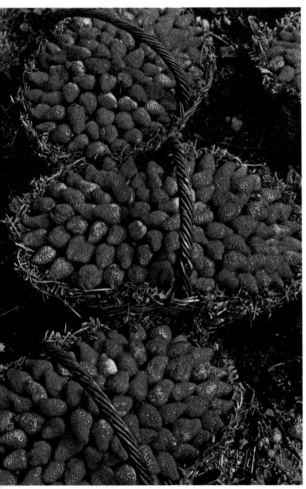

In spite of its dry climate and rugged terrain, Spain produces fruit in dazzling variety. From all corners of the land the harvest of orchards, vineyards and truck gardens pours into the cities daily. Housewives in the Barcelona market (*right*) may choose among grapes from the province of Almería, oranges from Valencia, lemons from Murcia, apples from Oviedo, figs from Huesca, dates from Alicante, melons from the area around Madrid and bananas from the Canary Islands. From close by, the countryside around Calella near Barcelona sends a fine crop of deliciously flavored strawberries (*above*). So delicate are the berries that they must be gathered in baskets lined with *lentejas,* an evergreen weed. The Calella berries are a local treat, for they are highly perishable and are sold mostly in the Barcelona area.

Driving through Catalonia in summer, you see peaches, apricots, pears, cherries and grapes, all of them big, almost luminous in color and violent with flavor. These fruits make excellent summer desserts, and very early strawberries here are especially good when served with a light layer of sugar and tart orange juice. The nearly explosive late-summer taste of slightly overripe, sweet peaches in dry white wine also makes a fine dish that is testimony to the Catalonian balance of thrift and intelligence in combining flavors. But the best fruits of the season are the innumerable melons, which are so varied, so well grown and sweet that they are eaten all summer and later. The crisp deep sound of a ripe Catalonian melon being sliced is welcome anywhere along the coast and inland through the summer to the fall.

When the fall comes, the tables of Catalonia fill with large meaty mushrooms called *rovellons,* another example of free-wheeling Catalonian ingenuity in eating. These wild wood mushrooms are looked down on in most of the rest of Spain as unworthy of consumption. In Catalonia they are prized, and because their season is short and they cannot be cultivated, the finding of the *rovelló* is held to be a sort of awesome secret. Just before the fall begins, the *rovelló* seekers—often experts who gather them every year—walk back and forth in the woods looking for the protruding heads as they begin to grow. No expert tells what he has seen or where he has seen it. But as the fall progresses, they go back to collect the full-grown vegetables in baskets. This is the time of greatest secrecy: I talked to one man who had gone out in the morning knowing he was being followed and who had happily walked about two miles out of his way to confuse the "spy." The *rovellons* he brought back were curly, reddish, earth-colored mushrooms, rosy underneath. They had to be washed several times to remove the sandy soil in which they had grown. But the efforts to find and clean them paid off in the eating. Broiled with finely chopped garlic and parsley the *rovellons* smelled of clean earth and woodland. They are firm and meaty and can be eaten as a first course, as an accompaniment to meat or fowl—or as a light main course. The meat-rich wild vegetable, overlooked by all but the Catalans, provides a good reason for everybody else to come to Catalonia.

Other hunters in the fall season bring game from the tablelands to the homes and restaurants of Catalonian cities. Partridge, quail and wild hare are among the best. A good place to eat them is Barcelona, Catalonia's principal city, which centuries ago vied with Venice as a port and today is the most prosperous city on the Mediterranean. In the heart of Barcelona lies the cool shaded Ramblas, an avenue whose wide center island is lined with stands selling books and flowers, birds and candy, as neatly placed and organized as everything else in a region where a kind of fierce tidiness sorts everything out. The restaurants leading off from the Ramblas run in style from an almost feudal elegance to the plainest undecorated back room of a bar. The expensive places are like mirror-lined halls filled with tables that in turn are filled with anything from shrimp or olives to pastry or ice cream. The poorer *barrio chino* (Chinese quarter), a place of winding small cobblestone streets and buildings waiting for the night, has several bars and restaurants that make up in food what they lack in finery. The streets reek of olive oil and cheap perfume, tobacco and port smells and wine-stained wood. One of the best dishes found here during the fall is roasted partridge with small croquettes of young cabbage and slices of carrots, cooked in white wine with other vegetables and flavored with cinnamon and bay leaf. It has a gamy wild taste tamed by the excellence of well-prepared garden vegetables. Also, anything that can be cooked over charcoal or thrown on a plain griddle is good here, and you can usually tell what is in season by just walking the streets. Smells of game with sausage, fish, or even mussels from the port steaming open on hot irons rise and mingle in these winding streets.

Between the very rich and very poor sections, deep in the center of Barcelona, are the students' bars. At the hour before dinner they fill with young people drinking glasses of beer or wine and eating appetizers of octopus tentacles cooked in almond sauce with a whiplash of hot spice and perhaps a few slices of grilled sausage. The low-beamed wooden ceilings are filled with names and messages and parts of poems that have been scratched on them over the years. By dinnertime the bars are packed with students, and there is a heavy layer of smoke caught by the ceiling beams—smoke of many cigarettes, smoke of charcoal, steam of frying fish. As the layer sinks, people's appetites rise to meet it, and a few of them begin to leave for dinner in their homes and cheap restaurants.

For dinner in Barcelona, the waterfront is a good place to go; autumn in Catalonia does not end the harvest of the sea. Here you walk past several restaurants placed side by side against the water, each displaying its raw materials next to its main entrance. There are big, flat, round baskets filled with fish intertwined with shellfish, carefully presented in geometric layers of many different seafoods bent into different shapes: dark green shells, shrimp, raw transparent-looking soles, long *langostinos, cigalas* (small Mediterranean lobsters), swirled squid, baby octopuses, curving purple eels, mussels, clams and oysters, all surrounded by strands of brown and green gleaming seaweed. The spider-web piles of seafood in the baskets are invitingly placed so near the entrance to the restaurants that anyone going close enough for a good look is nearly inside—at which point the spider, a waiter, appears out of the woodwork to finish the job. Of the seafood dishes that are best in autumn, one made with a chewy white fish called *rape* (pronounced rah-pay) is unusually good. This is a fish not found in waters where English is spoken and there is no English word for the fish, so the name appears in Spanish on the English columns of all menus. In this international port businesslike restaurant owners are given to translating their menus into several languages in an effort to lure foreign clients from all ships. The result has frozen many English and American clients to their chairs, where they are to be found staring silently at large efficiently translated menus on which there is one recommended dish with a single word left in the original language, the other two in English: "Rape with Onions." So be it: visitors are herewith advised to overcome their initial shock and order it. *Rape con cebollas,* to call it by its full Spanish name, is a dish of firm white fish whose texture and delicate sea taste go very well with thin wide slices of evenly browned onions in a sharp aromatic wine sauce that is no thicker than water. The fish and onions are a combination that makes a wonderful meal.

There are many other sea dishes worth ordering here, two of which I very much like. One is the Catalonian *bullabesa,* which rivals the Marseillaise bouillabaisse in its delicacy and strength. The other is a dish called *parrillada de pes-*

Continued on page 94

91

Barcelona's Nocturnal Sea Harvest

Barcelona is home to a fleet of 152 fishing boats that bring in nearly 5,000 tons of fish each year. Most of their catch is sardines. Barcelona's fishermen go out in the evening and form a circle with their boats, which are brightly lighted with oil lanterns. Attracted by the lights, the sardines are caught in a ring of nets. The fishermen return in the early morning to auction off the catch. In off hours during the day, the men usually repair their nets, but sometimes the women take over this job, forming the mosaic of net menders seen at right.

cado, a mixed grill of fish and other seafoods served steaming hot with slices of lemon. It is one of the simplest and best foods in all of Spain.

Tourist offices usually warn visitors away from the city of Barcelona during the winter season in favor of more temperate climates and picturesque views. I think they are wrong. Climates and views are not hard to find in the rest of Spain. But there is something special, almost mysterious about this city that seems to come to life in the early winter months and makes walking in bad weather worthwhile because its strange quality improves in the rain.

I went to a restaurant in the Gothic quarter of Barcelona one December when the first chilly winds came, cold but not brutal, the wet air lapping like waves over the city. It was only cold enough for a raincoat, and I had been through the dark, stone streets of the Gothic quarter only a few other times, between high walls and arches, gray inside gray, stone over flat stone. Walking there, you are followed by the echoes of footsteps that do not seem to be your own. If you do not know the quarter well, it is easy to get lost. The walls appear endlessly high on either side; everything is larger than life. Like the exit of a maze, the end of the quarter seems always around the next corner. I found myself in a wide dark patio of stone with a trickling fountain in the center and a church on one side. I had not seen anyone since entering the quarter and I was tired and hungry. There was a light coming from somewhere on the far side of the patio and I followed it. When I turned the corner, I nearly knocked over an old woman dressed in black coming in the opposite direction. I jumped hard, and the old woman, instead of screaming, threw her head back and laughed till her voice sang up high and resounded off the stone walls. I asked for directions to a restaurant, and she gave them to me. "Hungry?" she asked. Then she reached behind her, as if into the wall, and pulled out a little girl dressed in stone-blue eating a sandwich. The old woman tore off a tip of the sandwich and pushed it at me. "Something for the road," she said in Catalan and the two figures disappeared around a building. She was still laughing. I could hear her as I walked. I went on to the restaurant, only a few streets away, and ate the bread she had given me. It contained nothing. But the taste of veal was soaked into the bread and there was a green taste, like parsley ground with peppers, and the smell of tomato. The tip of the roll was only about half an inch long, an inch wide, and very stale, but with the fresh warm gravy-taste and the greenness it made the best first course I have ever eaten. I almost went back to tell her so, but instead I went on to dinner.

The Agut d'Avignon restaurant near the Gothic quarter is an excellent winter eating place. It is built, as are many rustic homes in this region, around a large fireplace that has two wide arms thrusting out into the room. In their homes, people sit on either arm of the fireplace, a plain wooden table between them, and eat foods cooked on a grill over the hearth or in an oven in the back of the fireplace. In the restaurant, of course, there are tables placed all over, but the hearth remains the focus of the big room. I found a table facing it and asked for a little of several dishes. There was a plate of dark green spinach cooked with pine nuts and almonds *(Recipe Index)*. With a glass of full-bodied dry red wine from the Torres vineyard it made a good first course that was warming after the winter air outside. Stuffed pigs' feet were being served and eaten in individual casseroles at the table next to mine; the meat

94

and meat-soaked vegetables smelled so good I was sorry I had not ordered it. Then came what I had ordered, a steak of bull meat, and I was not sorry any more. The steak was darker than any I had eaten and the meat was strong, finely seasoned and tender. With it I had a dish of *xató*, a winter salad of white endive soaked in a sauce of vinegar and oil, garlic, almonds and hot red peppers. *Xató* is classically Catalonian in ignoring the general Spanish distaste for spice-hot foods. It is filling enough to eat at midday with only the addition of marinated fish or sausages served on the side. It was almost too much at dinner with the steak, but the taste combination of spicy salad with the simple, broiled, rich meat was fine. Dessert was ice-cold, faintly salty white goat's cheese with thick fresh honey. You could not ask for a better finish to a warming winter meal.

After dinner I walked back along the loud echoing streets, past windows of chickens and other birds turning over coals on spits. The Catalans limit their roasting largely to fowl; their roast chicken is incomparable, crisp and juicy with sweet firm meat. The next day I bought one for lunch and carried it with me back into the Gothic quarter, for you do not tire easily of walking between those high walls. It began to rain and I stood under the stone eaves of a building, protected except for the spray of water that gathered and spilled and spurted in a wide stream between the grimacing gargoyles high over me. The water splashed high, and I ate the warm crisp chicken and wondered why people are warned away from this city in winter—and then I nearly dropped the paper with the chicken in it. Across the shivering water-filled air on the other side of the narrow street was a distorted image set in flat stone on the opposite wall, visible only because of the pouring rain and the mutilation of light through water, and probably aided by my own winter dreams. The carving in the stone was magnified and distorted through the rain and it was worn away with weather and time, but you could easily see the figure of an old woman with her mouth open, standing next to a little girl.

Spring appears suddenly in Catalonia and winter is soon forgotten, wiped out with light. This is the time of gardens. There are fresh young vegetables cooked in many ways, all of which are good. There are good omelets of baby artichokes and others of young white asparagus, best eaten when the vegetables come fresh from the damp earth and the farm hens are really laying. The tender garden taste is elegant and the omelets are smooth, warm and crisp on the outside. In spring a dish called *faves a la catalana*, broad beans (*habas* in Castilian), smothered with pork sausage, makes a main course for lunch or dinner; the rich sausage and bean taste is made lighter by the addition of sprigs of mint, parsley, cinnamon, tomatoes and garlic. Vegetables are eaten at all meals now, for the thrifty Catalans use everything they can grow in their gardens, throughout the season.

One spring morning I visited the Torres vineyards near Barcelona to see where the good wines came from. I drove through the heavy morning mist shrouding a range of hills and came down on the opposite side, to a vineyard that stretched as far as I could see. Grapes have been grown and wine made in and around the town of Villafranca del Panadés since the time of the Romans. The vines pushed out of the landscape like thatches of bubbles all the way to the vineyard. I stopped the car and went into the wide cool building of the Torres *bodega*, which smelled of many wines and grape products, dark rich and light dry reds, dry white and sweet dessert wines, pink rosés given their color by the grape peels that are allowed to float in the young wine for a time, aging amber brandies in huge wood casks. The smell of a good winery is heady and hunger-making, and some of the workmen were eating from the wide, slightly concave tops of two of the closed casks. The food was a simple one, *botifarra amb mongetes*, and I shared some of it. *Mongetes* are white beans and they are cooked with the same red wine contained in the *botifarra* sausage; they make a rich workman's breakfast on a misty, chilly spring morning. Eaten with a glass of the dry red Torres wine called *Sangre de Toro* (bull's blood), and the smells of the wine-soaked wood and all the surrounding wines, the dish was piercing and warm.

Later, in the country spring evening, I had a dish of hot grilled snails, tangy and sharp, and with it a full-bodied white wine and a plate of mixed, grilled vegetables called *escalibada*, sweet peppers and onions and young eggplant that had been put on a grid over charcoal and allowed to roast in the open air, then peeled, salted and served together, at first warm, and later cold. In the village of Villafranca there was a fair, and the *sardana* was danced —the Catalonian dance believed to be of Greek origin that is as different from flamenco as cold mixed grills are from hot fried fish. The *sardana* is almost like a modern Greek folk dance, performed in a group, for the Catalans break still another Spanish custom by knowing how to do things together rather than as individuals, each expressing the wounds of a culture in terms of his or her private pain. In fact, there is no pain in the *sardana*, but rather a happy floating circle of precise dancers who flow and move and turn as one to the right or left. It is said that no one but a Catalan can dance the *sardana* without counting out loud. The dance seems as unemotional as it is graceful, and if it lacks the deeply moving thrust of flamenco, it has a pleasant, effortless quality all its own. After the dance was finished, a dessert was served that I like best of all the sweets in Catalonia. It is *crema catalana*, a Catalonian custard made from fresh eggs and rich country milk and covered with a tissue-thin crust of crystallized burnt sugar. The custard is served in a wide flat layer on a plate. When you eat, you break the bittersweet burnt crust into the rich thick custard below. The crust cuts the sweetness and richness of it, and before leaving Catalonia, you may find yourself eating more platefuls of *crema catalana* than anybody should.

Every Sunday morning, scores of Catalans join in a centuries-old tradition as they gather before the Cathedral of Barcelona *(opposite)*, and in plazas of other Catalonian towns, to clasp hands for the *sardana*, the dance of Catalonia. Behind the dancers, out of view in the picture, a band provides accompaniment.

Ali-oli
GARLIC MAYONNAISE

To make about 2 cups

4 to 8 medium-sized garlic cloves, peeled and coarsely chopped
¼ teaspoon salt
1 tablespoon fresh lemon juice
2 egg yolks
1½ cups olive oil
1 to 2 tablespoons cold water

With a mortar and pestle or with the back of a wooden spoon, vigorously mash the garlic, salt and lemon juice to a smooth paste. Beat in the egg yolks, one at a time, continuing to beat until the mixture is thick. Now transfer it to a mixing bowl and with a whisk or a rotary or electric beater, beat in the oil, ½ teaspoon at a time; make sure each ½ teaspoon is absorbed before adding more. When about ½ cup of oil has been beaten in, the sauce should have thickened to a thick cream. Add the remaining oil by teaspoonfuls, beating constantly. If the mayonnaise becomes too thick to beat easily, thin it from time to time with 1 teaspoon of cold water, using up to 2 tablespoons if necessary. The finished sauce should be thick enough to hold its shape solidly in a spoon. Taste for seasoning.

Ali-oli is traditionally served, from a separate bowl or sauceboat, as an accompaniment to grilled or boiled meats and fish.

Romescu
ALMOND AND HOT PEPPER SAUCE

To make about 1½ cups

¼ cup blanched slivered almonds
1 teaspoon finely chopped garlic
½ teaspoon cayenne pepper
1 teaspoon salt
1 small tomato, peeled, seeded and finely chopped (*see huevos a la flamenca, page 16*)
¼ cup red wine vinegar
1 cup olive oil

Preheat the oven to 350°. Place the almonds on a baking sheet and toast them in the middle of the oven for about 10 minutes, or until they color lightly. Then pulverize them in an electric blender or with a nut grinder or mortar and pestle.

Crush the almonds, garlic, cayenne pepper and salt together with a large mortar and pestle or in a small bowl with the back of a large spoon. Add the tomato and vinegar and mash the mixture vigorously to a smooth paste.

Then transfer it to a mixing bowl and, with a whisk or a rotary or electric beater, beat in the oil a teaspoon at a time. Make sure each teaspoon is absorbed before adding more. When about ½ cup of the oil has been beaten in, the sauce should be thick and creamy. Beating constantly, pour in the remaining oil in a slow thin stream.

The finished sauce should be thick enough to hold its shape almost solidly in a spoon. Taste for seasoning and serve with grilled or boiled meats, shellfish or fish.

NOTE: In Catalonia *romescu* is often served with a bowl of *ali-oli (above)*, and the two are then combined to taste at the table.

Salpicón de Mariscos
SHRIMP AND LOBSTER SALAD

To serve 6

1 large onion, peeled and cut into quarters
¼ cup wine vinegar
1 teaspoon olive oil
1 large bay leaf
1 tablespoon salt
1½ pounds raw shrimp, in their shells
A 1½- to 2-pound live lobster

In a 6- to 8-quart casserole, combine the quartered onion, vinegar, 1 teaspoon olive oil, bay leaf and 1 tablespoon of salt with 2 quarts of water. Bring to a boil over high heat, drop in the shrimp and reduce the heat to low. Simmer uncovered for 3 or 4 minutes or until the shrimp turn pink. Then remove them with a slotted spoon and set the shrimp aside.

Bring the liquid remaining in the casserole to a boil again. Plunge the lobster head first into the liquid, cover and boil briskly for 10 to 15 minutes or until the shell turns bright red. Remove the lobster to a plate and let it cool to room temperature.

Shell the shrimp. Devein them by making a shallow incision down their backs with a small, sharp knife, and lifting out their intestinal veins with the point of the knife. Cut the shrimp into ½-inch dice.

Twist off the large claws of the lobster at the point where they meet the body and crack each claw in two or three places with a nutcracker. Split the lobster in half and remove all of the meat from the claws, body and tail. Remove and save the greenish brown tomalley (liver) and the red coral (roe). Cut the lobster into ½-inch dice and refrigerate the lobster and shrimp for at least 1 hour or until thoroughly chilled.

To make the mayonnaise, warm a large mixing bowl in hot water, dry it quickly but thoroughly, and drop in the egg yolks. With a whisk, or a rotary or electric beater, beat the yolks vigorously for about 2 minutes until they thicken and cling to the beater. Add a teaspoon of the lemon juice, ½ teaspoon of salt and the white pepper. Then beat in ½ cup of the oil, ½ teaspoon at a time; make sure each addition is absorbed before adding more. By the time ½ cup of oil has been beaten in, the sauce should be the consistency of very thick cream.

Pour in the remaining oil in a slow, thin stream, beating constantly. Beat in the remaining 2 teaspoons of lemon juice, the 3 tablespoons of white wine vinegar, and the parsley. With the back of a spoon, force the lobster tomalley and coral (if any) through a fine sieve into the mayonnaise. Mix thoroughly, then taste for seasoning.

Just before serving, toss the shrimp, lobster, lettuce, tomato, chopped onions and sieved egg yolks together thoroughly in a large chilled bowl. Add about ½ cup of the mayonnaise and turn the shellfish and vegetables about with a spoon to coat them evenly. Garnish the salad with chopped egg whites and serve the remaining mayonnaise separately in a sauceboat.

Merluza Marinera

POACHED HAKE FILLETS WITH TOMATO AND ALMOND SAUCE

To make the *sofrito*, heat the olive oil over moderate heat in a heavy 8- to 10-inch skillet until a light haze forms above it. Add the onions and garlic and, stirring frequently, cook for 5 minutes, or until the onions are soft and transparent but not brown. Add the almonds and bread, stir for a minute or so, then add the tomatoes. Raise the heat and cook briskly, uncovered, until most of the liquid in the pan evaporates and the mixture is thick enough to hold its shape almost solidly in a spoon.

In a heavy 10- to 12-inch skillet, bring 6 cups of water, 3 teaspoons of the fresh lemon juice and the 1 teaspoon of salt to a boil over high heat. Reduce the heat to low, add the fish steaks and simmer uncovered for 5 to 8 minutes, or until the fish flakes easily when it is prodded gently with a fork.

With a slotted spatula, transfer the fish to a heated serving platter. Bring the *sofrito* to a boil over moderate heat, stir in the remaining teaspoon of lemon juice and add up to ½ cup of the fish stock, 1 or 2 tablespoons at a time. The *sofrito* should be just thick enough to coat the spoon lightly. Taste for seasoning. Pour the sauce over the fish, garnish with slivered almonds and parsley, and serve at once.

MAYONNAISE

2 egg yolks
3 teaspoons lemon juice
½ teaspoon salt
¼ teaspoon white pepper
1 cup olive oil
3 tablespoons white wine vinegar
1 tablespoon finely chopped parsley
1½ cups finely chopped crisp lettuce, preferably romaine
1 medium-sized tomato, peeled, seeded and finely chopped *(see huevos a la flamenca, page 16)*
½ cup finely chopped onions
2 hard-cooked eggs, the yolks forced through a sieve and the whites separated and finely chopped

To serve 4

¼ cup olive oil
½ cup finely chopped onions
1 tablespoon finely chopped garlic
⅓ cup blanched almonds, pulverized in a blender or with a nut grinder or mortar and pestle
¼ cup coarsely crumbled French or Italian bread, trimmed of all crusts
4 medium-sized tomatoes, peeled, seeded and finely chopped *(see huevos a la flamenca, page 16)*, or substitute 1½ cups chopped, drained, canned tomatoes
4 teaspoons fresh lemon juice
1 teaspoon salt
2 pounds hake, haddock or cod fillets
¼ cup slivered and lightly toasted blanched almonds *(see romescu, opposite)*
2 tablespoons finely chopped parsley

To serve 4 to 6

1 pound *chorizos*, or other garlic-
    seasoned smoked pork sausage
1 tablespoon lard
¼ pound salt pork, finely diced
½ cup finely chopped scallions
1 teaspoon finely chopped garlic
½ cup dry white wine
½ cup water
1 tablespoon finely cut fresh mint
1 small bay leaf, crumbled
½ teaspoon salt
Freshly ground black pepper
4 cups cooked, fresh fava beans or
    substitute drained, canned favas
    or frozen baby lima beans
2 tablespoons finely chopped parsley

To serve 6

A 1½ pound live lobster
12 large raw shrimp, in their shells
¼ cup olive oil
1 cup finely chopped onions
1 tablespoon finely chopped garlic
2 small sweet red or green peppers,
    deribbed, seeded and finely chopped
2 tablespoons finely chopped *serrano*
    ham or substitute prosciutto or
    other lean smoked ham
6 medium-sized tomatoes, peeled,
    seeded and finely chopped *(see
    huevos a la flamenca, page 16)*
½ cup blanched almonds, pulverized
    in a blender or with a nut grinder
    or mortar and pestle
1 large bay leaf, crumbled
⅛ teaspoon ground saffron or saffron
    threads crushed with a mortar and
    pestle or with the back of a spoon
1 teaspoon salt
Freshly ground black pepper
3 cups water
½ cup dry white wine
1 tablespoon fresh lemon juice
12 mussels, washed, scrubbed and
    with black tufts removed
12 small clams, washed and
    thoroughly scrubbed
½ pound sea scallops, cut in half

Habas a la Catalana
FAVA BEANS WITH SAUSAGES AND MINT

Place the sausages in an 8- to 10-inch skillet and prick them in two or three places with the point of a small, sharp knife. Add enough cold water to cover them completely and bring to a boil over high heat. Reduce the heat to low and simmer uncovered for 5 minutes. Drain on paper towels, then slice the sausages into ¼-inch-thick rounds.

In a heavy 3- to 4-quart casserole, melt the lard over moderate heat. Add the salt pork and, stirring frequently, cook until the pieces have rendered all their fat and become crisp and golden brown. With a slotted spoon, transfer them to paper towels to drain.

Add the scallions and garlic to the fat in the pan and cook for about 5 minutes, or until the scallions are soft but not brown. Pour in the wine and water and add the sliced sausages, pork dice, mint, bay leaf, salt and a few grindings of pepper. Bring to a boil over high heat, reduce the heat to low and simmer partially covered for 20 minutes.

Add the beans and parsley and simmer uncovered, stirring frequently, for about 10 minutes longer, or until the beans are heated through.

Taste the *habas a la catalana* for seasoning and serve at once from a heated bowl or a deep heated platter.

Zarzuela de Mariscos
CATALONIAN SHELLFISH STEW

With a cleaver or large, heavy knife, chop off the tail section of the lobster at the point where it joins the body. Then cut the tail crosswise into 1-inch-thick slices. Twist or cut off the large claws, and cut the body of the lobster in half lengthwise. Remove and discard the gelatinous sac (stomach) in the head and the long white intestinal vein which is attached to it, but leave the greenish brown tomalley (liver) and the black coral (roe) if there is any.

Shell the shrimp but leave the tail shell attached. With a small, sharp knife, devein them by making a shallow incision down their backs and lifting out the intestinal vein with the point of the knife. Set the lobster and shrimp aside.

In a heavy 6- to 8-quart casserole, heat the olive oil over moderate heat until a light haze forms above it. Add the onions, garlic, and red or green peppers and, stirring frequently, cook for 5 minutes, or until the vegetables are soft but not brown.

Stir in the ham and cook for a minute or two. Then add the tomatoes, pulverized almonds, bay leaf, saffron, salt and a few grindings of pepper, raise the heat and bring to a boil. Cook briskly for about 5 minutes, or until most of the liquid in the pan evaporates and the mixture is thick enough to hold its shape lightly in a spoon.

Add the water, wine and lemon juice and bring to a boil. Stir thoroughly, then drop in the lobster, mussels and clams. Cover the casserole tightly, reduce the heat to moderate and cook for 10 minutes. Add the shrimp and scallops, cover, and cook 5 minutes longer. Discard any clams or mussels that have not opened.

Taste the *zarzuela* for seasoning and serve it directly from the casserole, sprinkled with parsley if you like.

The rhapsodic blend of flavors in this Catalonian shellfish stew gave it the name *zarzuela*, Spanish for a light operetta.

VI

A Winning Way with Sauces

Nestled in the Pyrenees near San Sebastián, these ancestral Basque homesteads are separated by geography from the rest of Spain and the outer world. In the seclusion of their rugged homeland, the Basques have zealously maintained their own identity—retaining their own dances, games and music, speaking a language that is unrelated to any other on earth and clinging to their excellent, distinctive cuisine.

The cooking of northeastern Spain is almost as concerned with sauces as that of the Levante is concerned with rice—though at first glance the visitor may not realize this, for the kitchens of northeastern Spain do not recognize the distinction others make between the two terms, *sauce* and *gravy*. For most cooks, gravy is based on the liquid juices of food, while a sauce is more or less an additive, usually served separately. But here, the two are one and the same: juices and separate ingredients are nearly always cooked together with the food itself until they are indistinguishably mixed. And if the key term in the dining rooms of this culinary zone is sauce, which refers to the final product, the magic word in the kitchens is blend—the process by which the product is achieved.

The first taste of the gentle art of blending may be found in the two ancient kingdoms extending from Catalonia to the northwest, called Aragon and Navarre, that mark the beginning of the zone of sauces and lead directly into the sharp, green, glittering land of the Basques *(Las Vascongadas)*, which contains the simplest and the finest cooking of Spain. Aragon produces the excellent *chilindrón* sauces, combining tomatoes, onions, garlic, *serrano* ham and roasted fresh peppers. The best of these is perhaps the version found in the central province. This province and its capital city are called Saragossa; the name itself is a kind of blending of all the syllables in Caesarea Augusta, the city's ancient name, after the Roman emperor who made it his headquarters. In their kitchens, Saragossans blend dishes containing vegetables and chicken *(pollo a la chilindrón, Recipe Index)*, lamb, rabbit, kid or veal—any of which can be prepared with *chilindrón* sauce. Try a meal in one of the old city's light gray bar-restaurants near the huge, sliding waters of the Ebro, the longest river entirely in Spain. The taste of a good *chilindrón* has a sharpness and a fresh sudden pungence that appears to grow from the meat itself rather than from anything that has been ladled onto it. Even the steam that rises like a small fissure cloud from a *chilindrón* dish smells more sweetly of the meat than of the sauce alone. Choice, young, tender meat is the rule, but it is said that anything edible will taste better *a la chilindrón*, a statement that is easy to verify if you finish a dish by mopping up the pungent remains of the sauce with a crust of thick light Aragonese bread. The only people who eat without bread in this part of Spain are weight-watching travelers from foreign lands, and even they have trouble. In the zone of sauces, bread is an integral part of every meal from beginning to end, and in the northern Spanish vocabulary there is no more difference between dunking and mopping than there is between sauce and gravy.

The use of bread for texture as well as taste can be seen in the preparation of a food called *migas*—a national Spanish dish with regional variants throughout the Peninsula, but which I happen to like best the way it is cooked in Aragon. *Migas* are fried bread chunks, referred to in English by the French word croutons, which does not do justice in either language to the dish that is prepared in Spain. It has been said that *migas* constitute the most ancient dish in the whole Peninsula, tracing back to early Iberian or Celtiberian cooking. A modern Aragonese woman may tell you, jokingly but proudly, that countless generations ago some ancient ancestor was already simmering sauces so well that her mate took to dropping bits of bread not only in the finished dish but in the food while it was being cooked—or even in the oil that was being heated before cooking had begun. That is the way *migas* are prepared in Aragon today, from two-day-old bread that has been cut or broken into very small chunks about the size of chick-peas and soaked overnight in a wet, salted cloth. In the morning, garlic is heated in oil and then discarded, and the *migas* are dropped in the oil. Bits of ham are sometimes added and the bread is left to brown until it is the color of rust.

Migas are eaten in all of Spain with almost anything from fried eggplant to hot chocolate. But the best *migas* I have tasted were served in a Saragossan bar as small as a walk-in closet, with tables so close together that it sometimes seemed that all the clients would have to stand up if one more came in. The *migas* here were cooked together with small bits of dark, salty *serrano* ham and served, still sizzling, with a ripe bunch of sweet white grapes. The salty *migas* and ham were almost too hot to chew and the sweet grapes were ice-cold. The blending of temperatures and tastes produced a sauce made, not in the kitchen, or even at the table, but in the mouth itself while the food was being eaten. *Migas* at that little Saragossan bar, with a dry red wine, functioned as appetizer, main course and dessert. The least known Spanish food outside of Spain, *migas* are the Spaniards' private delight.

When you leave Saragossa for the small villages of the provinces of Huesca or Teruel, you will find a kind, quiet people who do not lock their larders at night; who sing, dance and eat with a gentle awareness of their neighbors, which itself is quite rare in Spain. Compare it to the bordering region: if you have stopped in a Catalonian city or town to ask directions, you may have found that the industrious Catalans are too busy to listen. Here in Aragon, ask a strange old man on the street how to get to a restaurant or food bar. He will not tell you how to find a place where good food is served; he will take you, sit with you, order for you, eat with you and more likely than not insist on paying the bill. He will be very careful of what he orders. It may be a *cochifrito* or fricassee of lamb *(Recipe Index)*, fried with finely minced onion and garlic, lemon juice and chopped fresh parsley. In this dish, the faint sharpness and the sour hint of the sauce heighten the flavor of the young lamb, which seems like a new kind of meat altogether. The old man may suggest veal tongue *a la aragonesa*. If you say yes, he will hover over you a little when a casserole arrives containing the tongue and tomatoes, carrots, potatoes and turnips—all in a brown, smooth sauce produced by the juices of the tongue and vegetables simmering with a chunk of rich melted chocolate. The sauce holds and sharpens the taste of the food, and what is added instantly becomes a part of the whole so that, again, the slight sweetness seems to come out of the meat; you will think tongue always had a mysterious chocolate savor that you never noticed before. The old man will grin with a certain pride before he leaves you and goes on about his business.

The region of Navarre to the northwest of Aragon also uses chocolate in the kitchen, most interestingly together with small, glazed white onions in a fine sauce that accompanies partridge or squab *(pichones estofados, Recipe Index)*. The gamy meat of the wild fowl blends wonderfully with the tame tang and aftertaste of the dark chocolate.

Despite its size, Navarre has given Spain several other dishes which themselves seem to blend Aragonese cooking with the first traces of the great Basque kitchens. Navarre was the smallest of the five medieval Christian kingdoms in the north of Spain when the Moors held the south, and it was so small that it produced only one modern province. The capital is not called after the province it serves, as is the usual rule; its name is Pamplona. In the San Fermín festival of July, made internationally famous by Hemingway, a channel of bulls surges through Pamplona's narrow streets behind the stumbling, running men of the city, who are lunging toward the comparative safety of the bull ring. At night, during San Fermín, a *pastel de conejo* (rabbit pie) is served, the meat sunk in a light potato paste that has been tinged with the flavors of wild rosemary and thyme. A strong, sharp, excellent sheep's cheese is sent in from the Roncal Valley, tangy with the herbs that grow in the green Navarrese mountains.

After the festival, go in August far into the mountains and valleys of Navarre's rolling Pyrenean scenery. Quick, clear, glistening mountain streams slice and bubble white through the roots of trees and out between heavy, green grasses, over cliffs, sliding and splashing into the valleys below, carrying with them the trout that fishermen and gourmets from all over the world come here to find. The flesh of Navarrese trout is juicier, more tender and lighter than that of any other trout. It is cooked in many ways, among the best of which calls for a long soaking in dry, full-bodied wine containing peppercorns, fresh mint, thyme, mountain rosemary and bay leaf, chopped onion and aromatic dried herbs *(truchas a la navarra, Recipe Index)*. After marinating, the trout is poached in this same liquid and then served with hot boiled potatoes and a sauce made of the poaching liquid and beaten egg yolks. The blended tastes of the fish and aromatic herbs in the dry

Practicing a traditional vocation of his people, a Basque shepherd guards his flock on the slopes of the Sierra de Aralar in the province of Guipúzcoa. The sheep he tends are called *lachas,* and are raised for their milk rather than their wool.

wine have a sparkling sweetness even rarer than the mountain trout itself.

But for purists who like the natural taste of fresh trout, the basic Spanish kitchen rule holds as true in Navarre as it does anywhere else in the Peninsula: the simplest way of cooking is the best way. Another dish, also called *truchas a la navarra,* known throughout Spain and served in the most sophisticated restaurants of Europe, is believed to have been invented in the mountain meadows of Navarre. Shepherds tending their flocks here caught trout from nearby streams; over fires of rosemary and thyme branches, they heated frying pans, rubbing them inside with the fat from chunks of *serrano* ham they had carried in knapsacks from home. Into these hot skillets the shepherds threw the whole fresh trout, cleaned but unscaled, cooking them well on both sides before picking the seared flesh from the bones. Salt from the gleaming snow-cured ham fat was the only seasoning. Sometimes bits of ham accidentally stayed in the pan with the fat; and eventually ham bits were left there on purpose, then scooped on top of the fish as a kind of simple sauce. Finally, it became customary to place some ham bits inside the fish before cooking. *Truchas a la navarra,* the shepherd's practical concoction, is simply trout that has been slit open, stuffed with *serrano* ham, and pan fried. This time the sauce is found not under or over the food, but within it.

The aged, cured ham and the mountain trout produce a single delicate taste subtle enough to be credited to the chef who serves it at the most elegant New York or Paris restaurant, rather than to the inventive shepherd who cooked and ate it out of the cooking pan under the blazing white sun of the Navarrese mountains.

From Navarre you can easily enter the Basque region whose kitchens are now known for the finest Spanish cooking. Walk into a Basque kitchen abruptly, for there is no proper introduction to Basque food. Like the Basque peoples and like their language, Basque cooking seems to come out of nowhere, a part of the earth, a thing in itself.

The history of the people who live in the three Spanish Basque provinces of Guipúzcoa, Vizcaya and Álava is covered by a haze like one of those sudden, blinding fogs that sweep south from the fish-laden Bay of Biscay to hide the land and the people—shining and clear in the sun one minute, gone the next. No one knows exactly who the Basques are or where they came from. There are many theories; the one currently in vogue claims that the Basque peoples trace back to the original Iberians who first came to the Peninsula. The biting, fractured syllables of the rounded Basque language, Euskera, are not even vaguely similar to the sounds of Castilian, Catalan or even Portuguese—for Basque is not a Romance language and therefore does not have the same root. It is as foreign to the ears of any other Spaniard as Castilian would be to a Japanese. The brilliant white, traditional native Basque costume—with its white canvas-and-rope shoes called *alpargatas,* the wide line of crimson from the sash at the waist, the *makila,* which is a combination walking stick and weapon, and the *boina* or world-famous beret—is the same for both men and women; it is approximately as different from the Andalusian folk costumes as an Indian sari is from Western tennis garb. Yet, paradoxically, Basque cooking is not foreign or alien to other Spanish palates. Its distinction is not in its strangeness, for, unlike the language and the many unique Basque traits, Basque food is not removed from the rest of the Peninsula by history or custom. Falling as it does within the Spanish zone of sauces, the Basque kitchen is not the most individual of the Spanish kitchens. It is merely the best.

The fierce excellence of Basque cooking is at least partly due to the masculine energy, exuberance and fire of the Basques themselves, who make the industrious Catalans, the closest peoples in temperament as well as in separatist tendencies, seem like sluggards. But while the Catalan guards his individuality, the Basque is so sure of *his* uniqueness he does not need to consider it. He simply goes out and practices living in what is the most natural way for him—a way that has become as apparent in his kitchen as anywhere else he happens to go. His true purpose is not to be different, but only to excel, and he does so in everything from cooking to outdoor sports. In serving any kind of food, the Basque demonstrates his excellence to such a degree that the menus of all the restaurants in Spain echo his foods. Any dish followed by the phrase *a la vasca* (in the Basque manner) is worth ordering if the cook has used the original recipe. So are dishes marked *a la vasconia, a la vizcaína, a la vascongada* (all of which are variations of *a la vasca*). Dishes that bear the markings *a la bilbaína, a la iruñesa, a la donostiarra, a la vergarense, a la guipuzcoana, a la tolosana* or *a la easo* are from Basque towns or

Idiázabal cheese is made by Basques from the milk of their long-haired *lacha* sheep. Cured and smoked mostly on the farms of sheep growers, the cheese has a delicate tang, but varies in taste and quality.

provinces. Whatever the name, if it is an authentic Basque dish, order it in any restaurant; you cannot really go wrong.

But if you are introduced to Basque cooking in one of the private Basque gastronomic societies themselves, you will be served the kind of meal not to be found anywhere else in the world. The great gastronomic societies are set apart for those who truly like fine food and cooking; membership is limited, and a young Basque wishing to join must usually wait until an older member's departure for the kitchens of the next world has left a space in this one. San Sebastián, capital of Guipúzcoa, is the city where the first gastronomic society was founded in 1870. Today there are societies in nearly all the cities of the Basque provinces as well as in some of the villages and towns. If you want to see inside one, there are only two requirements. First, you must be invited by a member as his guest. Second, you must be a man, for food and cooking in the Basque provinces is and has always been solely man's work. Basque women are respected, loved, and treated with infinite attention and kindness—in their proper place. Their proper place is not the kitchen. The only occasions during the year on which women are allowed to walk into the gatherings of the gastronomic societies are on the eve of Assumption Day, August 15, and on Saint Sebastian's Day, January 20. Otherwise, no woman is allowed to enter the food sanctuaries except, possibly, a cleaning woman—that is, if no man can be found to wash the pots, pans and dishes at the end of the day.

When inviting you, your host will look guardedly to his right and his left, and, with something faintly like a leer, will ask, "Are you a man who likes food . . .?" in the tone of voice usually reserved by men for another kind of question. Say yes, and walk with him down the brown-gray cobblestone streets of San Sebastián's old quarter on the evening of a spring day, through the gusts and sharp sea breezes. The white city, backed by low hills, is cupped around the sparkling blue Bay of Biscay. Stop in a bar on the way and invite your host to a glass of *txakoli*, the tart, ciderlike, white wine that exists only here; it spoils if it travels even to another region of Spain. Order a before-dinner *ración* of fresh grilled anchovies, and another of grilled sardines just in from the boats. With the iced, bubbly *txakoli* the crisp strips of warm, unsalted anchovy make the canned variety seem like a different fish. But have a few canned ones here too, served on either raw or roasted sweet red peppers that counteract and blend with the salt to make one of Spain's best appetizers. The steaming, grilled sardines eaten on every coast of Spain are sweeter and lighter here than anywhere else, for it is said that no fish or seafood tastes quite as good as when it comes from the cold Bay of Biscay. The Basques are snobbish about seafood, no matter how fresh, that is taken from other waters. A fish, they claim, relaxes too much in the warm Mediterranean and loses its vitality and taste; too far north in the Atlantic the fish, except for cod, are so cold they lose their taste through rigidity. But catch a fish in the blue-gray waters of the Bay of Biscay, and it will be vibrant and alive with taste, ready for the kitchens of Basque chefs who give it the treatment it deserves.

Walk now up a steep hill ending at a building with a large oak door, and your host will pull out a large key and unlock the sanctuary. Every member has such a key, and when the door is unlocked you enter through the foyer

The three principal ingredients of the Basque dish *bacalao al pil-pil*, are salt cod, garlic and olive oil. Other ingredients, such as the peppers and parsley included above, may be used as garnishes. *Bacalao al pil-pil* is served in the earthenware pot in which it cooks. When placed on the table at the Guria restaurant in Bilbao *(opposite)*, it is accompanied by a glass of *txakoli*, a local white wine. A wedge of cheese made from sheep's milk serves as dessert.

On a restaurant terrace overlooking the Basque fishing port of Bermeo, a chef grills savory red bream along with two veal chops.

into the single big room that is thick with the smells of simmering seafoods and herbs, fresh country vegetables and fowl and meat. This is the banquet room, living room and reading room combined; in fact, it is the only room. Long, solid, dark tables line the clean white walls, benches on one side, chairs on the other. The room is functional and comfortable, but there is none of the attempt at luxury of the usual men's club; men come here to sit up and eat well, not to sink into the leather cushions and doze. Here the general rule is that no man wears a necktie, let alone a jacket. On the left as you walk in is a wall-niche containing a round object that looks like a roulette wheel with slits that empty into a big communal cup at the center. This is the money till, where at the end of the week each member pays for what he has eaten or drunk. The honor system reigns. No man checks up on other members, no one asks to see what anyone else puts in the till, and each man keeps his own accounts. Life here is democratic; as you walk in, you will see lawyers, bankers, fishermen and salesmen sitting together and talking or reading their newspapers before dinner, side by side at the wooden tables. To the right is an alcove where liqueurs and apéritifs are kept, but there is no bartender; each man helps himself and his neighbors, remembering what he has taken so that he can drop the money into the till before the week is over. Wine is bought in barrels and bottled on the premises; beer comes in vast kegs. At the far end of the room, with no separation, is the kitchen: 2 huge refrigerators, 5 ovens, 5 sinks, 20 or 25 gas ranges, 4 chopping blocks, hundreds of cooking utensils and drawers full of aprons and every other kitchen accessory. A robust man of about 55 is cleaning and washing several large soles; another younger man is cutting up a chicken and preparing to brown it in oil after dotting it with garlic, parsley and paprika; another can be seen chopping onions and keeping an eye on a steaming casserole that smells of lobster and white wine. Any of them will show you what he is doing, how he is doing it, or why there is not any other way of doing it that will come out exactly right. There are no secrets here. But you are a guest, and you must quickly sit down at one of the tables and wait to be served.

Being a guest at one of the Basque gastronomic societies is like being the only nonfamous person at a Hollywood cocktail party: everybody talks to you. Each chef here is a star, and a man who cannot cook at all is very much in demand because everybody else can cook for him. Your host had better keep a tight hold on you if you are not a born chef, for you are a rare commodity. The minute you sit down, someone will come up asking you just to try this or only to taste that. It may be a crab or lobster soup, thick or thin, intensely blended with flavors of the Bay of Biscay; or possibly a first course egg dish—a *piperade* of fresh-roasted, peeled, green peppers, sliced white onions, tomatoes and *serrano* ham, sautéed together as a sauce and then filled with beaten country eggs that are given a few fast swirls before the dish is emptied onto a warm plate, smelling and tasting of fresh flavors from the Basque farm land and the clean, rising country air. Or perhaps the eggs have been scrambled in a skillet full of bright leaves of sweet, green spinach mingled with pink Biscay shrimp like juice-containers of the sea. Someone will have cooked *changurro (Recipe Index)*, the dish made from a large round crab of this coast—cut up and simmered in oil with puréed tomatoes, onions, leeks, garlic and parsley, and then possibly flamed with brandy before being put back into its shell to bake a few minutes in a hot oven until it appears, sizzling red and gold, a kind of sauce-of-crab, an essence that manages to taste more like pure crab than the original crab did. There will be platters of different fish, simmered in different sauces, and small bowls of cold, boiled shellfish in the center to be shared by all. The Basque kitchen is at its best in cooking seafood, and every variety is to be found, prepared in more ways than would seem possible.

While you are eating, your next-table neighbor-host will want you to try a casserole of *kokotxas*, the long, translucent, gelatinous part cut from the throat of hake, the most prized and delicate part of this fish, which is sometimes still used instead of money to pay fishermen for their work. *Kokotxas* spoil before the rest of the hake, and are removed before the fish is taken inland; Basque morning markets are often lined with baskets of them piled high in the blowing sea air. They are cooked with peas and parsley and a little garlic in an earthenware casserole, swimming in one of the specially fine Basque sauces, called simply green sauce—the same sauce your neighbor on the other side is eating with a thick, tender slice of the hake itself. The Basque green sauce contains parsley and peas and gets its name from these ingredients. They are combined with garlic and oil and the juices of the fish, but the dish is never stirred. In the Basque kitchen, a casserole is more often gently shaken or jiggled during cooking to prevent the food from sticking, and it is simmered very slowly until the fish juices have blended perfectly with the olive oil to make the sauce—the taste of which, in this land of sauces, might be described as what the fish meant by being a fish. As a rule, the Basques do not believe in adding things to a sauce that will suddenly change its taste, for they do not want the taste changed. The texture and flavor of a sauce grow gradually out of the basic ingredients; little seasoning if any is used. Asparagus tips or other vegetables are included for flavor, but rarely any spices. The Basques believe that taste, texture, color and the *wholeness* of the sauce must be a subtle combination of simple ingredients blended by the hands of a master chef who respects the natural flavors of the foods enough not to disguise them, but rather to work to bring them out as strongly as possible. That perhaps is the single aim of all fine cooking in the zone of sauces. The level of quality is high because of it.

The ability of the Basque to consume food in quantity as well as quality is famous throughout Spain; it makes anything the Madrileño thinks of as a large meal seem paltry by comparison. After the egg course and the fish course, your Basque host will expect you to have something from a fowl dish —chicken or duck cooked in a light, fragrant, wine sauce tasting of almonds and citrus fruit. Then, naturally, you will go on to a lean veal stew, or the prospect of choosing a section from an entire roast kid with sauce-gravy. It is said that two Basques can eat a small roast lamb between the fowl course and the cheese. They even lay bets as to who can eat more.

There are good Basque cheeses, among the best of which is one that can only be made from the milk of the long-haired *lacha* sheep, which graze on the high slopes of the Pyrenees. This cheese has an incredibly delicate flavor redolent of mountain herbs, and goes very well after the meat course—that is to say, before dessert. The Basque version of the dessert, *natillas*, a liquid custard, is wonderfully sweet, edged with the tastes of lemon and cinnamon.

A Santander chef shreds cabbage for *olla podrida*, a hearty stew known to Don Quixote. Closely related to Madrid's *cocido (Recipe Index)*, *olla podrida* contains cabbage, beans, onions, leeks, garlic, tomatoes and five meats: ham, blood sausage, *chorizo* sausage, pork shoulder and bacon. The Bodega del Riojano restaurant in Santander (*opposite*) serves an *olla podrida* in the pot in which it was cooked, accompanied by bread and red wine.

There are pastries, and there are baskets of light and dark grapes and ripe pink-green pears and bright orange peaches if you prefer. Then comes black coffee, or you might like—or need—an *infusión de manzanilla,* camomile tea, said to be a soothing aid to digestion. But your host will probably suggest a fine brandy or a glass of sweet *anís* just to top things off.

The meal you have eaten was dinner rather than lunch, for the Basques take work seriously enough not to destroy their working hours by banqueting through the day. Unlike the American businessman, a Basque often goes home to eat with his family at midday, and goes out—to the gastronomic societies—at night, when there is time to prepare a meal properly and enjoy it. After dinner, your host will take you for a digestive stroll around the winding narrow streets of the old quarter; he may stop here or there to visit a friend in one or two of the other societies. Rivalry among the societies exists only minimally, for it is their culture as a whole that the Basques are proudest of: the provinces that have kept personality, food and customs, as well as much of their independence, intact despite 30 years of constant threats and innumerable repressive acts from the military dictatorship of the Franco regime. Still, if you happen to see a familiar dish in one of the *other* gastronomic societies, your host may remark quietly that you have already tasted that dish cooked at its best once and so need not pay too much attention. Then he will accompany you back to your hotel silently under the blue-black, glittering sky.

On weekends, Basque men may spend part of an evening with their wives and families, going for a walk, taking a drive in the country, or attending local festivals. In summer, there are many outdoor festivals, not of the religious variety so common in the rest of Spain, but given over to dancing and games. Competition is at the heart of this culture, and Basque men of all ages are expected to prove their abilities in sports at least once a year. Summer festivals often take place outside the towns in the sleek hills that turn as evenly green as good Basque sauces. August heat on the northern coast is not paralyzing, as it can be in the south of Spain, and there are always fresh cool breezes blowing in from the Bay of Biscay.

The Basque dances that may precede a summer festival are no more like other folk dances of the north than the spoken language is like Castilian, or the Basque food like the fried fish and cold soups of the south. Shining in the brilliant white Basque costumes, men as a rule perform the dances without female partners; the warlike dances themselves are of an even rhythm and a kind of unhurried aggression that is masculine and endless. High kicks with unbended knee are repeated in a thrusting series of movements.

The audience sits outside under a blazing blue sky, watching the dancers, who will join them at tables now and then for a glass of wine and a plate of the pencil-thin Basque sausages that are the best of all *chorizos* for an appetizer or snack, with crisp skins and finely chopped, dark, tangy pork inside.

Many people in the audience will also order individual casseroles of *angulas,* needlelike baby eels that are so tiny they are eaten whole. It may take 40 or 50 *angulas* to make a serving. They are now considered a great delicacy, though they were once so plentiful that Basque farmers carelessly fed them to their pigs instead of grain. When it became known that Basque gourmets would pay high prices for *angulas,* certain fishermen went out at night

Pantortillas de Reinosa (above), a popoverlike pastry named for the Santander village in which it originated, are made of flour and water. These simple pastries are popular the year round. *Opposite:* A baker in a Reinosa shop decorates a baked candy dragon with almond-studded jaws. In the foreground a three-headed monster with two hitchhikers aboard awaits its turn at the oven. Made of marzipan and filled with dried fruits, the toothsome dragons are especially popular in Spain at Christmastime.

A miniature candy menagerie beckons customers at a pastry shop in Reinosa near the northern coast of Spain. The little stylized creatures are made of marzipan, that internationally famous confection composed of almonds, egg whites and sugar. They were sculpted by hand and colored with vegetable dye.

in the strong moonlight to trail fine-meshed nets along the rivers and inlets where the young eels swam. Soon the dish became so popular in all of Spain that the *angulas* began to disappear; and today they come from *criaderos* (breeding vats) where they are nurtured until ready for eating. Preparatory to cooking, the *angulas* are killed in a special way—with tobacco placed in the water. The tobacco may be sprinkled over the surface of an entire *criadero;* at home in the privacy of a kitchen sink, the tobacco may just be what is left of grandfather's cigar. The tobacco both kills and relieves the *angulas* of all stickiness so that they are washed clean before being placed by the handful into an earthenware casserole of blistering hot oil in which garlic and one or two slices of *guindilla* (hot red pepper) have been browning. The casserole is immediately covered by an upside-down plate to keep it from spattering, and after no more than half a minute it is brought to the table. You uncover the casserole gingerly, with a napkin around your neck, for the oil still sputters. You use a thick wooden fork, for the tiny *angulas* would slip off the prongs of a metal one. First you give them a few careful swirls and folds in the hot oil; when they are cool enough you bring a forkful to your mouth over a crust of bread to keep the oil from dripping. The taste is sharp and strong with garlic, pricked by the taste of the peppers—not quite land and not quite sea, but between, wonderful with a dry white wine.

After the dances, many Basque sports may take place: rowing, wood-chopping, tug of war, jai alai, shot-putting, bowling or racing, among others.

The barrel-chested, short, strongly muscled Basques look as if they have been built for competition in sports. If there are many children at the festival, you will sometimes see in the background of the sportsmen the gigantic figure of Gargantua seated on an enormous basket. His open mouth is the start of a twisting toboggan chute down which boys and girls slide out of sight —"eaten" by the giant, who is called by the name "Trigantua," or Swallower. Whatever he is called, he does not drink. Wine is the exclusive property of another huge figure, Celedon, whose bulbous red nose indicates his bottomless capacity for *txakoli,* the famous Rioja wines and other regional wines drunk all year. The two figures are also guardians of many Basque restaurants, taverns and inns that overlook ports of the coast where squid, herring, conger eels, bonito, sole, flatfish, tunny, lobster, spiny lobster, giant sea-crab and literally hundreds of other varieties of fish and shellfish are brought ashore.

In the early autumn at an outdoor bar at one of the small Basque ports on the northern coast of Spain, you can watch the white and pastel fishing fleets go out. Here you may order a dish of squid cooked in its own ink and sip a glass of strong white wine in the sweeping sea air. The dish is called *Chipirones en su tinta* in Basque country and *Calamares en su tinta* in the rest of Spain *(Recipe Index).* Squid are caught in nets by the boats, but also individually by hand, as you will see if you watch one of the men or boys fishing with a rod and line at the end of the piers. Ask what he is using for bait and you will be shown a strange object like the head of a mop, about two inches long, made of multicolored rubber bands with bright pieces of shells for eyes, and a sharp hook hidden deep inside. Is the strange bait edible? No. Not even to a squid. What is it? It is another squid, a make-believe one that is a real squid's fantasy of the perfect playmate, who bounces and flirts, teases and attracts him into a quick hug, to be followed by a cloud of ink in the water, and death. Not fair play, you say? "But why not?" the fisherboy asks. Fair is fair, fishing is fishing is fishing. You might as well bait your hook with love as with food.

Go back to your table where the white-coated waiter is signaling that the squid dish is ready to eat. Sit and be served a small, earthenware casserole; inside is a substance that looks as if the contents of a tar pool had been boiled with pieces of white rubber. Do not look at it if it bothers you. But do eat it. There are a few Spanish dishes designed to be tasted unseen, and this is one of them. *Chipirones en su tinta* is the general anathema of many tourists who order it by mistake and send it back without trying it. But the shimmering taste of the thick, rich black sauce makes it worth getting past the first look of the ink. And after you have eaten enough for your mind to connect the taste of the food with its appearance, even the gleaming reflections of the sky above you, like strips of silver in the sauce, begin to look fine. It takes a Basque to make a black sauce appetizing.

The fishing boats you can see in the distance will be gone a short or a long time, depending on what each is after. The Basques were the earliest whalers in Spain; at first they kept watch from high towers, and harpooned whales from shore. Then they went out after them, as far as Newfoundland, the banks of which became regular Basque fishing grounds. Eventually, cod replaced whale as the most desirable catch; dried salt cod, the only fish easily available in the interior of Spain before there were railroads, became a fun-

Continued on page 120

A Manly Gathering of Convivial Cooks

In Spanish-speaking countries the quality called *machismo*, or total masculinity, is held in supreme regard. It dictates the style of whatever men do—from fighting bulls to dancing flamenco. Male gatherings devoted to cooking and carousing, and redolent with *machismo*, are a popular social form in Spain. The men prepare their own repasts, accompanying the cooking and eating with singing, dancing, drinking and male talk. Such gatherings range from formal Basque gastronomic societies, which turn out some of Spain's finest dishes, to casual get-togethers of neighbors like those at left in a farmhouse in Palencia province. First, the men cooked a chick-pea stew *(potaje de titos)*, shown simmering below beside a brace of veal chops. When it was done, they served themselves huge portions of it, washing it down with red wine; then they danced and sang to the music of the antique violins, shown hanging from a rafter, until the wineskins ran dry.

Draped in garlic and dried hot red peppers, an itinerant vendor peddles his wares door-to-door in Reinosa. A common sight in much of northern Spain, such merchants travel about for four or five days at a time, supplying households and restaurants with popular seasonings.

damental part of the economy in much of the Peninsula. Today, the best Spanish recipes for cooking cod are all Basque: *bacalao al pil-pil, bacalao a la vizcaína* or *bacalao al ajo arriero (Recipe Index)*. Before cooking, the dried cod must be soaked for 12 hours in several changes of water to remove the salt. Then it is blended with oil and garlic, *al pil-pil,* an onomatopoetic term referring to the sound of slowly simmering oil; cooked *a la vizcaína,* the classic way with onion, garlic, pimientos, parsley, salt pork, hard-boiled eggs, *migas* and almonds—most recipes now also include tomatoes; or made *ajo arriero,* a workman's garlicky concoction which is at its best with chunks of fresh lobster mixed in. Properly prepared, simple cod dishes become superior gourmet feasts that taste of sweet, rich, fresh, Basque farm vegetables blended with the still faintly salty, gum-textured fish of northern seas. These three very pleasant cod dishes are all served at the finest and most expensive restaurants of all Spain, all year round. It is hard for any restaurant owner to keep up with Basque inventiveness for recipes, and there are always new dishes to be found in all of the Basque provinces, suitable for the poor and for the rich. One Basque chef, Don José María Busca Isusi, whom I know, specializes (in his spare time) in inventing fine tasting and attractive looking meals which cost so little there is almost no Basque family that cannot afford them. One of his best recipes, *arroz blanco con mejillones* (white rice with mussels), won the regional gastronomy contest in Guipúzcoa two years ago. Such contests are common in the Basque country, and the recipe that won is one that can well compete with any expensive dish the world over. Fresh mussels are prepared with a bright red sauce containing tomatoes, onion, carrots and leeks, all strained and then enlivened with a touch of brandy, a splash of white wine and a little cayenne. The mussels and sauce are placed inside the glistening ring of white rice on a long platter, and the rice is then adorned on top with ten or twelve shells still containing mussels. The result looks good and tastes even better; the mussels and the red sauce provide a thick and very pungent taste that softens when mixed with the rice; the whole makes a colorful, complete shellfish meal. The cost of this dish in Guipúzcoa is seven pesetas (10 cents) per serving. Add three pesetas and Señor Busca Isusi will happily throw in dessert, brandy and a cigar.

From Guipúzcoa, drive west along the Biscayan shore, and you will see some of Spain's most elegant, little-known scenery—white beaches separating the blue sea from gently plunging, verdant hills—under skies like inverted bowls of weightless white clabber over the land. *Las Vascongadas,* the Basque provinces, contain landscapes as full and varied as their dishes, a fact that has not escaped the attention of many fine Basque chefs, one of whom has recently left home to open a superb, as yet obscure Basque restaurant in Madrid, called Gure-Etxea (Our House). This gentleman, Don Ignacio Loinaz Echaniz Galarraga Arrizabalaga Garmendia Alcorta, whose Basque name sounds more like a Basque pedigree, has invented a dish that he calls *tierra, aire y mar* (land, air and sea). In it slices of veal, chicken and lobster are marvelously blended in a biting, rich, brandy-tomato sauce; the resulting dish has a single flavor quite unlike any one of its three main ingredients alone. Its inventor explains that he only wished to present to the rest of the world a taste-impression of all the Basque provinces in one simple dish.

West of these provinces lie the billowy, green regions of Asturias and Galicia, the last and least known reaches of the varied country called Spain.

Calamares en su Tinta

SQUID IN ITS OWN INK

Following the directions given in the diagrams below, clean the squid and carefully reserve the ink sacs in a small fine sieve set over a bowl. Wash the tail cone, fins and tentacles under cold running water and pat them completely dry with paper towels. Then slice the tail crosswise into ½-inch-wide rings. Cut the tentacles from the base, cut the base and each tentacle into 2 or 3 pieces, and slice each fin in half.

In a heavy 10- to 12-inch skillet, heat the olive oil over high heat until a light haze forms above it. Add the squid, onions, garlic and parsley and cook briskly uncovered for 5 or 6 minutes, stirring frequently. Add the nutmeg, salt and pepper, reduce the heat to low, cover the skillet tightly, and simmer for 20 minutes.

Meanwhile, mash the ink sacs in the sieve with the back of a spoon and press out as much of the ink as possible. Pour the water over the sacs and mash again to extract any remaining ink. The ink is usually black but may be brown, and in either case the water should become dark and opaque. With a whisk beat the flour into the ink and continue to beat until the mixture is smooth.

When the squid has simmered its allotted 20 minutes, pour the ink over it and, stirring constantly, bring to a boil over high heat. Immediately reduce the heat to its lowest point, cover and simmer for 5 minutes. Remove the pan from the heat and, without removing the cover, let the squid rest for about 5 minutes before serving. Taste for seasoning and serve hot, accompanied if you like by hot boiled rice.

To serve 6

3 pounds small fresh whole squid
   with ink sacs
½ cup olive oil
1 cup finely chopped onions
1 teaspoon finely chopped garlic
¼ cup finely chopped parsley
⅛ teaspoon ground nutmeg,
   preferably freshly grated
1 teaspoon salt
¼ teaspoon freshly ground black
   pepper
1 cup cold water
2 tablespoons flour

These drawings show how to take apart and clean a fresh squid (1). First, grasp the tail and head sections firmly in your hands and pull the fin and outer part of the tail away from the head and tentacles (2). Then (3) carefully lift the silvery gray ink sac (if there is one) from the inner section of the tail and set it aside in a fine sieve. Next (4), use a sharp knife to cut the tentacles free, just beyond the eyes of the squid. Discard the innards and eye section. With your fingers, pop out the small round cartilage from the core of the tentacle base. Pull the transparent icicle-shaped pen or tail skeleton from the inside of the tail cone (5) and discard it. Pull the fins away from the cone-shaped tail and set aside (6). Under cold running water, peel the red, lacy outer membrane away from the fins and the cone with your fingers, and remove as much of the membrane as possible from the tentacles. Gently invert the cone and then wash it thoroughly.

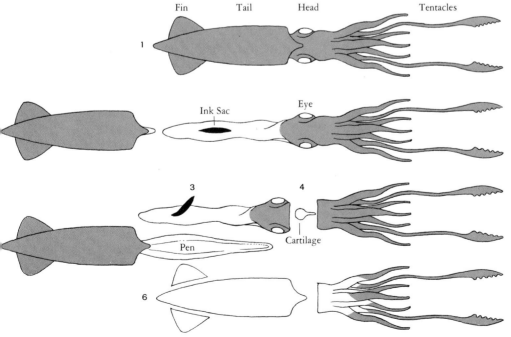

Fin   Tail   Head   Tentacles

Ink Sac   Eye

Pen   Cartilage

To serve 4

½ cup dry red wine
¼ cup olive oil
¼ cup water
½ cup finely chopped onions
1 tablespoon finely cut fresh mint
 or ½ teaspoon crumbled dried
 mint
½ teaspoon dried rosemary
½ teaspoon dried thyme
1 small bay leaf, crumbled
15 to 20 whole black peppercorns
1 teaspoon salt
4 trout, 8 to 12 ounces each, cleaned
 but with heads and tails left on
3 egg yolks, lightly beaten

Truchas a la Navarra
MARINATED TROUT BAKED WITH RED WINE AND HERBS

In a flameproof glass, enamel or stainless-steel baking dish large enough to hold the fish in one layer, combine the red wine, olive oil, water, onions, mint, rosemary, thyme, bay leaf, peppercorns and salt, and stir thoroughly. Wash the trout under cold running water and dry them completely with paper towels. Then place them in the marinade, turning them about to coat them thoroughly. Marinate at room temperature for about 30 minutes, turning the trout over after 15 minutes.

Preheat the oven to 350°. On top of the stove bring the marinade to a simmer, then lay a sheet of wax paper or foil lightly over the baking dish. Bake in the middle of the oven for 20 minutes, or until the fish is firm to the touch. Be careful not to overcook.

With a slotted spatula, transfer the fish to a heated serving platter and cover loosely with foil to keep them warm. Strain the cooking liquid through a fine sieve into a small saucepan, pressing down hard on the onions and herbs with the back of a spoon before discarding them. Whisk about ¼ cup of the liquid into the beaten egg yolks, then whisk the mixture into the remaining liquid in the pan. Heat slowly, whisking constantly, until the sauce thickens lightly. (Do not let it come anywhere near a boil or it will curdle.) Taste for seasoning.

Pour the sauce over the trout or serve the sauce separately. Traditionally the trout are accompanied by hot, freshly boiled potatoes.

To serve 4

4 one-pound oven-ready squabs, or
 substitute 4 one-pound partridge,
 quail, pheasant or other small
 game birds
Salt
Freshly ground black pepper
½ cup plus 1 tablespoon flour
⅓ cup olive oil
12 whole peeled white onions, each
 about 1 inch in diameter
2 medium-sized garlic cloves, peeled
 and finely sliced
¼ cup dry white wine
1 cup chicken stock, fresh or canned
2 teaspoons finely grated
 unsweetened baking chocolate
1 lemon, cut lengthwise into 8
 wedges (optional)

Pichones Estofados
BRAISED SQUABS WITH CHOCOLATE SAUCE

Pat the birds completely dry with paper towels, and sprinkle them liberally with salt and a few grindings of pepper. Then turn them about in ½ cup of flour and shake each one vigorously to remove the excess.

In a heavy casserole large enough to hold the birds comfortably, heat the olive oil over high heat until it splutters. Brown the birds in the oil, turning them with tongs and regulating the heat so that they color quickly and evenly on all sides without burning. Then transfer them to a plate and add the onions to the fat remaining in the casserole. Brown them over high heat, shaking the pan so that the onions roll around and color evenly. Remove them with a slotted spoon and set aside with the squabs.

Drop the garlic into the casserole and cook over moderate heat for a minute or two. Then stir in the remaining 1 tablespoon of flour. Pour in the wine and stock and, stirring constantly with a whisk, cook over high heat until the sauce comes to a boil and thickens lightly. Return the squabs to the casserole, baste them well with the sauce and cover the casserole tightly. Simmer over low heat for 40 minutes. Then add the onions, ½ teaspoon of salt and ¼ teaspoon of pepper. Cover again and simmer for 20 minutes longer, or until the onions are tender and the birds fully cooked.

With a slotted spoon, transfer the squabs to a heated platter and place the onions around them. Skim the sauce in the casserole of most of its fat and add the chocolate. Stirring constantly, cook over moderate heat for 2 or 3 minutes but do not let the chocolate boil. Taste for seasoning. Pour the sauce over the squabs and serve at once, garnished if you like with lemon.

The colorful and flavorful *pollo a la chilindrón* combines chicken with peppers, onions, black and green olives, and tomatoes.

Pollo a la Chilindrón

SAUTÉED CHICKEN WITH PEPPERS, TOMATOES AND OLIVES

Pat the chicken pieces dry with paper towels and sprinkle them liberally with salt and a few grindings of pepper. In a heavy 10- to 12-inch skillet, heat the oil over moderate heat until a light haze forms above it. Brown the chicken a few pieces at a time, starting them skin side down and turning them with tongs. Regulate the heat so that the chicken colors quickly and evenly without burning. As the pieces become a rich brown, transfer them to a plate.

Add the onions, garlic, peppers and ham to the fat remaining in the skillet. Stirring frequently, cook for 8 to 10 minutes over moderate heat until the vegetables are soft but not brown. Add the tomatoes, raise the heat and cook briskly until most of the liquid in the pan evaporates and the mixture is thick enough to hold its shape lightly in a spoon. Return the chicken to the skillet, turning the pieces about with a spoon to coat them evenly with the sauce. Then cover tightly and simmer over low heat for 25 to 30 minutes, or until the chicken is tender but not falling apart. Stir in the olives and taste for seasoning. Transfer the entire contents of the skillet to a heated serving bowl or deep platter and serve at once.

To serve 4

A 2½-to 3-pound chicken, cut into 6 to 8 serving pieces
Salt
Freshly ground black pepper
¼ cup olive oil
2 large onions, cut lengthwise in half, then into ¼-inch-wide strips
1 teaspoon finely chopped garlic
3 small sweet red or green peppers, seeded, deribbed, and cut lengthwise into ¼-inch-wide strips
½ cup finely chopped *serrano* ham or substitute other lean smoked ham
6 medium-sized tomatoes, peeled, seeded and finely chopped *(page 16)*
6 pitted black olives, cut in half
6 pitted green olives, cut in half

American red snapper is much like Mediterranean red bream *(besugo)* when baked Spanish style with seasoned crumbs on top.

Besugo al Horno

RED SNAPPER BAKED WITH POTATOES

To serve 4 to 6

2 two-pound red snappers, cleaned
   but with heads and tails left on,
   or substitute any firm white fish
1½ teaspoons salt
1 lemon, cut into 6 wedges
2 small black olives
¾ cup soft crumbs made from
   French or Italian bread, pulverized
   in a blender or with a fork
1 teaspoon finely chopped garlic
1 tablespoon finely chopped parsley
2 tablespoons paprika
3 medium-sized boiling potatoes,
   peeled and cut into ¼-inch rounds
Freshly ground black pepper
1 cup water
½ cup olive oil

Preheat the oven to 350°. Wash the fish under cold running water and pat them dry, inside and out, with paper towels. Sprinkle the fish with 1 teaspoon of the salt, then place them side by side on a board or plate.

With a small, sharp knife, score each fish, by making three crosswise parallel cuts about ¼ inch deep, 2 inches long and 1½ inches apart. Insert a wedge of lemon skin side up in each cut. Insert a black olive in the exposed eye socket of each fish.

In a small bowl, combine the bread crumbs, garlic, parsley and paprika. Spread the potato slices evenly on the bottom of a 16-by-10-by-2-inch baking-serving dish. Sprinkle them with the remaining ½ teaspoon of salt and a few grindings of pepper and place the fish side by side on top. Pour the water down the side of the baking dish and pour the olive oil over the fish. Sprinkle them evenly with the bread-crumb mixture.

Bake in the middle of the oven for 30 minutes, or until the fish feels firm when pressed lightly with a finger and the potatoes beneath them are done. Serve at once, directly from the baking dish.

Patatas en Salsa Verde
POTATOES IN PARSLEY SAUCE

In a heavy 10- to 12-inch skillet, heat the olive oil over high heat until a light haze forms above it. Add the potatoes. Turning them frequently with a metal spatula, cook for 10 minutes, or until they are a light golden brown on all sides.

Scatter the onions, garlic, parsley, salt and pepper on top of the potatoes and pour in the boiling water. Do not stir. Instead, shake the pan back and forth for a minute or two to distribute the water evenly.

Cover the skillet tightly and simmer over low heat for about 20 minutes, or until the potatoes are tender but not falling apart. Shake the skillet back and forth occasionally to prevent the potatoes from sticking to the bottom of the pan.

With a slotted spatula transfer the potatoes to a platter and pour a few teaspoonsful of their cooking liquid over them. Serve the remaining liquid separately in a sauceboat.

To serve 4 to 6

5 tablespoons olive oil
6 small boiling potatoes (about 2 pounds), peeled and sliced crosswise into ½-inch rounds
½ cup finely chopped onions
1 teaspoon finely chopped garlic
2 tablespoons finely chopped parsley
1 teaspoon salt
¼ teaspoon freshly ground black pepper
1½ cups boiling water

Limonada
BASQUE RED AND WHITE WINE "LEMONADE"

With a small, sharp knife or a vegetable peeler with rotating blade, remove the yellow peel from three of the lemons, being careful not to cut into the bitter white pith underneath it. Cut the peel into strips about 2 inches long and ½ inch wide. Set them aside. Squeeze the juice from one of the peeled lemons and then slice the remaining 3 unpeeled lemons crosswise into ¼-inch-thick rounds.

Combine the strips of lemon peel, the lemon juice, lemon slices and sugar in a 3- to 4-quart serving pitcher. Pour in the red and white wine and stir with a bar spoon or other long-handled spoon until well mixed. Refrigerate for at least 8 hours, stirring two or three times.

To serve, stir again, taste and add more sugar if you prefer the drink sweeter. Serve in chilled wine glasses or tumblers. If you like, the glasses may be filled with ice cubes before adding the *limonada*.

To serve 8

6 lemons
1 cup superfine sugar
1 bottle dry red wine, preferably imported Spanish wine
1 bottle dry white wine, preferably imported Spanish wine

Natillas
SOFT CUSTARD

In a heavy 1- to 1½-quart saucepan, heat the milk with the cinnamon sticks until small bubbles begin to form around the edge of the pan. Remove from the heat.

With a whisk or a rotary or electric beater, beat the eggs, egg yolks and sugar in a mixing bowl for 3 or 4 minutes, or until pale yellow and slightly thickened. Beating constantly, slowly pour in the hot milk in a thin stream. Return the mixture to the saucepan. Stirring constantly, cook over low heat until the custard thickens enough to lightly coat the spoon. Do not let the custard come anywhere near a boil or it will curdle. Cool the custard to room temperature.

Just before serving, spoon the custard into six individual dessert dishes, place a ladyfinger in each dish, and sprinkle the custard lightly with ground cinnamon.

To serve 6

3 cups milk
2 cinnamon sticks each 4 inches long
4 eggs
2 egg yolks
½ cup sugar
6 ladyfingers (*Recipe Booklet*)
Ground cinnamon

VII

Hearty Land Dishes and Fine Seafood

At a Sunday market near Santiago de Compostela, Galician farmers haggle over prices for sturdy oxen, animals that are indispensable to their way of life. In this agricultural section of Spain, oxen are still used to plow fields and to pull primitive carts over rutted roads.

The people of the northwest area of the Peninsula—the two regions of Asturias and Galicia that lead into Portugal—do not resemble in temperament any of their Spanish neighbors, far or near. They are not like the Basques, the Castilians or the Catalans—nor is there any similarity to the Levantines and Andalusians. It was the Celts who came to dominate here; the rugged mountain ranges and the heavy rains prevented the Moors from achieving a foothold. The northwesterners therefore think of themselves as "pure" Spaniards—while the rest of the world claims that a Celtic temperament is distinctly *un*-Spanish. In common with certain of their Portuguese neighbors, they are marked by a Celtic melancholy they call *saudade,* a sadness and nostalgia for things past and a yearning for things that will never be. There is no agony or melodrama, but a kind of lyric genius.

These Celtic roots go back in Spain to the very earliest part of its history, as can be seen in all northwest Spanish folklore. The open, sometimes solemn *muñeira* dance that is bright and sharp in Asturias, a bit more solemn in Galicia, is fully as different from the Basque dances as those are from Catalonian or flamenco dances. There are many traditional dances here in the northwest, ranging from the free rising *pericote* to the *vaqueira,* a kind of formal herdsmen's dance, to the *danza prima,* said to trace as far back as the Bronze Age. Most are accompanied by a musical instrument that is unknown in the rest of Spain, though it is used by other Celtic peoples: the bagpipe. But the bagpipe is as purely Spanish in the northwest of Spain as castanets are in the south. Folk festivals here also include fire rituals, said to be rooted in prehistoric times when magic was called upon to ripen the

In Galicia and Asturias, Spain's chief corn-producing regions, specially designed granaries called *hórreos* are used to store the corn. Built of stone, wood, or sometimes wicker, *hórreos* squat on tall columns that are topped with flat round stones to prevent rats from climbing into the storage space.

earth. And there are festivals in which young men and women sing and dance and carry food in from the shining fields to honor the harvesting not only of corn but of chestnuts, big and sweet as small apples in Asturias, eaten raw in the streets or candied and sold in shops.

Just as the festivals and dances of the northwest strongly reflect its history, so does the cooking of this part of Spain. A certain resemblance to the cooking of Celtic Brittany and Normandy in France is noticeable; both Spain and France from time to time accuse each other of rifling their kitchens. But if tripe *a la ovetense* and *tripe à la mode de Caen* seem somewhat similar (they are basically the same dish), it is because they have the same Celtic origin. From these ancient roots northwestern Spain has developed a superb cuisine that divides itself easily into two parts, almost like two distinct ways of coping with the dampness of the climate. The hearty land dishes warm the body, preparing it for the incredibly complete and varied array of shellfish—as the wild mountains of Asturias protect the more gentle and tranquil mystery of Galicia, so shimmering-soft in the moonlight, so rich in delicate foods of the sea.

Of all the fine dishes that Asturias produces, the most memorable perhaps is a fine body-warming bean stew, known as *fabada,* which has been called the most "solid" single dish in Spain. The stew's name comes from a thick, curved local white bean called *faba.* In the *fabada asturiana (Recipe Index),* these beans are simmered slowly with pork shoulder or ham, bacon and Asturian blood sausage, pig's ears and pig's feet; an oven-cured pork sausage called *longaniza* may also be included. The tastes of the differently cured forms of cooked pork mingle and mix in cooking until they are absorbed by the rich white beans of the stew. The beans are meaty in texture, never mealy, and fresh in taste; they hold the meat juices in a special savor. The beans sustain their heat long after they are eaten, like highly flavored small white-hot coals inside the body. Cooked and served in an earthenware casserole, the rich, nourishing *fabada* maintains the body heat of Asturian miners in snow-blanketed mining towns and of brave fishermen setting out from the quiet of cliff-coves into Atlantic gales.

With any hearty dish like the *fabada*, the country people of both Asturias and Galicia eat cornbread in preference to bread made from any other grain. A rarity in Spain and in most of Europe, the golden cornbread of the northwest is as spongy and yellow as cake. It is not at all sweet, and it goes well with heat-containing food like a bean stew. The corn for it is grown all over northwest Spain. If you drive through Asturian mountain passes or along the coast, you will see the storehouses, structures built on curious mushroom-shaped pillars for protection against dampness and mice. In Galicia, too, there is hardly a single home that doesn't have a grain house next to it; called *hórreos*, they are smaller and longer than the Asturian granaries.

Along with cornbread, another fine complement to the *fabada* is a drink that replaces wine in Asturias, and is peculiar to this area of Spain. Asturias has been called the land of cider. The ancient Greek geographer, Strabo, once spoke of Asturian cider; today about six million gallons are produced yearly, nearly all of which is consumed in this area. Amber in color, the frothy, faintly effervescent cider has a sour tang. Its effervescence is a trick produced by sleight of hand, for cider in Asturias is poured in a special way. The bottle is held high over the head with a straight arm; the glass is held in the other hand, so low that it almost touches the floor. Any Asturian can pour cider so deftly that in bars you regularly see waiters pouring behind their backs without looking. The thin amber stream falls in a long glittering arc onto the side of the glass, and the pressure of the fall produces a high foam like thick gold lace. You drink it quickly, for it is the foam that is best; sparkling and tickling inside the mouth, it is the lightest of drinks. Most Asturians throw the remains of the cider out of the glass once they have drunk off the foam; they throw it in such a way that it rinses out the glass for the next man, and the glass is then passed around the table. In the Asturian country kitchen, cider is often used instead of white wine for cooking as well as drinking, and many dishes are improved by this simple substitution.

In addition to the *fabada*, Asturian cooking produces another fine heat-containing dish that deserves mention here. This one—derived from sea rather than land—is the *caldereta asturiana*, a kind of Biscayan bouillabaisse, said by some gourmets to be better than all other versions of seafood stew because of the superiority of the fish in these waters. Many solid-fleshed fish are used in the *caldereta*, either as small whole fish or as chunks and slices of larger ones. A few special local shellfish are also added, among them Biscayan *langostinos* and a small rock barnacle called *lapa*. The main ingredients are put into a deep pot with water, a little oil, chopped onion, paprika and a few other spices. While these ingredients are boiling, fresh parsley is mixed

Galicians usually dry their corn next to the *hórreo* in which it will be stored. But the family that lives in this house near Bayona has found a sunny spot on the walk just outside the front door. When the corn is dry, they will move it to the *hórreo* and later use it for cornbread or as feed for livestock in the winter months.

Continued on page 132

A Gourmet Cheese from Mountain Caves

The shaft of sunlight probing into a mountain cave in Asturias (*opposite*) reveals a prized cheese ripening under ideal conditions. Called *Queso de Cabrales*, it is made by combining goat's milk, for a sharp flavor, sheep's milk, for an extra tang, and cow's milk, for smoothness. The curds are pressed into round shapes in country kitchens, then salted and dried for a week or two. Later they are stored in limestone caves and kept under lock and key by farm owners, like the woman at left. The cheeses age for two or three months, at 41° to 46°, acquiring a red-green mold and a Roquefortlike flavor. More than half of the cheese is consumed locally, often with goatskins of red wine (*below*). The rest is wrapped in *plagamo* leaves—to preserve it—and sold in gourmet shops all over Spain.

with peppercorns, sherry, nutmeg and a very small hot red pepper. This mixture is added to the main ingredients. The resulting stew is one of those rare dishes—like ripe olives or salted peanuts—that are almost impossible to stop eating once you have tasted them. *Caldereta* is usually made in quantity by Asturian country women, but visitors to Asturias are advised not to order any other food with it; *caldereta asturiana* is a meal in itself.

Across the mountain ranges from Asturias, in the farthest reaches of the northwest where the Atlantic joins the Bay of Biscay, is the place once called Finisterre, "end of the earth," before the discovery of America. Now it is called Galicia. Here all roads lead not to Rome but to another Christian burial place and shrine, the town of Santiago de Compostela—for centuries the goal of thousands upon thousands of people who slowly tramped the roads of Europe down into Spain, then westward to see and touch the tomb of St. James the Apostle.

Santiago de Compostela was an important city for all of medieval Christendom. Today it is still the goal of many travelers, for James is the patron saint of Spain and the cathedral that holds his shrine is one of the most magnificent on the Continent. The original tomb is said to have been found in the Ninth Century by a Galician peasant whose dark vision took him out of his home one night, to walk over the wet country earth following a bright star to a primitive sort of burial place, the first tomb of the Apostle James. Miracle legend, in which Galicia is richer than all the rest of Spain put together, had already told that the body of James was somewhere nearby, having been washed in from the Atlantic and onto Galician shores. The tomb was quickly found, and the cathedral built around and over it in the same way that the Vatican was constructed over the bones of St. Peter. The Cathedral of Santiago today is a high thrust of powerful Romanesque architecture—with Gothic and Baroque additions—set over the primitive tomb. The old people of Santiago say that you should see the cathedral for the first time through the rain. In the darkened watery light, the stones themselves seem to move. If you watch from a bar-restaurant nearby, drinking half a bottle of red Ribero wine, so thick with tannin it is almost purple, the cathedral looms above you taller and taller, weaving now a little in the rain. But a waiter will come and explain quickly that the vast gray, shimmering stone can make you drunker than the wine. He will suggest that you eat something in a hurry—a dish of *pimientos de Padrón*, very small roasted green peppers that are sharp and sometimes hot on the tongue. Then, when you have finished this dish, you will certainly need more wine, and after that, as an unsolicited gift, the waiter will bring you a slice of a thick *empanada (Recipe Index)*, the meat or seafood pastry for which Galicia is famous.

An *empanada* is a pie with a gold crust that can be soft and flaky at the same time. It can be made with *pasta,* a bread dough, or with a sheath of *hojaldre,* a flaky pastry containing fresh pork lard. It is served more often cold than hot in Galicia—either in an individual pastry triangle or as a wedge from a larger pie. An *empanada* can contain almost anything, and the ingredients vary through the Galician provinces. In Santiago the best *empanadas* are filled with pork shoulder and possibly other kinds of meat or codfish; on the coasts, with shellfish or fresh sardines; in the province of Orense with river eel or lamprey. The lamprey, a carnivorous animal that looks like an eel, takes a bit of getting used to if you happen to see it raw first—particularly as any lore-and-legend-loving Galician will happily tell you that ancient Romans threw slaves into Galician lakes to feed them. But the lamprey *empanadas* here are pungent and strong, especially good with the tannin-filled Ribero wine. And *empanadas* made with scallops, which are brought to Santiago from the Galician coast, have a sweet fresh taste that's like a first inland hint of the open seas.

When you have finished eating your *empanada,* go back for a last look inside the cathedral; wander through the Romanesque and Baroque stone. And at the top of one of the pillars you will see a 12th Century carved stone figure of a man eating. In his hand is an *empanada* identical to the one you have just been served.

Spend some time visiting the shops close to the cathedral. You will see many objects made from scallop shells. Wide pink and gray scallop shells were common in the city of Santiago centuries ago when pilgrims coming to the shrine pinned them to their capes and hats or nailed them to their staffs as symbols of their devotion to St. James. Today, the fresh scallop is more widely eaten on the coast than here, but the shell is identified with Santiago, where it often serves as a sign of welcome to the visitor. If you walk out of the city over cobblestones worn smooth by the feet of pilgrims coming to the cathedral, you will see a single big scallop shell marking hostels, inns and other sleeping places ready to welcome the tired traveler from any land. Stop in one for the night before you leave Santiago for the eerie beauty of the Galician countryside. In the early morning you may drink a cup of blistering coffee and eat a sweet, rich almond pastry called *tarta de Santiago.* The pastry is good for breakfast or dessert, fine to carry with you when you drive out from the city in the early morning mist that begins to thicken and turn to rain as you come out near open country.

Any Galician will tell you that it rains for an hour or so every day in Galicia, except perhaps in the summer. Again, rain here is not like rain in any other land. The sweeping water magnifies and sharpens the look of the countryside. The earth of Galicia is big, swollen, foggy and lush. Geologically, this is by far the oldest part of the Iberian Peninsula; Galicia bulged fresh out of the sea millions of years before any of the rest, and soon half the new earth fell back into the water and disappeared, causing the strange wonderful look of the coast we will see later. Here in inland country many mountains were left, but by now they are smooth, rounded and green, worn and eroded by the constant rain. Broad crumbling valleys have been ravaged by centuries of erosion. Forested places and long, gentle green hills loom all over, like waves of earth between the mountains and valleys. Gray stone villages and country houses dot the land. From sunrise till late afternoon you see them through a low-lying, very thin mist like a veil that is bluish green, opaque and trembling over the earth. Galicia, the least known region of Spain, is perhaps the most astonishingly beautiful.

When the rain comes, stop in a country house. Any one will take you in, and you will quickly be offered a steaming bowl of *caldo gallego (Recipe Index),* Galician broth, the liquid from the *pote gallego,* the Galician version of the *cocido.* The *pote* can be found simmering all day and night in a pot over the kitchen hearth, winter and summer. It is made with *lacón,* or cured pork shoulder, and a piece of *unto*—aged salt pork that has been allowed to spoil—plus turnip greens, potatoes and dried white beans. The *caldo* is as thin as consommé; it is rich and dark in flavor and can be as strong as fire. It is just what you want, coming in from the thick misty air and the chilly morning rain of Galicia. One earthenware bowl of this steaming broth will dry you out and kindle a new glowing heat in the body.

The *caldo* acquires a special flavor from the fiercely strong *unto* and the fresh turnip greens. *Unto* is a strange taste—most foreigners reel back from it the first time—and for this reason many good Galician city restaurants leave it out. It is so pungent it can make the eyes water, and I happen to like it very much. The turnip greens are special here too—for in Galicia, thanks to the humidity, the green top of the turnip grows more abundantly than the vegetable itself. The top has two names: *naviza* when it is young and tender; *grelo* when it is full grown, lush and leafy dark in flavor. *Lacón con grelos*—pork shoulder with turnip greens—makes a wonderful dish served after the *caldo*, or simply eaten by itself. The smoky dark flavor of the pork mixes very well with the green, slightly bitter taste of the *grelos*.

Finish eating the *grelos* slowly, sitting in a window seat of a country house before the misty blue and green of the land as the day fades. The oldest woman of the house will surely come to sit across from you and talk in a voice like a throaty whisper. Her conversations will soon turn to shades and mystery, for the Galician country people believe so strongly in the supernatural that it is never far from their consciousness. As you eat the rich food, listen to the old woman, who is speaking in Castilian for your benefit rather than in her own Galician dialect. Witches are prevalent in Galicia, you will have heard. The old woman will smile in a distant way and get up to fill your plate with more *grelos* or your white cup with more dark red wine—lifting the cup for an instant and giving it a swirl as if it contained something else besides the wine. Yes, she will say, witches exist here. Naturally, she doesn't know anything about them *personally* . . . but they exist . . . oh, yes; she has a very good friend who once spoke of a friend who practices the black art just over that other hill. . . . Only, she asks, you wouldn't want to know too much about a thing like that, would you? She doesn't wait for an answer and she doesn't look at you. She goes on talking. . . .

But if it is late afternoon, and if you ask her about ghosts, the old woman will not smile at all. She will stop speaking for a while at least. By 6 o'clock you will be sipping coffee and eating a piece of white Galician cheese. The late afternoon light in Galicia is strange and marvelous. It is a hard yellow filter over the earth, over everything, and when it comes all noises seem to stop; it is the kind of thick light that appears to absorb sound. The blue-green fields turn to yellow, the mist in the air is yellow, the glass panes in the window of the country kitchen are suddenly yellow. This is the magic time of day; the wild Celtic twilight brings a blanket of wet blackness in which the only light will come from spirits walking the hushed earth. Then, on certain nights, the *Santa Compaña*, a procession of the dead, can be seen—and there are almost no Galician country folk who have not seen it at least once. No one likes to talk about it. Dressed in black and carrying torches, the spirits of the dead walk high on the dark Galician hills under the blue-black sky. They go soundlessly in a row toward some hidden place no man knows. They look straight ahead and they make no footprints in the wet earth. But if one of them turns abruptly and looks at you . . . well, try not to meet his eyes. Turn away and walk. That may help.

And if you have listened to ghost stories through the glowing yellow end of the day and night has come and it is too late to leave, however skeptical you are, you will do well to accept Galician hospitality and spend the night inside the country house by the fierce fire where there is more *caldo,* more good hot food and plenty of wine. When the fire turns to coals, a Galician peasant omelet, made of *chorizo,* a few vegetables and thin slices of potato will make a fine supper. It tastes of country-fresh eggs and pork sausage mixed with the bittersweet green of lush turnip tops. Later, when you have finished supper, you can sleep the wine off on a strangely comfortable pallet-bed and leave in the morning.

If you drive toward the northern coast at dawn, you will pass oxcarts with screeching wheels that are never oiled. The carts must pass over roads so deep in mud that the surrounding hills and fields block the view, and only the screeching of the wheels warns oncoming traffic of their approach. Many of the drivers are women, for in most places the land here will not grow anything but an occasional crop of corn, and the men have emigrated to other lands to make their fortunes. The wives and children are often left behind, even though the men may not return until 20 years have passed and they have accumulated enough money to provide another kind of life for their families. While the men are gone, the women grow as strong as their oxen, and braver. Often you will see them driving the oxcarts into the rivers to collect huge loads of soft-shelled crabs no bigger than chestnuts. The crabs are too tiny for food but they serve another useful purpose; the women spread them over the fields as fertilizer. Other strong women in the country villages walk erect and proud, carrying on their heads enormous pots as big as bathtubs on end, weighing far more than the women themselves. They wear wooden shoes built on small stilts to enable them to walk in the muddy fields in the rain. And they go home at the end of the working day to cook potatoes and pork, bake cornbread and boil greens—to provide dry, life-sustaining heat for their children. With a pot of water, a little oil, a small piece of meat and a handful of vegetables, these women can work miracles.

Leave them now and drive on to the coast—to La Coruña, a crag of land jutting into the sea. Here the mist is mingled with sea spray from the Atlantic as the ocean surges to the Bay of Biscay, bursting over the high stone walls, sparkling, fluttering high in the early morning sun. There is no place where the crashing surf cannot be heard. In La Coruña each house within view of it has a gallery enclosed with glass panes that connects to the gallery of the next house. Seen from the sea in the sun, the thousands of glass panes explode with light, as though the whole town was on fire. The people of La Coruña sing and dance by the sea, by the wild winter surf and the gentle summer swells, and in rain or sun they walk the streets of the misty city through the day and halfway into the night.

Walk along with the people at lunchtime and you will find yourself suddenly in a square where four connecting streets are called La Estrella, Los Olmos, La Galera and La Franja. These streets have one thing in common. Look to the right and left as you walk: Every building on both sides has a ground-floor window, each window displays seafood. One after another the windows are full, each trying to outdo the next, for all of them adjoin the entrances of restaurants, bars or taverns. Fish and shellfish fill these windows in strokes and splashes of color, so intense and varied that you will think you are surrounded by rows of aquariums. You will see lobsters huge and tiny; pink and purple crabs of every size, shape and sheen are grouped delicately on white platters with gray and brown oysters. Clams of every species stand next to black and rose mussels. There are rainbow trout and swollen pink king salmon from Galician rivers. Ringed layers of pink shrimp cascade down onto rows of red *langostinos* and form a halo around a pile of vast fluted scallops carefully stacked above heaping platters of more scallops and shellfish. Crayfish, prawns, gray and pink goose barnacles, mauve bulbous octopus and opalescent squid surround convoluted conger eels, delicate thin pale soles, black bass, red mullet and silvery sardines. The windows are like still-life orchards of the sea.

Some say there is nothing that swims in ocean, sea or river that cannot be found along the Galician coast, for Galicia is the most important fishing region in all of Spain; the catch here is worth more than that of the whole Mediterranean coast. And the best of this catch is offered here along these four narrow streets. Join now with the milling people here in La Coruña as they stop at a bar for a glass of acid-dry white wine to wash down a plate of icy flat oysters and another of tart mussels steamed open, with parsley and garlic in more of the same white wine, flicked with lemon, smelling and tasting of the freshest sea spray.

Cross the street to a bar-restaurant and have a plate of the justly famous Galician baked scallops, served always on the half shell and topped with a bit of parsley and garlic and a sprinkling of bread crumbs. The hot scallops have a smooth sweet taste unlike any other scallops the world over, strongest when they are freshly cooked. Swap your neighbor a scallop for a sampling from his plate of *nécoras,* small orange boiled crabs that are said to bring luck because each carries the cross of St. James in the shell formation of its head. The meat of the *nécora* is flaky and white when boiled, tender in texture, subtle in flavor. The Galicians are all masters of the apparently simple business of boiling. They know exactly how long any food must cook without being too tough or too soft, and how to extract the taste from it.

The mastery applies to steaming as well as boiling. *Merluza,* hake, is steamed here to perfection with potatoes, paprika and garlic. The white flesh of the fish remains firm, and the sweet taste is not overwhelmed by liquid, for the fish is set on a rack in the pot above the boiling potatoes and never touches the water, which is so carefully measured it can boil around the potatoes until it evaporates entirely.

Nowhere is this special talent of Galician cooks displayed so wonderfully and so simply as in the boiling of the goose barnacles called *percebes,* which are peculiar to this particular coast of Spain and Portugal. If up to now you haven't found a convincing reason to come to Iberia's northern coasts, *percebes* alone are worth the trip, for it is not likely that you will find them anywhere else in the world. Shaped like small fingers, sheathed in a dark-gray sea leather that is like elephant skin, and topped with pointed, triangular, shingled black shells for mouths, the *percebes* grow in clusters in pools among

the sharply cut inlets of the Galician coastline. The *percebes* are boiled with only a bay leaf until they are tender, and they are equally good to eat hot or cold. Served a plate of them, you break one off from the cluster and peel the thick skin from the small triangular shell-mouth. The skin then slips off like a slippery glove and underneath is the pink flesh ready to be bitten from the shell top by which it is held. Tinged with salt and iodine, cleaned by soaring waves, sweet and juicy as they are tender, *percebes* are another of those foods that you cannot stop eating; but unlike most shellfish, too many of them will not do you much harm.

Many fish and shellfish, among them the *percebes* and the best lobsters, are caught in the high and low *rías* that line the coast of Galicia. In the geologic infancy of this land, before the rest of the Iberian Peninsula rose from the sea —when the first terrific earth bubble burst and half of what is now Galicia slid back into the waters—the *rías* were formed. (There is no exact translation for *ría;* the closest perhaps would be fjord.) They are places where the ocean cuts and slashes very deep into the high land; they are like wounds in the earth. Great gaping channels of ocean water slide in and out of the *rías* every six hours with the tide. When the tide is at its lowest, men and women wade into them, netting fish, raking shellfish, groping with their bare hands

The hearty meat pie above, called an *empanada,* brims with a savory mixture of chicken, onions and sweet red pepper. The *empanada* shown here serves four to six, but these pasties are also made as individual portions and may be filled with almost any kind of meat, fish and vegetables, singly or in combination. They are eaten in many parts of Spain and Latin America, and have long been a specialty of Galicia— where the damp, frequently harsh climate encourages robust diets.

for seaweed to fertilize their fields. The fisherfolk must time their work carefully, to be sure they reach the safety of the shore before the waters come rushing back into the *rías* with the locomotive violence of the returning tide.

Because of the importance of the *rías* in the economy and daily life of the people, it is often said that all life on the coasts of Galicia revolves around the tide-regulating cycles of the moon. If the first of October, the opening day of the shellfish season, happens to coincide with a neap tide, the very low tide that occurs at the first and the third quarter of the moon, literally everybody on the coast goes shellfishing to celebrate. Men, women and childen walk the now shallow waters of the *rías* with deep pots and wide baskets to hold and collect anything they can find. Lobster traps are emptied; the *rías* are robbed of everything they contain, and they contain a great variety of fine seafood. Then, as the tide turns, the celebrating people lift their children and clamber up the sides of earth and rock away from the returning waters. They take the lobsters home alive and cook them in sea water, often with no other seasoning than a few strands of seaweed, and serve them steaming and tasting purely of the sea.

As you leave Galicia, traveling south along the Atlantic coast from La Coruña, at the southern foot of the province you will come to a strip of land running east and west that is about three miles long and 200 yards wide. Here you will find a grape that produces a wine called Rosal. It is a white wine, golden in color, sharp as silver on the tongue, and it is naturally effervescent. It is one of the most appropriate wines as an accompaniment for any of the fine fish or shellfish from this coast. Walk across the thin strip of land where it is produced and you will be standing at the mouth of a river known as the Miño here—but spelled Minho on its far bank. Cross to that bank by ferry, and you will be standing on the foggy northern shore of a place that spreads far south below you: a dimly seen carpet of colors and savors, bright sights and high sounds, called Portugal.

When tourists and townsmen pause for cakes and tea on the sunswept terrace before the cathedral in Santiago de Compostela *(opposite)*, they are surrounded by reminders of St. James, the patron saint of Spain. The name of the town—Santiago—means St. James, while the massive cathedral was erected on the spot where, according to legend, the saint's bones were discovered in the Ninth Century. The sugar-topped almond cake in the foreground, served with other confections on the terrace, is embellished with the saint's own cross and called *tarta de Santiago*—the cake of St. James.

CHAPTER VII RECIPES

To serve 4 to 6

BREAD DOUGH

1 package or cake of active dry or
    compressed yeast
½ teaspoon sugar
½ cup lukewarm water (110° to
    115°)
2½ to 3 cups all-purpose flour
1½ teaspoons salt
½ cup lukewarm milk (110° to 115°)
1 tablespoon olive oil
1 egg, lightly beaten

FILLING

A 2- to 2½-pound chicken, cut into
    6 to 8 serving pieces
1 large onion, quartered
3 tablespoons olive oil
½ cup finely chopped onions
½ teaspoon finely chopped garlic
1 medium-sized sweet red or green
    pepper, deribbed, seeded and cut
    into ¼-inch squares
½ cup finely chopped *serrano* ham
    or substitute prosciutto or other
    lean smoked ham
3 medium-sized tomatoes peeled,
    seeded and finely chopped *(see
    huevos a la flamenca, page 16)*, or
    substitute 1 cup chopped, drained,
    canned tomatoes
½ teaspoon salt
¼ teaspoon freshly ground black
    pepper

Empanada Gallega
CHICKEN-FILLED BREAD PIE

In a small bowl, sprinkle the yeast and sugar over ¼ cup of the lukewarm water. Let it stand for 2 or 3 minutes, then stir to dissolve the yeast completely. Set the bowl in a warm, draft-free place, such as an unlighted oven, for 8 to 10 minutes, or until the mixture doubles in volume.

Combine 2 cups of the flour and the salt in a deep mixing bowl, make a well in the center, and pour in the yeast, milk and remaining ¼ cup of lukewarm water. Slowly stir together, adding up to 1 cup more flour, a few tablespoons at a time, until the mixture becomes a medium-firm dough that can be lifted up in a moist, solid mass.

Place the dough on a lightly floured surface and knead it by pressing down, pushing it forward several times with the heel of your hand. Fold it back on itself and knead for at least 10 minutes, or until the dough is smooth and elastic. Sprinkle a little flour over and under the dough when necessary to prevent it from sticking to the board.

Gather the dough into a ball and place it in a large, lightly buttered bowl. Dust the top with flour, drape a towel over it, and set in the warm place for 1½ hours or until the dough doubles in bulk. Punch it down with one blow of your fist, cover with a towel and let it rise again for 45 minutes.

To prepare the filling: Place the chicken and quartered onion in a 3- to 4-quart saucepan and add enough water to cover them by 1 inch. Bring to a boil over high heat, meanwhile skimming off the foam and scum as they rise to the surface. Reduce the heat to low, cover and cook the chicken for 30 minutes or until tender but not falling apart. Transfer the chicken to a plate.

When the chicken is cool enough to handle, remove the skin with a small knife or your fingers. Cut or pull the meat away from the bones. Discard the skin and bones, and cut the chicken meat into ½-inch cubes. Set aside.

In a 10- to 12-inch skillet, heat the oil over moderate heat until a light haze forms above it. Add the onions, garlic and red or green pepper and, stirring frequently, cook for 8 to 10 minutes, or until the vegetables are soft but not brown. Stir in the ham, then add the tomatoes, raise the heat and cook briskly until most of the liquid in the pan evaporates and the mixture is thick enough to hold its shape lightly in a spoon. Add the chicken, salt and pepper, taste for seasoning and cool to room temperature.

Preheat the oven to 375°. With a pastry brush, coat a large baking sheet with 1 tablespoon of olive oil.

To assemble the pie, divide the dough into halves. On a lightly floured surface, roll each half into a circle about 12 inches in diameter and ¼-inch thick. Place one of the circles on the baking sheet and spoon the filling on top, spreading it to within about 1 inch of the outside edges. Place the second circle of dough over the filling, pressing it down firmly around the edges. Then fold up the entire rim of the pie by about ½ inch and press all around the outer edges with your fingertips or the tines of a fork to seal them securely. Let the pie rise in the warm place for about 20 minutes.

Brush the pie with the beaten egg and bake in the middle of the oven for 45 minutes, or until the top is golden. Serve hot, or at room temperature.

Tortilla de Patata

POTATO AND ONION OMELET

To serve 4 to 6

In a heavy 10- to 12-inch skillet, heat 1 cup of olive oil over high heat until hot but not smoking. Add the potatoes, sprinkle them with 1 teaspoon of the salt and turn them about in the pan to coat them well with oil. Continue cooking, turning occasionally, until the potatoes brown lightly; then add the onions, reduce the heat and cook for about 10 minutes, stirring every now and then until the potatoes and onions are tender. Transfer the entire contents of the skillet to a large sieve or colander and drain the potatoes and onions of all their excess oil.

With a whisk or a rotary or electric beater, beat the eggs and the remaining 1 teaspoon of salt until frothy. Gently stir in the potatoes and onions. Heat the remaining 3 tablespoons of oil in a heavy 8-inch skillet until a light haze forms above it. Pour in the omelet mixture, spread it out with a spatula and cook over moderate heat for 2 minutes. Shake the pan periodically to keep the eggs from sticking. When the omelet is firm but not dry, cover the skillet with a flat plate and, grasping the plate and skillet firmly together, invert them and turn the omelet out in the plate. Then carefully slide the omelet back into the pan. Cook for 3 minutes longer to brown the underside, and serve at once.

NOTE: If you like, you may add previously fried chopped *chorizo* or other sausage to the omelet along with the potatoes.

Ingredients

1 cup plus 3 tablespoons olive oil
3 large potatoes (about 2 pounds), peeled and sliced into ⅛-inch-thick rounds
2 teaspoons salt
½ cup finely chopped onions
4 eggs

Fabada Asturiana

BEAN SOUP WITH SAUSAGES

To serve 6

In a heavy 8- to 10-quart casserole, bring 2 quarts of the water to a boil over high heat. Drop in the beans and boil them briskly uncovered for 2 minutes. Then remove the casserole from the heat and let the beans soak for 1 hour. Drain the beans in a sieve or colander set over a large bowl and return them to the casserole. Measure the bean-soaking liquid, add to it enough additional water to make 4 quarts and pour it into the casserole. Add the onions, garlic, and salt pork and bring to a boil over high heat, meanwhile skimming off the foam as it rises to the surface. Reduce the heat to low and simmer partially covered for 1 hour. Add the ham and simmer about 1 hour longer, or until the beans are barely tender.

Meanwhile, place the *chorizos* in an 8- to 10-inch skillet and prick them in two or three places with the point of a small, sharp knife. Add enough cold water to cover them completely and bring to a boil over high heat. Then reduce the heat to low and simmer uncovered for 5 minutes. Drain the sausages on paper towels.

When the soup has cooked for its allotted 2 hours, drop in the *chorizos* and *morcillas,* stir in the saffron, and cook 30 minutes longer. Taste and season liberally with salt and a few grindings of pepper. Then with a slotted spoon, transfer the salt pork, ham and sausages to a plate. Cut the pork and ham into ½-inch cubes and slice the sausages into ½-inch-thick rounds. Return the meat to the soup and simmer for 2 or 3 minutes. Traditionally, *fabada* is accompanied by a cornbread similar to the Portuguese *broa (Recipe Index)* and glasses of sparkling apple cider.

Ingredients

4 to 5 quarts water
2 cups (1 pound) dried fava beans or dried white kidney beans
2 cups coarsely chopped onions
1 tablespoon finely chopped garlic
¼ pound lean salt pork, in one piece with rind removed
½ pound *serrano* ham, or substitute prosciutto or other lean smoked ham, in one piece
3 *chorizos,* or substitute ½ pound other garlic-seasoned smoked pork sausage
3 *morcillas,* or substitute ½ pound other blood sausage
⅛ teaspoon ground saffron or saffron threads crushed with a mortar and pestle or with the back of a spoon
Salt
Freshly ground black pepper

Two Galician dishes use the sausages, smoked pork, turnip greens, potatoes, and broth shown at right. The broth and vegetables may be the base for the soup known as *caldo gallego (below)*. The meats and vegetables may be served as a main course called *lacón con grelos* (pork shoulder with turnip greens).

To serve 6

1 cup dried white beans, preferably white kidney or Great Northern
2 to 3 quarts water
½ pound *serrano* ham, cut into ½-inch cubes, or substitute prosciutto or other lean smoked ham or pork butt
2 ounces salt pork in one piece, with rind removed
½ cup finely chopped onions
2 teaspoons salt
2 *chorizos*, or substitute ⅓ pound other garlic-seasoned smoked pork sausage
½ pound turnip greens, washed, trimmed and coarsely shredded
2 small potatoes, peeled and cut into ¼-inch dice

Caldo Gallego
WHITE BEAN, TURNIP GREEN AND POTATO SOUP

In a heavy 3- to 4-quart casserole, bring 2 quarts of water to a boil over high heat. Drop in the beans and boil them briskly for 2 minutes. Then remove the pot from the heat and let the beans soak for 1 hour.

Drain the beans in a sieve or colander set over a bowl and return them to the casserole. Measure the soaking liquid and add enough fresh water to make 2 quarts. Pour the water into the casserole, add the ham, salt pork, onions and salt, and bring to a boil over high heat. Reduce the heat to low and simmer partially covered for 1½ hours.

When the beans have cooked their allotted 1½ hours, add the sausages, turnip greens and potatoes and continue to cook, partially covered for 30 minutes longer, or until the beans and potatoes are tender. With a slotted spoon, remove the sausages and salt pork. Slice the sausages into ¼-inch-thick rounds and return them to the soup. Discard the pork. Taste for seasoning and serve at once from a heated tureen or individual soup plates.

NOTE: This is one version of a classic Galician dish. In other versions,

142

smoked pork shoulder and salt pork are boiled together; sausage is added during the last part of the cooking. The meats are then removed and set aside, and chopped turnip greens, white beans, and diced potatoes are simmered in the remaining broth. The soup that results is served as *caldo gallego*.

The reserved smoked pork and sausages are sliced and served with cooked whole turnip greens and boiled potatoes as a main course known as *lacón con grelos*. The Galician version of the *cocido*, called *pote gallego*, is made with all the above ingredients plus veal and chicken.

Merluza a la Gallega
POACHED HAKE WITH POTATOES AND TOMATO SAUCE

To serve 4

In a heavy 12-inch skillet at least 2 inches deep, bring 2 quarts of water to a boil over high heat. Drop in the potatoes, onion, and bay leaf. There should be enough water to cover them completely; if necessary, add more. Boil briskly uncovered until the potatoes are tender but not falling apart. With a slotted spoon, transfer the potatoes to a plate. Add the fish fillets to the liquid remaining in the pan and reduce the heat to low. Cover the skillet tightly and simmer for 8 to 10 minutes, or until the fish flakes easily when prodded gently with a fork.

Meanwhile, heat the oil in a heavy 8- to 10-inch skillet over moderate heat until a light haze forms above it. Add the garlic cloves and, stirring frequently, cook them for about 5 minutes, or until light brown. With a slotted spoon, remove and discard them, then add the tomatoes and salt. Cook briskly, stirring and mashing the tomatoes with a large spoon, until the mixture is thick enough to hold its shape almost solidly in the spoon. Stir in the paprika and set aside.

Pour off all but 1 cup of liquid from the fish, discard the onion and bay leaf and return the potatoes to the skillet. With the back of a spoon, force the tomato mixture through a fine sieve, directly over the fish. Simmer over low heat for 5 minutes, basting the fish and potatoes frequently with the sauce. Sprinkle with the vinegar and serve at once, directly from the skillet or from a deep heated platter.

- 12 small firm boiling-type potatoes, each about 1½ inches in diameter, peeled
- 1 small onion, peeled and cut in half
- 1 small bay leaf
- 1½ pounds of hake, haddock or cod fillets
- 6 tablespoons olive oil
- 6 medium-sized garlic cloves, peeled and gently bruised with the flat of a knife
- 3 medium-sized tomatoes, peeled, seeded and coarsely chopped (*huevos a la flamenca, page 16*)
- ½ teaspoon salt
- 1 tablespoon paprika
- 1 teaspoon red wine vinegar

Pastel de Manzana
APPLE-MINT CRISP

To serve 6

Preheat the oven to 350°. With a pastry brush, coat the bottom and sides of an 8-by-8-by-2-inch baking dish with softened butter. Set aside. Combine the sugar, flour and baking powder and sift them into a mixing bowl. Make a well in the center and drop in the egg. Mix together with two table knives until the flour has thoroughly absorbed the egg.

In a large mixing bowl, stir the mint leaves and cinnamon together. Add the apples and toss them about with a large spoon until the slices are evenly coated on all sides. Arrange the slices in the baking dish and scatter the flour mixture over them, spreading and pressing it gently into a smooth layer to cover the apples completely. Bake in the middle of the oven for 45 minutes, or until the topping is crusty. Remove the dish from the oven, cover it tightly with a lid or foil, and set aside to cool. Serve, at room temperature, accompanied if you like with a bowl of whipped cream.

- 1 tablespoon butter, softened
- 1 cup sugar
- 1 cup all-purpose flour
- ½ teaspoon double-acting baking powder
- 1 egg
- 1 tablespoon dried mint leaves
- 1 tablespoon ground cinnamon
- 4 medium-sized tart cooking apples (about 2 pounds), peeled, quartered, cored and cut lengthwise into ¼-inch slices
- 1 cup heavy cream, whipped (optional)

VIII

Portugal: The Rugged North

In the southwestern corner of Europe lies a slender patch of land 360 miles at its longest by 140 miles at its widest, isolated from the rest of the continent by Spain, and isolated from Spain by jagged mountains. Stroked onto the sea like the afterthought of a wine-happy painter who returned to his canvas with the conviction that *something* was missing, Portugal stands alone; it is related to Spain but separate from it—and totally exposed to the harsh winds and waves of the Atlantic Ocean, which stretches westward like a desert of water as far as the setting sun. If things are not done in Portugal today quite as they are done in Spain, this may be not so much a matter of taste as of historical necessity: what Spain denied her, Portugal *had* to find in the mysterious, apparently endless stretches of gray water from which an occasional strange leaf or tropical fruit or oddly carved bit of wood washed onto her shores. From the first, Portugal missed much of the agony and torture of her sister country; instead, she found other qualities. Brave curiosity, flagrant nostalgia, a kind of innocence, youth, a lyric sadness over a lurking brightness, all of these are to be found today in Portugal in bold focus. They can be seen in everything from its most sophisticated urban architecture to the faces of its peasants. But nowhere are its unique qualities and achievements so clearly illustrated as in all things related to its food and cooking.

For those who approach the subject as we have, after visiting Spain region by region, it is important to realize that Portuguese cooking is *not* Spanish cooking. It is rather another type of Iberian cooking, as different from any one of the regional kitchens we have seen as each of them is from all the others. Like all Iberian food, it is basically simple and a food of the people; yet

145

spices and herbs are more widely used here, and taste combinations that would be astonishing to most Spanish palates are common in Portugal.

From north to south the kitchens of Portugal share a wide variety of ingredients. Fresh herbs like coriander as well as preserved foods like salt-dried cod are often found. Fresh lemon juice is squeezed on meat, which is also cooked with sweet rich port or Madeira. Fresh and dried figs, nuts, rice, egg yolks, vanilla and even curry are used throughout the country, along with many other foods and ingredients already familiar to us in Spain. More noticeable is the number of ways in which these ingredients are used—for the diversity of taste combinations is what makes Portuguese cooking most special. If you travel south from the Spanish frontier in Galicia, you can find in the 11 Portuguese provinces enough different juxtapositions of flavors to fill an encyclopedia. Go fairly slowly, starting from the three provinces of the north and winding back and forth, east to west, but always keeping in a general southerly direction, visiting coastal towns and cities as well as inland farms and country inns. Follow the map in a winding line from top to bottom and in each area you will be able to choose dishes that tell something about the place where they are served and the people who serve them.

The three northern provinces—Minho, Trás-os-Montes e Alto Douro and Douro Litoral, contain, paradoxically, some of the poorest and most ragged land and some of the finest cooking in Portugal. One of the first things you notice in this country is the ability of all of its people to respond to the harshest living conditions with the gayest costumes, the brightest festivals and the best food—as if they wanted to grace the earth with their presence. The fertile province of Minho is a good example. This sister province to Spain's Galicia (where a nearly identical dialect is spoken) has become a region of poverty; its rich earth has been divided among its sons and daughters so minutely that it can no longer feed all of them. In the early decades of this century many left for Venezuela or Brazil to make a living; more recently others have gone to Germany and France. Those who have remained behind cultivate every inch of the soil, plan elaborate holidays, sing and dance and turn the dreariest work into the liveliest of occasions. They chant in chorus as they shuck corn from the fields to be kept in storehouses near their homes; they make a bright cornbread called *broa (Recipe Index),* which is nearly sweet, spongier and more filling than the cornbread of Galicia, and especially good when eaten with a Minho soup called *caldo verde (Recipe Index).*

Minho's *caldo verde* or green broth is to Portugal what onion soup is to France—it has become a kind of national food. Wherever you go in the country, at any time of day, you see women dressed in black, seated and standing, shredding kale for *caldo verde.* The deep green, strongly flavored Portuguese kale is different from the vegetable grown in other countries. Not only is kale superb in Minho, all vegetables seem stronger in color, leafier and bigger than anywhere else in Portugal.

Caldo verde is made simply. First, Minho potatoes, which because of the richness of the soil here are the best in the country, are boiled, lightly mashed, and then put back into the cooking water with olive oil and strips of kale shredded so uniformly thin they appear to be machine-made. One or two slices of garlic pork sausage, *linguiça* or *chouriço,* are placed at the bottom of a bowl and the steaming soup is poured over them. "Drink it while it's hot"

is a cliché that might have been invented for *caldo verde,* which can be drunk any time of the day or night all year, but is best in the cold wet weather of the Minho winters. Just slightly thick in texture, whitish green in color with deep vibrant green kale-strips floating on the surface and dark purple sausage slices swimming underneath, *caldo verde* has a delicately edged rich taste that matches the look of Minho's fresh vegetables blooming on the land. Offset by the taste of the sweetish yellow country cornbread, it should be drunk with one of tart red *vinhos verdes* that are produced in this region.

Vinho verde, green wine, refers not to the color of the wine in Minho—it is white or red—but to the state of the young grape that is crushed to make it. Faintly effervescent, the green wine has a tart light flavor that gives an extra tinge to *caldo verde* and to another fine local dish—lamprey stew.

While Minho river waters provide the same lamprey that is found in Galicia, Minho cooks give it a new taste. Here the slices of tender lamprey are prepared with a deep yellow gravy that often smells and tastes of curry, an ingredient that would not ordinarily be expected in any part of Iberia. First brought back from India by Vasco da Gama in 1497 as a sort of tasteful preservative, curry has by now taken its place as a useful spice in some of the poorest peasant homes and country taverns of Portugal. It is more often used purely for flavor than as a "hot" spice, and it blends well with the dark, almost meaty taste of the river lamprey.

Minho also produces a variety of fine rice dishes, combining the rice with rabbit, duck or partridge, which are usually cooked with *presunto,* the Portuguese mountain-cured ham; *chouriço* or possibly *linguiça;* and fresh lemon

Turning the thin soil of Portugal's Douro Litoral province with a primitive plow, two farmers and their oxen prepare a field for planting. They will sow it with wheat, a crop that grows even in this barren and hilly region outside the village of Chãos (*background*).

Continued on page 150

Ribatejan picnickers enjoy the codfish cakes and wine they have brought to Vila Franca for a post-bullfight supper.

A More Relaxed Way of Fighting Bulls

Bullfighting in Portugal is not like bullfighting in Spain:
Portuguese bullfighters may be on foot or horseback,
and they do not kill the bulls. As a gentler sport,
mainly a display of grace and adeptness, Portuguese
bullfighting is family entertainment—the main event
in a festival called a *festa brava*. The most famous *festa
brava* is held at Vila Franca de Xira in Ribatejo for
two days in October. On the first day, the bulls are
driven through the streets of the town by *campinos*, the
men who train the bulls and the horses. In colorful
costumes with red trimmed green caps, the *campinos*
are watched (and sometimes handed a snack, as at
left) by admiring throngs. When the bullfighting is
over, families set their picnic fare out on long tables
in shaded pavilions. Those who come unprepared may
use charcoal grills to cook fresh sardines *(right),* which
are eaten between slices of country bread.

juice. Often made during the gay pilgrimage-fair or *romaria* in the town of Viana do Castelo during the latter part of August, country rice dishes of Minho have become city foods and are enjoyed during the hundreds of festivals that take place throughout Portugal every year. Go there any time during Viana's *romaria*. There will be parades and bullfights and light, floating country dancing in which blonde Minho peasant women wearing colorful, bright folk costumes and single-strand gold necklaces step in unison through the streets over carpets of flowers. In the evening you will see figures from legend and the Bible roaming the city in honor of Our Lady of Agony. Fireworks glitter over the gentle slow river Lima, once called the River of Forgetfulness. You walk past cool granite houses under curving windows and sit in a small tavern where you will be served a dish of Minho rice. The rich sweet meat of roast duck has been combined with just enough lemon juice to bring out the lean taste, then brushed with butter and baked on a bed of rice. It is served steaming and juicy in the same casserole in which it was cooked.

Even the briefest visit to this *romaria* will suggest that things in Portugal do not run to extremes as they do in Spain; this is a country of gentler customs and softer traditions. The bull is not killed in the bullfight; the folkdancing is placid, lighter and easier and more carefree, less stark than in Spain. Meal hours here are earlier, with lunch at about 1:30 or 2 p.m. and dinner at about 8 or 9 p.m. Nowhere is this a country of extremes; even the houses themselves in rural villages and cities take on the tints of a predominantly pastel prism that will stay with you throughout your visit.

Go now to the ocean along Minho's coast for a first taste of one of the many superlative seafood dishes of Portugal that are best with one of the white green wines. Guidebooks often tell you to stick to large restaurants in sizable Portuguese cities; I find the opposite rule works best. With a few marked exceptions, Portuguese cooking, always a food of the people, is better in the kitchens of country homes or village taverns where the fare is sometimes so limited there is no choice—but the cooking is always superb.

Stop at an inn or tavern on this northern coast for a shellfish *açorda*, a dish that—like most Portuguese achievements—has been overlooked by foreigners. In Portugal the term *açorda* refers to any one of a collection of dry bready soups that are largely unknown elsewhere. An *açorda* is a dish of softened bread with a little oil, crushed garlic and anything from vegetables to pork or chicken, fish or snails. The shellfish *açorda*, the one I happen to like best, is prepared and served in a small earthenware dish. Bread is soaked in the hot liquid that has been used to boil mussels, clams, shrimp, squid and whatever other shellfish have been caught in the fishermen's nets the day the dish is made. Chopped fresh coriander is added—and just before the steaming *açorda* is served it is topped by the hot shellfish and then by raw eggs that poach as they are stirred slowly into the blistering mixture. Again, the combination of tastes is wonderful. Fresh coriander in steaming liquid has a pungent, sharp taste that blends gently and marvelously with the tangy shellfish, the fresh poached farm eggs and the sweet country bread.

Travel a short distance down the coast from Minho and you will find yourself in Porto, the capital of the province of Douro Litoral. Portugal's second largest city, Porto was a prospering business town when Lisbon was only a resort. Today it is almost a definition of a middle-class provincial business city

Like other Portuguese convents, the one at Aveiro is famous for its sweets, including the confections shown here. At left is *morcelas oces de Arouca* or sweet "sausages" and at right, a variety of *ovos moles*, an egg-yolk and sugar mixture molded into fish and shell shapes.

—a place of odd visual contrasts, of old stone and neon lights, roses and river water often washed into pastel streaks by thin sweeping rain. Famous the world over for the port wines that are bottled here (though the grapes come from another province), Porto is just as famous in its own country, as the place to eat tripe. The citizens are, in fact, called "tripe-eaters" in the rest of Portugal. There are several legends to explain this; the most popular tells of Prince Henry the Navigator who in 1415 slaughtered all the cattle of the region to feed the troops of his crusader fleet, leaving only tripe for the citizens of Porto. Today tripe is hardly the only food in town but it is prepared here simply and perhaps better than anywhere else in the world. Again, it is best when made either in a home or in one of the *tascas* or taverns hidden in the old quarters; the big fine restaurants tend to modify it out of existence. Look near the docks for a small *tasca* of six or eight tables and order a dish of tripe with beans. The casserole will be brought in with a trail of steam— the beans cooked with the tripe, the rice served separately. This may be your first introduction to a rigid standard of Portuguese restaurants, large or small: At least two kinds of starch are served at every meal, often three or four, as we shall see later. The tripe stew in front of you is seasoned with cumin, pepper and bay leaf. The ingredients of the dish *(Recipe Index)*—fine tripe, beans, veal, garlicky *chouriço* or *linguiça*, dark-cured *presunto*, chicken, onion, carrots and fresh parsley—combine to season themselves into a peppery, dappled taste, that is best when eaten with a red sparkling *vinho verde*. Follow the tripe and beans with fresh fruit, or if you can manage it, a bowl of dried fruit and nuts. Walnuts are wonderful in Portugal; they are especially fine when broken into bits and stuffed, by the diner, into a long slit made in a chewy dried fig. The tastes mingle well, and are heightened by a glass of one of the city's vintage tawny ports.

As you go east from Porto, inland through Douro Litoral and toward Trás-os-Montes e Alto Douro, you will see the grapes grown for port hanging heavy in thick purple and ruby clusters on hillsides of dark lava soil. At harvest time men carry the ripe grapes in huge baskets looped by leather thongs to their foreheads; leaning forward precariously they go down the gray-green hillsides to vats where the grapes are crushed. Here the grapes begin to ferment into new wine, surrounded by men and women who chant, sing and dance until the air appears to take on a dark purple glow.

Drive on through the country and stop in the small city of Amarante to have a jellylike egg sweet, called the sweet of São Gonçalo. There are literally thousands of egg-yolk sweets made in Portugal, and this one is a good introduction; egg yolk and sugar will become a familiar taste as you travel; it is best offset by a glass of ruby port.

The name of Amarante's version of this sweet honors the patron saint of spinsters, as does the *romaria* held here the first weekend in June. Special cakes are baked all over the town in the shape of a phallus and given by men to women and women to men in a Catholic vestige of what once must have been a pagan fertility rite. In Portugal it is not unusual for the most ancient pagan custom to mingle with a relatively modern tradition. Prehistoric statues of boars are seen in this same area, from the "Pig of Murça" in the town of that name, to the great stone boar of Bragança. Legend has it that the ancient statues were made as magic charms to protect the countryside that was once terrorized by the attacks of an immense wild boar; but it seems more likely that the popular stone boar symbol was worshipped as a god.

From this landlocked province, you turn naturally back to the sea. It is as if the earth itself reminds you that Portugal belongs to the ocean and you are drawn back to the beach almost as often as the tides. You journey now to Aveiro, in the province of Beira Litoral. Aveiro is a coastal city where you are always aware of the ocean's mastery over the land. It sits on the edge of an oddly shaped lagoon where birdlike boats seem to float over the green meadows; here you see canals and ponds, ditches and sand bars swept by ocean waters. Aveiro's port was choked in 1575 by a savage storm and was not reopened until another storm broke the barrier in 1808; so the city has learned to live by land as well as by sea. In her amoeba-shaped lagoon, its form altering from year to year with the violence of tides, sea birds soar, fresh-water fish swim over salt-water shellfish, and men and oxen rake in crabs, eels and clams as well as seaweed for fertilizer. In the earliest part of the day these men, stripped to the waist like bronze figures in the pastel morning mist, pole their swan's-neck boats through the lagoon, returning home with the catch. Then their wives, mixing these ingredients with one or two river and salt-water fish they have obtained at the market that day, are able to make the local version of the *caldeirada (Recipe Index)*—the fish and shellfish stew that is prepared in all coastal cities and towns of Portugal.

Aveiro's *caldeirada* is special, tasting of both ocean and lagoon. It combines salt-water with fresh-water ingredients in a thick stew that includes chunks of ocean mullet, inland river eel, red snapper, sole, octopus, crabs, shrimp, possibly squid and perhaps a few clams and mussels. The result, cooked in a thick sauce the color of oak, sharp with cumin and chopped parsley and sometimes fresh coriander, bright with slices of carrot and onion, is as solid as a meat stew. It is hot and filling but not heavy—the taste is a deep reminder of the sea-land life that sustains the city. I like it with a cold, full dry wine like the white Dão made in Beira Alta, and it should be followed by any one of the fabulous collection of Aveiro sweets.

If you walk through Aveiro in the paling morning mist you will find two, three and sometimes even four sweet shops next to each other; each has a big window piled high with freshly baked pastries, sweets and cakes of astounding variety. They look like displays of edible gold in every shape and shade. The Aveiro specialty is called *ovos moles (Recipe Index)*, sold in tiny wooden barrels. It is a sort of paste of egg yolk cooked with sugar in rice water and the taste of yolk is so strong and sweet you must eat it sparingly, but even a little is a very good thing. A recipe for *ovos moles*, like many Iberian sweets, has been preserved in a nearby convent where nuns in past centuries provided visiting ecclesiastic dignitaries with the most elegant desserts. I like *ovos moles* with the bland taste of one of the sponge cakes from the same shop windows. It is best also when taken with a little port at an outdoor table in Aveiro during spring or summer, in the sea haze that softens and freshens the land.

With this new breath of ocean air, you turn back inland, heading southeast of Aveiro toward the hill-and-river city of Coimbra. Stop just before you get there for lunch or dinner at one of the towns north of the city and try the roast suckling pig. It is cooked in a stone oven, much the same as in Spain, but here it is more peppery on the outside and tangier with herbs on the inside because it is spitted on a whole branch of wild country thyme. The tender meat under the crisp skin is delicate in flavor and quite lean; it goes well with a green salad and the icy sparkling white wine of the region.

When you have finished eating here, drive on into Coimbra, breaking another guidebook rule by going in the late fall or early winter when rain is frequent. After a morning of rain when the clouds momentarily lift, the earth looks almost purple; olive trees are light silver in the gray swollen light, and the pink and gray buildings suddenly loom over a hill under a leaden but brightening sky. Steeped in stone on the banks of the Mondego River, this university city is a fine place in November, when the grays of stone, river and sky are like parts of one immense design. You will want to stay at least a day or two: Walking or eating or just being in this city is a pleasure.

Go in the afternoon to the top of Coimbra to visit the university that controls the pulse of the city's life; from these white and gray long buildings where Camões, Portugal's most famous poet, studied in the 16th Century, the city below looks like a maze of brown-topped houses and plunging streets that meet at the angular river. Go at night to one of the many *repúblicas* or fraternity houses where the university students live, and have a meal with them. You need not know them; a call from your hotel will suffice for an introduction; the students are friendly, hospitable and at least as curious about you as you are about them. One of these fraternity houses, the *República Pagode Chinês* (Chinese Pagoda) is a small dark building that was once a private house on a hill. It is now a home for Catholic-Monarchist uni-

In her tiled and pot-lined kitchen (*above*) at Arouca, a Portuguese housewife and her daughter prepare *caldo verde*, a hot soup made with fresh kale and potatoes. For her version, slices of a smoked ham roll called *salpicão* are simmered in the soup and served with it (*below*).

153

On the Vale Feitoso estate in the province of Beira Baixa, one oven serves the whole community. Over a glowing hearth in this cement and stone oven, the estate's baker, Dores, can bake a dozen or more loaves at a time, sliding them expertly into place on a long wooden baker's peel.

versity students who have painted a large figure of Buddha on the wall of their dining room: whoever touches him must suffer a punishment devised at the time by all the other students.

Go now with one or two of the students who will ask the woman who works for them—the only servant for cooking, cleaning and laundering in the whole house—to reheat a plate of something left over from dinner for their unexpected guest. While the food is being prepared, visit the students' rooms—small, dark, strangely cheerful cell-like places. The walls are crowded with geometric symbols and figures of Chinese masks and Chinese temples next to real American Indian tomahawks and posters of Monarchist leaders side by side with English and American rock 'n' roll singers. Books are spread open on desks, beds and floors next to papers and pens, and close by dark-shaded lamps; there is a kind of happy gloom and piercing interest in everything. When the cooking smells roll in strong from the kitchen, you go back through the dark hall with the students to the dining room for a plate of octopus and rice in a deep pink sauce set in front of a platter of cold turkey leftovers. Afterward, you are given a bowl of fresh fruit and a plate of sugar-coated cup cakes that are spongy, pale yellow and not too sweet. But for coffee, invite the students in turn to be your guests in one of Coimbra's late night snack-bar-restaurants.

When the university students go out in the city of Coimbra tradition requires that they wear long black capes over their coats. You will see many of them carrying guitars, and the melancholy strains of sentimental ballads and bawdy songs rise out of courtyards and patios along the steep streets and alleyways. The city itself is like a wonderfully twisted collection of cobblestone paths, steep steps and swooping roads that seem as aimless as the trickles and streams of water winding down toward the Mondego—the river Portuguese people are proudest of because it begins and ends in Portugal without ever touching Spanish soil. Below the city, poplars hang as if suspended from the sky along the banks of the Mondego. Women wash clothes here, and the river waters are used both to irrigate the fields and to transport fresh food from ocean to inland cities and towns. Fish, shellfish, octopus and squid are carried up this sea-vein to Coimbra, reminding city-dwellers in the interior that the Atlantic, even when invisible, still feeds the land.

At the foot of a steep flight of steps near the river is a bar-restaurant, open late, where students often gather with other citizens of Coimbra to swap stories and discuss the world. Everything is talked about here, but people are very careful about whom they are talking to when they discuss Portuguese politics—a reminder that Portugal, like Spain, is a dictatorship. In the student restaurant here, as the evening grows older, the air is thick with smoke from cigarettes and pipes, steam from coffee and tea, smells of beer and wine and broiling fish and meats. The walls are clean white and the tables weathered and plain with straight wooden chairs; the room is comfortable and nearly full, but there are few women at this hour. At one table, two men are eating a plate of hard boiled eggs with salt and pepper and drinking pints of golden Portuguese beer from frosted dark brown bottles. Next to them, a student has a cup of exquisitely bitter Angola coffee with a small plate of chocolate mousse made with sweet port. A white-coated waiter passes with a plate of eight different pastries and puts it down before another student who may eat one or at most two of the pastries along with a glass of *anis*. Behind this student three men share a platter of boiled, opaque white hake surrounded by hot boiled potatoes and cabbage so perfectly steamed it lies on the plate like a blowzy open flower. Try the most expensive dish on the menu, called a "Sputnik" because it disappears over the horizon of the table with the speed of a satellite. The price is just under a dollar, and a waiter will bring you a long, wide heated platter with two slices of juicy broiled veal steak topped by two fried eggs, all lying on a bed of crisp fried potatoes surrounded by small pyramids of rice and garnished with shells of lettuce and small, ripe, pitted black olives. The thin hot juice from the steak slides around the edges of the platter and seeps up into the rice and potatoes; the meat is fresh and sharp; nothing needs salt, and no mustard will be brought to the table unless requested, for Portuguese restaurants take as much pride in seasoning their food as in decorating and serving it.

In the morning, after your introduction to Coimbra, you will want to visit the shadowy alleys behind the big river-bank buildings to see the *tascas*, small taverns and tiny restaurants. The *tascas* hold just a few small tables where fine meals are served to workers and poor students on dates—and to all people who care more about what they are eating than about elegant décor. Take an umbrella and walk in the heavy late morning rain along the narrow cobblestone alleys, past small rooms with swinging doors closed against the water that splashes high off the stones and rushes loudly by in the shallow gutters. Here you will see steamed windows with sizzling meats and piles of tomatoes, onions, fresh vegetables and fish waiting to be cooked. Food smells fill the wet alley. Small blackboards and hand-lettered signs announce the plates of the day: *bife à portuguésa*, steak topped with slices of ham *(Recipe Index)*, or *sopa à portuguésa*, a special soup made of pork and veal with cabbage, white beans, carrots and macaroni—warming and nourishing in the cold rain. As the water suddenly falls heavier, like a dam bursting down into the little alley, you duck now into a *tasca* past a big glass cage of small gray-feathered birds. Inside, anybody from the only waitress to the cook-owner will rescue your dripping umbrella and seat you with a menu at a small square table. Ask for the menu of the day, which is bound to be good, and you will be served a four-course meal for about a dollar. First is a *canja* or chicken broth *(Recipe Index)*—another national dish of Portugal, prepared in many versions. This one contains rice, ham and lemon juice with chopped onions and almonds. With it you have a dry white house wine in a blue ceramic pitcher; the wine will serve for the entire meal. Next comes a dish of broiled tiny squid and scrambled eggs in a shallow earthenware dish with a thin scattering of pickles—usually small slices of pickled carrots, cauliflower and onions as well as two or three black olives—and, around the rim, a few fried potatoes. Afterward a broiled, split, whole quail is served with its thin skin crackling over light meat and tender bones. This is one of the birds from the glass case you passed as you came in; the small tavern has put its game in the window just as seafood restaurants sometimes put fish in tanks for customers to see. Iberians are not hypocritically sentimental about seeing baby birds prior to eating them: Food is food. The fragrant quail meat is firm and fine, and there are a few more fried potatoes and two small hillocks of rice and olives to go with it. Then for dessert you are served a juicy, slightly over-ripe pear with a thick piece of creamy sharp white *serra* or mountain cheese—another taste-texture combination that is produced as simply in Portugal as if the two ingredients had been invented to be eaten together.

On my last trip I left Coimbra on a wet autumn day, to visit Vale Feitoso farm about 75 miles to the southeast, deep in the interior of the province called Beira Baixa. The road took me past Conimbriga, the ruins of the ancient Roman city from which Coimbra took its name in the Middle Ages, where the remains of thermal baths and fountains, columns and glittering intricate mosaics shone and sparkled in the damp gleaming afternoon. The road led south and I took a shortcut to the east, twisting and turning over dirt roads on the edges of high pine-shadowed hills until the light began to dim. I stopped for the night at a white country inn, and in the morning I woke looking over smoky hills that sloped down to white and yellow houses with orange roofs and many-paned windows glittering in the early light. I had a breakfast of hot tea and rolls with fresh butter and thick, dark, aromatic honey—honey that was so suddenly sweet it was almost bitter and that smelled as strongly of flowers as if it were perfumed. I ate slowly, watching the long, cold, pink clouds lighten over the earth. Later in the chilly morning as I drove on, the sky turned steely blue and gold and then tarnished in the east as more rain clouds gathered over the hills.

I drove into the rain and stopped toward noon in a country village; I was damp and cold, and when the rain turned to a light drizzle I got out of the car and asked if there was a tavern anywhere. A woman carrying a basket of kale on her head shrugged and said that there was no place to eat in the noon-deserted village. She started away and then stopped for a second with her strong back still turned and pointed to a low building in another street. She said nothing, and the wet kale gleamed and shivered over her as she turned the corner and disappeared. My throat ached with the damp, and I went to the place she had pointed out. It was dark inside the one-story building and I could see only one room. There was a fierce smell of baking, and the glow of a dull orange fire in a corner to my right. Two women dressed in black were sitting in the dark around the glowing oven; they rose when I asked if there was anything to eat; one of them opened the oven, but it was too dark to make out the contents. The younger woman stooped over and gathered some dry brush from the earthen floor of the room. She set fire to it by touching it to a hot coal at the back of the oven; then she stood the brush just inside the oven to the left and it flared up almost immediately, sending a deep red light far into the dark hollow. The oven belonged to the village, and at the back of it was a flat layer of reddish-black coals like chunks of lava around ten or twelve round pie-sized loaves of brown bread. Half of the loaves had single short straws sticking out of their centers to identify them for the owners. The older woman took a long, flat, wooden spade from a row of utensils against the wall, slipped the spade under a loaf of bread and slid it out along the cement and stone oven floor. Then she waited until the loaf was cool enough to touch, and handed it to me; I broke a chunk off the edge. The heavy bread was the color of dark earth, dusty-dry with flour on the outside of the crust. On the inside it was very moist and chewy like a thick sponge, and too hot to touch at the center, as if it concealed a single red-hot coal from the oven. I ate a piece, letting the hot bread sear my throat open and burn away the feel of the dampness outside. The country bread was salt-sweet and it bloomed on the tongue, a taste to match the color of late sun in a wheatfield. People who think that all bread should be "light" should try this. It was the best bread I have ever eaten—the only bread that made a whole meal by itself without butter or cheese or even wine—and I finished half the loaf and took the other half with me, zippered inside my windbreaker and warm against my chest, the bread keeping a faint glow inside and outside the body for hours on into the damp day.

By 7 o'clock that night I reached the farm in Beira Baixa—12,000 hectares, or 28,000 acres, between the Portuguese city of Castelo Branco and the Spanish frontier. It belonged to Count da Ponte, a friend of a friend, and I had been told that it was entirely self-sufficient. I could find nothing on any map to indicate that the farm existed—not even a third-class road anywhere in the near vicinity. Now, at its edge, I drove along an ox path for half an hour in deserted rolling country both misty and dark. High trees gave a sense of green gloom to the night: it was a little like entering a world with another dimension of time. The trees closed behind the car like two halves of a curtain swinging together, shutting off the rest of the country. I slowed here and there for a stray cow or a deep rut in the road. The farm was huge, and looked more like what Americans might describe as a ranch in the woods. Surrounded by pine and eucalyptus trees and studded with long, one-storied buildings like white oblong blocks, the main house, in contrast, was made of high wooden beams with finished dark logs for walls. It had a rustic elegance and a sense of well-protected space.

I arrived at the farm in time to be welcomed for dinner. Count da Ponte was away on a trip, and in his absence I sat down with his grown sons in a dark-wood dining room at a round table.

In the center of the table there was a basket of fresh fruit surrounded by dishes of almonds, walnuts and figs. A bowl of *canja* was served, thickened with egg yolks, and after it came two platters filled with tender chunks of kid and gravy. The kid had been roasted with sweet red peppers, and around it on the platter was a ring of sautéed mashed potatoes. The meat was juicy and rich, good with the sweet-bitter taste of the peppers, and the po-

With centuries-old techniques, the Vale Feitoso estate produces its own cheese from the milk of its sheep. Cheese maker Maria Borrega presses the clabber (thick soured milk) firmly into metal molds, squeezing it to force the liquid whey out of the soft curds. Covered with cheesecloth, the new cheeses are then left to drain for a day or so before being put in a cool storage room to age and ripen.

Continued on page 160

157

Equipped with a parasol and a prod, farm hand Tio (uncle) Braz tends the Vale Feitoso's long-horned breeding cattle.

A Farm With No Need Of the Outside World

The people of Vale Feitoso, the 28,000-acre estate in eastern Portugal visited by the author of this book, could live there in comfort indefinitely without contact with the modern world around them. The estate is owned by the family of the Count da Ponte, whose ancestors received the property as a gift from Queen Dona Maria II in the middle of the 19th Century. The farm produces its own lumber, cereals, meat, dairy products, olives, olive oil, wine and fruits. The herds of cattle *(above)* and flocks of sheep and goats on the farm provide meat, wool and milk for cheese making. Wild game—partridges, hares, wild rabbits and foxes—is so abundant in the forests on the estate that two wings of the main house are equipped as lodges to accommodate visiting hunters. The herdsmen shown here also serve as guides.

Back from a day's hunting on the expansive Vale Feitoso estate in remote eastern Portugal, hosts and guests enjoy a hearty dinner: a rice-and-meat dish and a green salad, accompanied by red wine and followed by cheese, fruit and nuts. Manuel da Ponte, heir apparent to the estate, is at the far right. Manuel's brother, Diogo, is at his right.

tatoes were crisp, hot and smooth on the inside. There was another platter that looked like creamed spinach and turned out to be creamed turnip tops studded golden with wedges of fried bread. The turnip tops were wonderful, dark green mixed with white cream and faintly bitter—fine with the kid and the sweet peppers. For dessert there were two platters of small yellow egg cakes—called angels' breasts *(papos de anjo)* by the Portuguese—smothered with amber syrup *(Recipe Index)*. They had a dark flavor, alive with the syrup, and I ate three of them and could have eaten three more. I had heard about them before, and I asked Manuel, the eldest da Ponte son, who was acting as host, whether the same sweet wasn't called nuns' breasts elsewhere in Portugal. He grinned and said no, they weren't the same thing at all: these pastries were made with egg yolk and were therefore yellow; nuns' breasts, he explained, are white.

I slept in the big brown-and-white farmhouse, and the rain stopped sometime early in the morning. I got up early and ate a country breakfast of hot coffee, served in a fireproof pitcher over a burner with an open flame, chunks of fresh brown bread, white rolls, jam and heavy dark honey.

Then I walked around the farm. The land was white and thick with morning fog, dotted with the low eucalyptus and pine trees. I passed a long pile of yellow-red pumpkins gleaming in the mist; the earth was wet, and the bleating of many sheep came from somewhere deep out of the fog: voices torn from bodies and left floating, echoing in the rocky hills. The cook at the main house had told me proudly that the sheep all knew their names, and each came to be milked when called by the shepherd. I saw them finally, white blots like pieces of congealed fog held neatly together in the thick white air by two small yellow dogs that lay flat on the earth watching, or sliced back and forth at either end of the flock. I was trying to find the building where cheese was made from the sheeps' milk; it had been described to me, but all the low, white farm buildings looked alike and a little unreal in

160

the white air. I passed a man raking manure and asked him which building it was. He straightened and pointed to his right with the surety of a compass; I asked how he could tell which building was which when the fog was so thick I could hardly see my own shoes. He laughed loudly and said that he knew all the buildings and paths as well as every inch of road in all the nearly 50 square miles of farmland. I thanked him and went on. There was something strange about the way he had stared at me in the fog, but it wasn't until I got back to the main house later and asked about him that I knew for certain the man was blind.

The building where the *serra* cheeses were made consisted of a single damp room with a steep wooden ladder going down through the floor to a larger basement. The room smelled sour and old and wet. A woman was dipping clabber out of a large metal container shaped like a Greek amphora and packing the clabber into a long circular strip of metal full of draining holes. The metal circle lay on its side on a wooden trough, which was tilted at a slight angle so that the watery whey could spill off into a bucket placed underneath. The woman packed the clabber tightly, squeezing as much whey as she could by hand, covering it with cheesecloth and then kneeling on it with one knee for more pressure. She explained that the bucket of pale white whey below would not be thrown out, but would be mixed with pumpkins and potatoes as food for the pigs: nothing was wasted on the farm. After she had made four new cheeses about the size of large Camemberts, she covered them with cheesecloth, left them on the board to drain for the rest of the day, and led me down the ladder to see the basement. It was damper and cooler below, and there was no light except from a single bulb overhead. There was a sharp ammonia smell in the air and the feel of mildew. The cheeses were laid in rows on shelves that covered all the walls. There were cheeses in every stage of development, from the freshly squeezed clabber I had seen above to the finished products from which the cloth and metal strips had been removed: rindy, yellowish-brown, dry cakes that had shrunk a third smaller and were solid looking, crosshatched on top with the marks of the cheesecloth through which they had drained. The woman took a knife and cut into one. The slice she gave me was hard on the outside, slightly runny at the center; the look and the flavor were not unlike Camembert, a bit less sharp, creamier, and without the soapy tinged aftertaste of many Camemberts. I tried another slice from a cheese four months older; it was very hard, almost crumbly, the same consistency throughout and much more violent on the tongue. Both were considered ripe, and both were wonderful.

I walked a while longer in the fog and then went back to the main house for lunch, served to me alone because the others had gone shooting in the pines. It began with *caldo verde,* then went on to *bolinhos de bacalhau (Recipe Index),* a dish that other countries have come to know, in a much-distorted version, as codfish cakes.

This was my first taste of Portuguese-prepared cod; I had heard many things about it and was curious to try it. The preparation and eating of cod in Portugal is not a tradition so much as an addiction. Cod appears on most tables two or even three times a week. It is cooked everywhere in the country, from Minho all the way south, enjoyed inland as much if not more than in coastal areas, because it is salt-dried and can be kept all year, served any

Salt cod is a favorite Portuguese food that comes to the table baked, poached, broiled or fried, seasoned or sauced in hundreds of ways, or in the form of codfish cakes (*bolinhos de bacalhau, Recipe Index*). Preparing the cakes in the main kitchen of the Vale Feitoso estate, the goatherd's wife Conceição removes the skin and bones from well-soaked salt cod (*above*). She seasons the shredded cod with fresh coriander, mint and parsley and beats bread crumbs into it. The mixture is then shaped and fried in garlic-flavored oil. The finished cakes are served topped with freshly poached eggs (*opposite*).

place, any time. Paradoxically, a country that leads the world in varieties of fresh foods of the sea has chosen as its national fish one that is neither fresh nor obtainable locally. Cod is found only in faraway waters and with great difficulty (*pages 178-179*). The cooking of it in Portugal is always special; there is almost no family that does not pride itself on its own handed-down recipe. There are said to be 1,001 ways of preparing cod in this country, and the estimate seems conservative.

The first thing I noticed when I tasted the codfish cakes now was that the hamburger-shaped patties tasted not at all like dried preserved fish but like the freshest of foods. There was a strange, very good combination of flavors mixed with the cod, and I took my plate and went out to the kitchen to watch it being prepared while I ate. On a wooden table against the wall were three separate piles of shimmering fresh green leaves: coriander, parsley and mint. The cook was chopping them finely. Behind her in a clay bowl I could see bread soaking in water to which she had added oil, minced garlic, salt and paprika. To one side was another bowl in which thick, yellowish chunks of cod had soaked all night. After the cook had finished chopping the greens, she shredded cod with her hands into paper-thin slivers; these she mixed with other ingredients into the soaked bread, shaping the mass into thick patties, which she fried lightly in a little hot oil over an oven fire of pine wood. While she allowed the cakes to drain, she carefully poached some eggs and then she deftly slid them over the cakes on the serving platter. Eating the result while it was very hot made me know that something had been done to the cod that was not quite as simple as it looked. Four things had happened: the water had soaked out the salt, leaving the pungent pure taste of the fish; the shredding had changed a chewy-tough texture to a delicate one; the three distinct, sharp flavors of green herbs had blended with the fish, giving it a garden freshness and a triple-edged delicacy;

and the soaked country bread combined and contained all the tastes, turning them into a many-faceted new flavor. When I mashed the egg into the cakes on my plate, the crisply fried surface splintered like shattered crystal, and the egg yolk flowed into the steaming center. It was the kind of fish that convinces a man he could live on cod for the rest of his life, which is not only possible but practical in Portugal, where the fish is boiled, broiled, fried, baked or simply marinated. A light, dry, fruity red wine was served with it, for cod is an exception to the rule that dictates white wine with fish.

After lunch at the cook's suggestion I slept for an hour, waking in time to walk again in the smoky hills, past fields of flax grown for hemp processed on the farm; past olive and grape presses and herds of pigs and fields of vegetables. Aside from a few chemicals, and one or two delicacies like cod, everything one needed was produced there on the farm.

In the evening, the hunters who had been shooting in the pines came back carrying bags heavy with game and looking mud-spattered, red-faced and contented. Rather than take their muddy boots off and eat in the house, they collapsed alongside the stable—at the forge where horseshoes were made—drying themselves and their clothes near the hot coals. As the coals in the forge turned white, pine wood was added, and jugs of strong red wine were brought out and passed around among the hunters while the cook in the kitchen skinned and cleaned several rabbits and hares from the bag. Much later, while the night outside turned cold, the fresh game was salted and roasted by the tired hunters over the glowing forge. The sputtering hot pieces of hare and rabbit were then dipped into a warm sauce of vinegar, oil and onion—and eaten, dripping, with long gulps of the cool red wine. The plain hunter's meal of gamy meat, burned by the coals and blended hot into the vinegar sauce, was as lovely as any I had in all of Portugal.

In the morning I took my car and started for a shortcut back to the main

A ceramic hen and chick hover over a tureen of *canja* (chicken soup) garnished with lemon and mint *(Recipe Index)*.

road that would lead me down to the town of Tomar and from there on into Lisbon. It was the rainy season, and it had been raining hard on and off for two days. The dirt road that I had taken to the farm was now temporarily blocked by rain and it looked like a slow-moving river. The cook had told me before I left the farm that the shortcut to the main road would take "about a half hour," and that it was "a little rough when it rains." It took me a bit over an hour to discover that there was no road of any kind except an ox path. Three hours later, having been caught in a blinding cloudburst in the fog-choked mountains and thrown with a small landslide down a steep hill into a newly formed rain-lake, I sat in my stalled car and wondered exactly what I had done wrong. There were no paths or houses in sight, the sides of the hills and valleys were only intermittently visible between the sheets of rain. I began to wish that I had taken along the blind farmhand to show me the way. I was learning the hard way a fundamental, unspoken Portuguese axiom: time doesn't exist. A job like cooking or walking or driving or living takes as long as it takes—a moment, a day, a year, a lifetime, a generation—but *time* as a quantitative measure remains alien to most Portuguese.

Waiting now alone in the flooded car, while the sheets and gushes of rain subsided outside, wondering what I would do next, I began to understand the blank looks I had seen on the faces of cooks when asked how long this or that dish took to prepare. "Only a minute or two" could mean a half hour—just as the guess of a half hour with an added warning about the rain in the mountains had meant "half a day if you get there at all." The cook at the farm had kindly given me a sandwich of *presunto* ham and a piece of cheese and country bread with a bottle of wine in case I got hungry driving, and now I knew she hadn't seriously believed I would make it before dark or even perhaps before morning.

There was nothing to do until the rain stopped or somebody passed by, and I watched the day darken from the car window. The high hills around me were gentle and stark in the heavy haze; the earth spilled in billows of rain-rutted red soil down to a valley far below, and from there sloped up again to a long flank of land that I knew to be the Spanish frontier. I ate a little of the pungent hard cheese and then a piece of deep, salty *presunto* on the nut-sweet brown bread, and drank some of the wine. The food and wine made me feel peculiarly warm and peaceful for a man trapped in a rain-lake. I was wearing boots over heavy pants and I got out of the car and stood thigh deep in the cold water. The rain had stopped now and the mist was hanging like a thin cloud over everything in the silver twilight. All around me, the place looked as timeless as the moon.

Just before dark I heard a sound above me and then I saw a man leading a pair of oxen on the hill. I called, and he came down and hitched his team to my car and pulled it out. The motor wouldn't start, and I walked with him two miles northeast to a two-room farmhouse where his wife made a place for me on the kitchen floor for the night. Then in the morning, when the rain clouds had cleared, the farmer went back with me and hitched the oxen to my car. The team of oxen towed it until the motor turned, and I drove again along the flooded oxen path, feeling strangely lighter and more alive for the rest of my trip through Portugal.

Canja
CHICKEN SOUP WITH LEMON AND MINT

To serve 6

A 3½- to 4-pound stewing fowl, securely trussed

The fowl's giblets—heart, gizzard and liver—finely chopped

2 quarts water

1 cup finely chopped onions

1½ teaspoons salt

3 tablespoons raw medium or long grain regular-milled rice, or imported short grain rice

¼ cup fresh lemon juice

6 tablespoons finely cut fresh mint

Place the chicken and its giblets in a heavy 3- to 4-quart casserole. Pour in the water and bring to a boil over high heat, meanwhile skimming off the foam and scum as they rise to the surface. Add the onions and salt and reduce the heat to low. Simmer partially covered for 2½ hours, then add the rice and simmer for 30 minutes or until the chicken and rice are tender.

Remove the casserole from the heat and transfer the chicken to a plate. When the bird is cool enough to handle, remove the skin with a small knife or your fingers. Cut or pull the meat away from the bones. Discard the skin and bones, and cut the meat into strips about ⅛ inch wide and 1 inch long.

Just before serving, return the chicken to the casserole, add the lemon juice and taste for seasoning. Bring to a simmer and cook only long enough to heat the chicken through. Place a tablespoon of the cut mint in each of six individual serving bowls, ladle the soup over it and serve at once.

Caldo Verde
POTATO AND KALE SOUP WITH SAUSAGE

To serve 4 to 6

½ pound fresh kale or collard greens

4 ounces *linguiça* or substitute 4 ounces of *chorizo* or any other garlic-seasoned smoked pork sausage

3 medium-sized potatoes (about 1 pound), peeled and sliced into ¼-inch-thick rounds

6 cups water

2 teaspoons salt

½ cup olive oil

¼ teaspoon freshly ground black pepper

Wash the greens under cold running water. With a sharp knife trim away any bruised or blemished spots and strip the leaves from their stems. Bunch the leaves together and shred them into the finest possible strips. Set aside.

Place the sausages in a small skillet and prick them in two or three places with the point of a knife. Add enough water to cover them and bring to a boil over high heat. Reduce the heat to low and simmer for 15 minutes. Drain the sausages on paper towels, slice into ¼-inch rounds, and set aside.

Combine the potatoes, water and salt in a 4- to 5-quart saucepan and bring to a boil over high heat. Reduce the heat to moderate and cook uncovered for 15 minutes, or until the potatoes when tested can be easily mashed against the sides of the pan. With a slotted spoon, transfer the potatoes to a bowl and mash them to a smooth purée with a fork. Return the potatoes to the liquid in the pan, stir in the olive oil and pepper and bring to a boil over high heat. Add the greens and boil uncovered for 3 or 4 minutes. Then drop in the reserved sausages and simmer for a minute or two to heat them through. Serve at once, accompanied by a plate of *broa (page 14)*.

Batatas à Portuguêsa
PORTUGUESE FRIED POTATOES

To serve 4

3 tablespoons butter

3 tablespoons olive oil

1½ pounds new potatoes, peeled and sliced into ¼-inch-thick rounds

½ teaspoon salt

Freshly ground black pepper

1 tablespoon finely chopped parsley

In a heavy 10- to 12-inch skillet, melt the butter in the olive oil over moderate heat. When the foam begins to subside, add the potatoes. Turning them frequently with a metal spatula, cook for 15 minutes or until they are tender and golden brown. Season with salt and a few grindings of pepper, then transfer the potatoes to a heated bowl or platter and serve at once, sprinkled with parsley if you like. When fried potatoes accompany *iscas (Recipe Index)* or *bife à portuguêsa (Recipe Index)*, they are traditionally arranged in a symmetrical ring around the meat.

Bolinhos de Bacalhau
CODFISH CAKES WITH PARSLEY, CORIANDER AND MINT

To serve 3 to 6

Starting a day ahead, place the cod in a glass, enamel or stainless-steel pan or bowl. Cover it with cold water and soak for at least 12 hours, changing the water 3 or 4 times.

Drain the cod, rinse under cold running water, place it in a saucepan and add enough fresh water to cover the fish by 1 inch. Bring to a boil over high heat. (Taste the water. If it seems excessively salty, drain, cover with fresh water, and bring to a boil again.) Reduce the heat to low and simmer uncovered for about 20 minutes, or until the fish flakes easily when prodded gently with a fork.

Meanwhile, in a large bowl, combine the bread and ½ cup of the olive oil. Beat and mash them together until the bread has absorbed all the oil, then set aside.

Drain the cod thoroughly. When it is cool enough to handle, remove and discard any skin and bones. Then shred the fish finely with your fingers or a table fork and place it in a mixing bowl. Add the coriander, chopped parsley, mint, paprika, salt, pepper and reserved bread, and beat vigorously with a large spoon until the ingredients are thoroughly combined. With lightly moistened hands shape the mixture into 6 flat round cakes, about 3½ inches in diameter and ½ inch thick.

In a heavy 12-inch skillet, heat the remaining ¼ cup of olive oil over moderate heat until a light haze forms above it. Add the garlic and, stirring frequently, cook for 2 or 3 minutes, or until golden brown. Then remove and discard them. Add the codfish cakes to the garlic-flavored oil and cook over moderate heat for about 3 minutes on each side turning them carefully with a metal spatula. When they are a golden brown on both sides, transfer them to a heated platter, garnish with parsley sprigs, and serve at once. Traditionally, each cake is topped with a freshly poached egg before serving.

1 pound salt cod
2 cups coarsely crumbled day-old French or Italian bread, trimmed of all crusts
¾ cup olive oil
¼ cup finely chopped fresh coriander (*cilantro*)
1 tablespoon finely chopped parsley
½ teaspoon finely chopped fresh mint
2 tablespoons paprika
1 teaspoon salt
⅛ teaspoon freshly ground black pepper
2 garlic cloves, peeled and cut lengthwise into halves
6 parsley sprigs
6 freshly poached eggs (optional)

Trouxa de Vitela
MARINATED VEAL ROAST WITH RED ONION

To serve 6 to 8

For the marinade, combine ¾ cup of the oil, the vinegar, onion, garlic, parsley, red pepper, salt and black pepper in a small bowl and stir well. Place the veal in a deep bowl just large enough to hold it comfortably, and pour in the marinade, turning the veal about with a large spoon until it is moistened on all sides. Marinate at room temperature for 4 hours or in the refrigerator for at least 8 hours, turning it over two or three times as it marinates.

Preheat the oven to 450°. Remove the veal from the marinade, brush off any bits of onion or spice clinging to it, and place it on a rack in a shallow roasting pan. Set the marinade aside in a small saucepan. Roast the veal in the middle of the oven for 20 minutes. Then baste it with a tablespoon or so of olive oil and reduce the heat to 350°. Basting two or three more times with the remaining olive oil, continue to roast for about 1½ hours longer, or until the veal is tender.

Then bring the reserved marinade to a boil over high heat, reduce the heat to low and simmer for 5 minutes. To serve, carve the veal into ¼-inch slices, arrange them attractively on a large heated platter and pour the simmering marinade over them. Serve at once.

1 cup olive oil
⅓ cup white wine vinegar
1 large red onion, peeled and finely chopped
½ teaspoon finely chopped garlic
2 tablespoons finely chopped parsley
¼ teaspoon crushed dried hot red pepper
2 teaspoons salt
½ teaspoon freshly ground black pepper
A 3½- to 4-pound boneless veal roast, preferably cut from the leg or rump and securely tied

To serve 2

¼ cup olive oil
¼ cup fresh lemon juice
Salt, preferably coarse salt
Freshly ground black pepper
1 head Boston, bibb, or romaine
   lettuce plus 2 or 3 chicory leaves,
   cut into small pieces
1 bunch water cress
1 large tomato, thinly sliced
1 large red onion, thinly sliced and
   separated into rings
8 ripe olives (optional)

To serve 4

4 large peeled garlic cloves, 2
   crushed with a cleaver or knife
   and 2 cut lengthwise into halves
1 tablespoon red wine vinegar
1 teaspoon salt
Freshly ground black pepper
4 beef tenderloin steaks, sliced about
   ¾ inch thick
2 tablespoons olive oil
2 tablespoons butter
1 large bay leaf, crumbled
8 thin slices *presunto* ham or
   prosciutto or other lean smoked
   ham
¼ cup dry red wine
1 teaspoon fresh lemon juice
2 teaspoons finely chopped parsley
1 lemon cut into 8 wedges

To serve 4

2 pounds lean boneless pork, cut
   into 1-inch cubes
1 tablespoon lard
¾ cup dry white wine
1½ teaspoons ground cumin seed
½ teaspoon finely chopped garlic
1 teaspoon salt
Freshly ground black pepper
5 thin lemon slices, quartered
2 tablespoons finely chopped fresh
   coriander (*cilantro*)

Uma Salada Portuguêsa
MIXED GREEN SALAD

Beat the oil and lemon juice together with a fork or whisk until they are well blended. Season liberally with salt and a few grindings of pepper.

Gently toss the lettuce and water cress together with the dressing and arrange the greens attractively on a large chilled serving plate. Place the tomato slices slightly overlapping on top and arrange the onion rings (and olives if you are using them) around them. Serve at once.

Bife à Portuguêsa
PORTUGUESE STEAK

Preheat the oven to 250°. Mash the crushed garlic, vinegar, salt and a few grindings of pepper to a smooth paste with a mortar and pestle or in a bowl with the back of a spoon. With your fingers, rub the paste into the steaks, pressing it firmly into both sides of the meat.

In a heavy 10- to 12-inch skillet, melt the butter in the olive oil over moderate heat. When the foam has almost subsided, add the garlic halves and bay leaf and cook for 1 minute, stirring constantly. Then with a slotted spoon, remove and discard the garlic and bay leaf. Add the steaks and cook for 2 or 3 minutes on each side, turning them with tongs, and regulating the heat so that they color quickly and evenly. The steaks should be well browned, but still pink inside.

Transfer the steaks to individual baking dishes or fairly deep plates and keep them warm in the oven. Add the slices of ham to the fat remaining in the skillet and cook over high heat, turning them frequently for 1 or 2 minutes. With the tongs, place 2 slices of ham on each steak. Pour off all but a thin film of fat from the skillet, add the wine and lemon juice and bring to a boil over high heat, meanwhile scraping in any brown particles clinging to the bottom and sides of the pan. Pour the sauce over the steaks, sprinkle them with parsley and garnish each serving with lemon wedges. Serve at once. *Bife à portuguêsa* is usually served with Portuguese fried potatoes *(Recipe Index)* carefully arranged around the edges of the serving dishes.

Rojões Cominho
BRAISED PORK WITH CUMIN, CORIANDER AND LEMON

Pat the pork cubes thoroughly dry with paper towels. In a heavy 10- to 12-inch skillet, melt the lard over high heat until it splutters. Add the pork cubes and brown them, turning the cubes frequently with a large spoon and regulating the heat so that they color quickly and evenly without burning. Stir in ½ cup of wine, the cumin, garlic, salt and a liberal grinding of pepper. Bring to a boil, then cover the skillet, reduce the heat to low and simmer for 25 minutes, or until the pork is tender and shows no resistance when pierced with the tip of a small, sharp knife. Add the remaining ¼ cup of wine and the lemon slices and cook over high heat, turning the meat and lemon pieces constantly, until the sauce thickens ever so slightly. Stir in the coriander and taste for seasoning.

Pour the pork mixture onto the center of a large heated platter and surround it if you like with Portuguese fried potatoes *(Recipe Index)*.

Ripe olives, lemon juice and coarse salt give a Portuguese green salad its extra measure of tartness and distinctive texture.

To serve 4

A 5- to 6-pound oven-ready duck
1 large garlic clove, peeled and
   bruised with the side of a cleaver
   or the blade of a large, heavy
   knife
Salt
Freshly ground black pepper
2 lemons
1 cup raw medium or long-grain
   regular-milled rice, or imported
   short-grain rice
2 tablespoons lard
¼ pound Portuguese *linguiça*, or
   substitute *chorizo* or any other
   garlic-seasoned smoked pork
   sausage
1 medium-sized carrot, scraped and
   finely chopped
1 medium-sized onion, finely
   chopped
¼ pound *presunto* ham, or substitute
   serrano, prosciutto or other lean
   smoked ham, sliced ⅛ inch thick
   and cut into 1-inch pieces
2 tablespoons fresh lemon juice
8 tablespoons finely chopped parsley

Arroz de Pato de Braga
ROAST DUCK WITH SAUSAGE-AND-HAM-FLAVORED RICE

Preheat the oven to 450°. Pat the duck completely dry with paper towels. Rub the bird inside and out with the crushed garlic clove, then sprinkle the cavity liberally with salt and a few grindings of pepper.

With a small, sharp knife or a vegetable peeler with a rotating blade, remove the peel from one of the lemons without cutting through to the bitter white pith beneath it. Place the peel inside the cavity of the duck, then close the opening securely by lacing it with skewers, or by sewing it with heavy white thread.

Fasten the neck skin to the back of the duck with a skewer and truss the bird securely. Slice the peeled lemon in half crosswise and rub its cut surface over the skin of the duck.

Place the duck breast side up on a rack set in a shallow open pan. Roast undisturbed in the middle of the oven about 20 minutes, or until the duck has begun to brown. Then reduce the heat to 350° and roast about 1½ hours longer. Basting is unnecessary.

To test for doneness, pierce the thigh of the duck with the tip of a small, sharp knife. The juices should run out a pale yellow; if tinged with pink, roast another 5 to 10 minutes.

While the duck is roasting, bring 2 quarts of water to a boil over high heat in a heavy 3- to 4-quart saucepan. Pour in the rice in a thin, slow stream so that the water keeps boiling. Reduce the heat to moderate and let the rice boil uncovered for 15 minutes, or until the grains are tender but still slightly firm to the bite. Drain the rice in a colander.

Place the sausages in an 8- to 10-inch skillet and prick them in two or three places with the point of a small, sharp knife. Add enough cold water to cover them completely and bring to a boil over high heat. Then reduce the heat to low and simmer uncovered for 5 minutes. Drain on paper towels, and slice the sausage into ⅛-inch-thick rounds.

In a heavy 12-inch skillet, melt the lard over high heat until it splutters. Drop in the sausage and cook, stirring frequently, for 3 or 4 minutes. Reduce the heat to low, add the carrot and onion and, stirring frequently, cook for about 5 minutes, or until the vegetables are soft but not brown. Add the ham and cook for 2 or 3 minutes longer. With a fork stir in the rice, lemon juice, and 6 tablespoons of parsley. Taste for seasoning and set aside, covered to keep warm.

Transfer the duck to a platter and, with a large spoon, skim as much of the fat as possible from the juices remaining in the roasting pan. Pour in ½ cup of water and bring it to a boil over high heat, meanwhile scraping in any brown particles clinging to the bottom and sides of the pan. Boil briskly, stirring frequently, until the liquid thickens lightly and is reduced to about ¼ cup. Taste for seasoning.

To assemble, spread the rice mixture evenly on the bottom of a large, shallow casserole or in a deep heated platter. Carve the duck into serving pieces and arrange the pieces attractively, skin side up, on the rice. Spoon the reduced cooking liquid over the duck, sprinkle with the remaining 2 tablespoons of parsley, and garnish the casserole with the remaining lemon cut lengthwise into 8 wedges. Serve the duck and rice at once directly from the casserole.

The sweetness of peppers melds with pungent garlic-marinated pork and tart lemon in *lombo de porco com pimentos vermelhos doces*.

Lombo de Porco com Pimentos Vermelhos Doces
MARINATED PORK LOIN WITH SWEET RED PEPPERS

With a mortar and pestle or the back of a large heavy spoon, mash the garlic, salt and pepper together to a smooth paste. Lightly spread the pork slices with the paste, place them in a bowl and toss with a spoon. Cover tightly and marinate at room temperature for 2 or 3 hours, or in the refrigerator for 6 hours, turning the pork about in the bowl from time to time.

In a heavy 10- to 12-inch skillet, melt the lard over high heat. Brown the pork in the hot fat (in two or three batches if necessary), turning the slices with tongs and regulating the heat so that the slices color quickly and evenly on both sides without burning. As they brown, transfer them to a plate.

Add the sweet red peppers (not the pimientos) to the fat remaining in the pan and, stirring frequently, cook for 5 minutes, or until they are coated with the fat but not brown. Transfer the peppers to the plate with the meat. Pour off all but a thin film of fat from the skillet and add the wine and stock. Bring to a boil over high heat, meanwhile scraping into the liquid any brown particles clinging to the bottom and sides of the pan.

Return the pork and sweet peppers to the skillet, cover tightly, and reduce the heat to low. Simmer for about 20 minutes, then add the canned pimientos if you are using them, and cook five minutes longer, or until the pork shows no resistance when pierced with a small knife.

With a slotted spoon, transfer the pork and peppers to a deep, heated platter. Bring the liquid remaining in the skillet to a boil over high heat, stirring constantly and cook briskly until it thickens lightly. Taste for seasoning, then pour the sauce over the meat. Serve garnished with lemon wedges.

To serve 4 to 6

1 tablespoon finely chopped garlic
1 teaspoon salt, preferably coarse salt
½ teaspoon freshly ground black pepper
2 pounds boneless pork loin, cut into ¼-inch-thick slices
¼ cup lard
4 medium-sized sweet red peppers, seeded, deribbed and cut lengthwise into ½-inch-wide strips, or substitute 1½ cups drained, canned pimientos, cut lengthwise into ½-inch strips
1 cup dry white wine
½ cup chicken stock, fresh or canned
1 lemon, cut lengthwise into 8 wedges

IX

Lisbon and the Gentle South

Pausing before the ornate Convent of Christ, a pretty girl of Tomar steadies her *tabuleiro*, the crown of bread loaves trimmed with wheat stalks and paper flowers that gives its name to one of the most spectacular festivals in Portugal. Her fiancé, who will help her with her massive headdress, holds her hand as they prepare to join a parade through Tomar's streets.

I came to Lisbon by a circuitous route, passing through the town of Tomar while continuing my trip through Portugal in a generally southerly direction. Tomar is a lovely place of contrasting buildings where the festival of *tabuleiros* is given. Literally, *tabuleiro* means tray; in this case it refers to a tall crown of bread adorned with sprigs of wheat and multicolored paper flowers, many of which are carried through the streets in perpetuation of a pagan rite. In different times, the rite has given thanks to the Roman goddess Ceres for a good harvest and to the Holy Spirit of the Christian faith in fulfillment of vows; today, as in Roman times, it celebrates a harvest feast.

This old and charming festival takes nearly four months to prepare and is presented every other year. Young virgins are chosen from the 15 neighboring parishes as well as the two parishes of Tomar. Their crowns, the *tabuleiros*, are elaborately made by hand; each weighs more than 30 pounds and must be as tall as its wearer. On the day of the festival the maidens parade through the town wearing their cumbersome crowns of bread, each accompanied by her fiancé, brother or father, who helps her keep her balance when the wind rocks her burden. Also in the parade go processions of bands, soldiers, standard bearers and bagpipers, drummers, oxen with gilded horns and little boys in green stockings driving wine carts. The boys aid the maidens by giving them an occasional drink of wine when their strength fails. In the evening, after the 17 most beautiful *tabuleiros* are chosen, the oxen are slaughtered and the people gather in front of the 15th Century Church of St. John the Baptist for a formal blessing of the bread, meat and wine. Then on the next day the poor people of Tomar come out to receive gifts of the blessed food; one

Continued on page 180

Wresting Treasure
from a Reluctant Sea

The Portuguese are heirs to a seafaring tradition that
goes back to the Phoenician sailors who first touched
Iberian shores around 1100 B.C., and in time produced
such intrepid explorers as Vasco da Gama and
Magellan. Every summer the tradition comes alive in
the town of Nazaré, 60 miles north of Lisbon on the
Atlantic coast. Here in gaily painted boats whose up-
curved prows suggest a Phoenician origin, fishermen
set out in the morning to row through the pounding
surf past Nazaré's dangerous barrier beach for a day's
fishing in the rough ocean waters. Other Nazaré
fishermen carry a huge net out to sea by boat in the
morning and laboriously haul it in toward evening.
By the end of the day the haul at Nazaré includes a
dozen different kinds of delicious fish—including
turbot, swordfish, bream and hake. Then the fish are
taken from the net or unloaded from the boats by the
women of Nazaré, who carry the sea's treasure ashore
(*following pages*) to clean and cook or to sell.

Barefoot, wearing traditional shawls and long skirts, the Nazaré women carry basketfuls of fish caught by their menfolk.

Bounty Hard Won from the Faraway Grand Banks

Every year for more than four centuries a fleet of Portuguese ships has set out from Lisbon for the Grand Banks, the iceberg-strewn fishing ground 2,800 miles away, near the coast of Newfoundland. On their decks these ships carry nests of dories—one-man rowboats in which the men set out alone to fish for cod. When the boats are full, the cod are taken back to the mother ships to be salted and stored. After six months at the Grand Banks, the Portuguese bring their salt-cured cargo back to Portugal, where it is sun dried at processing plants like the one near Lisbon shown below. Later, through the magic of Portuguese cooking, the dried salt cod are transformed into many of Portugal's finest dishes.

to two pounds of meat are presented to each family along with a liter of wine and loaves of bread from some of the *tabuleiros*. People accept these gifts with all the gravity and dignity due an ancient rite. The festival closes with donkey-cart races, bullfights, dancing and finally fireworks that glimmer over the tall gray-stone buildings of Tomar.

Continuing my progress to the south I followed the Peniche Peninsula past the resort towns of Cascais and Estoril, which stand like two pastel stage sets on the tossing waves. I stopped in Cascais to see the fishermen's auction. Stacked in tiers on the floor of the auction room were boxes full of every shape of fish to be found in the sea in shades of watery silver and pink that were different from any I had ever known. Long fish that looked like unsheathed scimitars were laid next to boxes of shivering needles; tarnished silver stars were piled over heaps of mingled pink squid, and opaque silver octopus and glimmers of herring were arranged in rectangular flat layers. The cement floor was slippery, silvered with scales, and boxes of lobsters and spider crabs slid quickly over them. Over everything the voice of the auctioneer boomed, calling his prices in a monotone until someone shouted "mine," or indicated with a gesture or a turn of the head that the box in question had been bought.

Outside the auction building, I walked through the clear, mist-free air of the port into a small restaurant for a plate of fresh lobster. The cook came out and asked how I wanted it—boiled or broiled, with or without a sauce he called *môlho à espanhola*, Spanish sauce. I said I would try it boiled, with some of the sauce on the side. When the lobster came it was still steaming, cooked in ocean water with a little seaweed, a few fresh herbs and half a lemon, full of that tinny sea tang that only the freshest shellfish have when just out of the pot. There was a light, dry white house wine, and a dish of the *môlho à espanhola*, the same red sauce—based on oil, tomato, garlic, onion and pimiento—that is called *salsa portuguesa* in Spain, *salsa americana* in the Basque country and Spanish-omelet sauce in America. Everybody for some reason has blamed it on somebody else, and each country accuses the others of using it to disguise the "natural" taste of good food. As a matter of fact, used in modest quantity it is amazingly good—particularly as a hot dip for fresh shellfish. I dipped the edges of a few pieces of lobster in the thick sauce and liked it very much; it was sharp and slightly acid but smooth, a good contrast to the fresh sea taste.

From Cascais I drove farther down the coast, past the quiet old houses and loud new hotels of the seaside resort of Estoril, detouring slightly to drive through the sudden lush greenery and florid stone masonry of Sintra, one of Portugal's most beautiful towns. Then in the late dustlike light of an autumn afternoon I reached Lisbon, as the city was paling in a looming haze like a mirage.

Lisbon—rolling, hanging and jutting through seven hills, dressed in pastel stone and pleated in green by the meandering Tagus River—is one of the loveliest capital cities in the world and one of the most consistently overlooked in recent times. The legendary shore touched by Ulysses, it was later the crown of an empire built on spices and numbered among the richest cities of the Western world. Aside from spices, cashmere and silk, ivory and porcelain, pearl, mother-of-pearl and other exotic riches from India, Africa and

Eggs, olives and parsley garnish *Bacalhau à Gomes de Sá*, a Portuguese dish with cod, potatoes and onions *(Recipe Index)*.

America all sailed into this port as if sucked in by centripetal force. Today the crush of riches is still reflected in the stone convolutions of convents, churches and monasteries built in an architectural style called Manueline because it was introduced by King Manuel I in the early 16th Century. Their grandeur is now the only reminder of the imperious city where all work was done by slaves—where favorite slaves wore silk and feathers and followed their masters on foot through the rolling, turning stone streets to eating places tucked like secret holes into the sides of hills.

Strolling through Lisbon at any time is enjoyable. At night in the misty autumn dark your footsteps echo and the streets gleam back at the sky. The buildings roll and tip together along many varied streets, from the narrow Alfama Moorish quarter to the broad, elegant newer avenues and the bustling business sections downtown. Lisbon, you will find, is no exception to the national rule for eating places: Victorian-elegant, fussy, overdecorated restaurants serve largely continental food; but if you want to taste pure Portuguese cooking, seek out the plainest, smallest, cleanest hole in the darkest wall where dim lights and clouds of steam lurk around many fine dishes. Stop in one of these *tascas* and try the roast chicken cut up in juicy chunks. Brush it lightly with a dark red sauce from a small ceramic keg on the table. It is called *piri-piri,* and is made from extremely hot small Angola peppers chopped and soaked in olive oil.

Late in the evening, about 11 or after, walk over to one of the spacious mirror-walled *cervejarias,* beer parlors that specialize in shellfish brought daily from the coast. By 11:30 or 12 there won't be an empty seat as Lisboans flock for glasses of foamy golden beer and plates heaped with shellfish. You can stand in front of the *cervejarias* windows before you go in and decide what you want. Layers of floating pale green live lobsters are strung one over another; there are cascades of clams in every size, of shiny black mussels and other mollusks, of shrimp so small you would think you need tweezers to peel them. Next to them are other shrimp so large their shells have begun to curl away from their bodies, and close by are scallops, coral-colored baby lobsters, rosy *langostims,* like the *langostinos* seen in Spain, and even black sea snails are to be found here.

If you find a table inside, try a glass of beer with a plate of *búsios,* the sea snails that come in black conch shells about 3 or 4 inches wide. The waiter will bring a dish of them accompanied by a flat piece of wood like a chopping block, and a long thin fork. When you have extracted all you can get out of the deep-curled snail shell with the fork, tap the pointed base of the shell hard on the wood a few times till the tail of the snail shakes loose and is visible. *Búsios* have a rich sea-bottom taste, and smell of seaweed and brine. They are among the best of Portuguese shellfish, excellent with the cool, smooth malt taste of Portuguese beer.

Still later at night, in Lisbon, at 1 or 2 in the morning, the crowds gather in the *fado* houses in the old quarters, the Alfama and the Bairro Alto, for a bottle of red wine, a grilled sausage and an hour of Lisbon song. The music is *fado* (the word means fate), a product of Lisbon that foreigners both love and hate. It is said to come originally from songs sung by homesick Portuguese sailors on ships that had been away from Portuguese shores months or even years in search of spices. Many *fados* eulogize Lisbon and the whole

Customers at the Monte-Mar Restaurant, at Guincho Beach 25 miles north of Lisbon, may order lobster cooked with rice and a brandy-and-liqueur-flavored sauce *(foreground),* or boiled lobster *(far side of the table).* For either dish they select their lobsters from a lattice-enclosed grotto *(opposite)* and a boy plucks them from the water.

country in the mournful tones of a singer who does not expect to live to see it again; other songs tell of lost loves and broken hearts; and still others are likely to be comic and almost raucous with a guilty, mournful wail, something like a man trying to tell a joke at a funeral. *Fado* is sometimes erroneously compared to Spanish flamenco singing; the only thing it has in common with that music is its misuse when presented in tourist-ridden, "typical" nightclubs visited by everyone except people who really like it. The gut-tearing agony and searing, visionary ecstasy of flamenco is not to be found in *fado,* which is lyrical and plaintive, purely Portuguese, and perhaps closer to what Americans call a torch song than anything Spanish.

In a *fado* house you sit at a small table in a dark smoke-filled room with dimmed lights and candles that flicker on the *azulejos* (tiles) along the wall and fade into dark corners. A waitress will bring you a very small charcoal grill and a piece of *linguiça* or *chouriço,* not too garlicky, on a prong. You grill the pungent hot sausage and eat it slowly in sizzling, small bites, washing it down with dark, dry, strong red wine that shines like molten garnet in the candlelight. There is the quick, mournful chord from a guitar, and then the rising sound of a *fado,* edged in darkness, falling off into a minor-keyed wail, one long effulgent cry that sweeps across the walls to fill the small house and shimmer in the heads of the listeners. A man or a woman will wander in from the streets, toss down a glass of wine or brandy, stand up to sing his or her own favorite *fado,* have another drink and leave. As the night progresses, the little room grows thick with the smoke of black tobacco, the smells of wine and sausage and the sharp mourning of song.

In Lisbon you will want to sample the coffee, for here the finest coffees from Angola, Mozambique and other Portuguese possessions mingle with the best fresh-ground brews from Brazil, the Orient or other parts of the world. You may, like most Portuguese, prefer to blend your own. The stores here reek with the richest perfumes of coffee to be found anywhere. Even an average shop offers a choice of 15 or 20 pure kinds and just as many standard blends. You can buy coffee beans, or the shop owner will grind several kinds for you into the same bag.

You may also want to visit one of the city's many coffeehouses for a cup of the brew and *pudim flan (Recipe Index).* This caramel custard is a national sweet in Portugal and the perfect dessert to have with coffee. Here, it is creamy and thick, richer with egg than it is in Spain. It may be made plain or with the added flavor of a sweet liqueur. Any way the Portuguese make it, they can't go wrong.

In the afternoon the Lisbon coffeehouses fill with women who meet women to gossip, men who meet men to gossip, and men who meet women for that quiet cup of coffee that starts all the gossip. Coffeehouses are places of raised eyebrows and passionate stares, of chuckles and assignations. Walk in alone, and the big room with its antique silver mirrors and Victorian swirls seems to adjust invisibly to your presence. Voices and eyes acknowledge you in a muted way as you sit at a table. A waiter in white tie brings you coffee, or if you prefer it, tea with Angola sugar and *pudim flan* or a platter of many small pastries—some soft and creamy inside, others that are flaky, crumbly, brittle and glazed—each on a paper doily. When you ask to pay, the number of empty pastry doilies will be counted and translated into

A sumptuous wedding feast is prepared in the spacious *Cozinha Velha (opposite),* an exclusive restaurant near Lisbon whose name, Old Kitchen, refers to its former role as the royal kitchen in Queluz Palace. Displayed in the foreground on the large table are a saddle of veal *(left),* a multi-tiered arrangement of boiled shrimplike *langostins (center)* and roast pheasant on a nest of *cineraria* leaves *(right).* The tree in the middle of the serving table is made of hydrangeas, carnations, roses and camellia leaves.

Continued on page 188

185

Roast kid for a special party is trimmed with paper frills and then garnished with slices of orange and sprigs of watercress.

A Noble Meal in a Palatial Home

When the guests include a marquis and marchioness plus a count and countess, as they do at the dinner party in Lisbon pictured at right, the usual simplicity of Portuguese food gives way to elegance. The host and hostess—Alfredo Roquette *(at far right)* and his wife *(facing the camera at the left)*—entertained in their 16th Century dining room, once part of a royal palace, with a dish that is often served on festive occasions, a *cabrito (whole roast kid, above)*. They also served dazzling *lampreia de ovos (below)*, an egg-yolk confection made to look like the seafood delicacy lamprey resting on fine threads of egg yolk.

Lampreia de ovos, or eggs lamprey, is a fancy dessert decorated to resemble a real lamprey, the eel-like creature prized in Portugal. Prepared with egg yolks, cooked in sugar syrup and cooled, it is decorated with sugar icing, candied cherries (used for the eyes) and a candied pear (for the tongue), and finally set on a bed of egg-yolk threads.

the bill. The coffee is rich, with a kind of hidden deepness, a nut-bitter hint and another mysterious extra edge of flavor, for many different beans have tinged its blend. Chances are, it will be the best coffee you have ever tasted, and no other cup outside of Portugal will ever quite match its full taste. One or two sweet, smooth pastries will balance the flavor, and before you leave the place you can light a cigarette, sit back and watch the next person come in just as you were watched when you came in.

The last time I was in Portugal I left Lisbon on the first of November, All Saints' Day. I had waited to see what that day was like here—the best-known day of the year in Lisbon, and the anniversary of an unforgettable event. In the year 1755, All Saints' Day was like a day of repentance for a giddy-gaudy year of overindulgence. By 10 o'clock that morning, most people were in the many Lisbon churches and High Mass had begun. When the rumbling sound began it left no time for thinking: in a sudden six-minute inferno, churches rocked and toppled, candle flames swam up tapestries. The earth heaved and tore itself open under falling buildings and spewing stone as the river foamed around it, a foretaste of the seismic sea wave that followed in its wake, rocked out of the ocean bed by one of the worst earthquakes in recorded history.

Now on All Saints' Day 200 years later, the morning was silent, as it must have been then; again all the churches were packed for High Mass. All Saints' Day in Lisbon is a time for remembering those who have lived and

Exquisite, finely wrought sweets like the confections shown here are a hallmark of the Portuguese cuisine, particularly in the province of Algarve, where almonds abound. Shaped like fruits, vegetables and even fish, the sweets are made from a tinted sugar and almond paste called *maçapão* (marzipan).

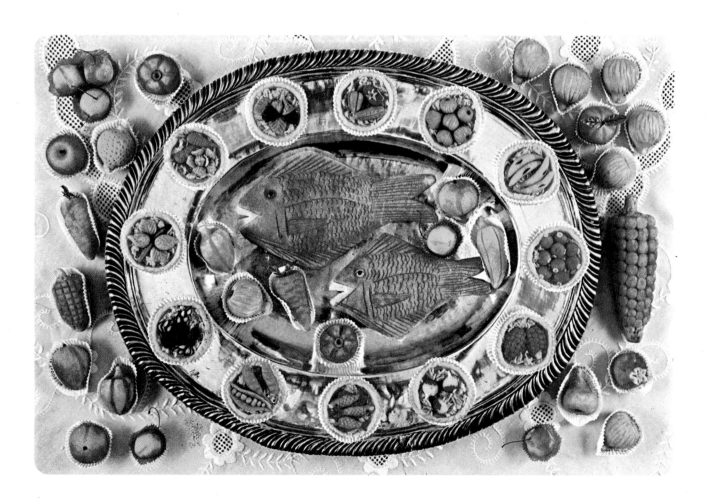

died not only in living memory but in much of the written history of man. Cemeteries turn into vast flower gardens; monuments are covered with blossoms. Streets outside churches are lined with vendors of candles, flowers and sweets. Inside, the churches are packed with people who kneel and pray and seem to be waiting. There is a great hushed underswell of whispering that disappears if you listen for it—like a wind through grass. You imagine the first deep rumbling noise and how it must have sounded when it began like a protestation of the earth itself under the whispering sheath of prayer. Now the earth is silent, and those who have prayed rise wearily, then shuffle toward the slices of sunlight at the ends of the stone-cool aisles. The church doors are thrown wide and the brilliant warm sun streaks in. Disaster has not struck. The people spill gratefully out into the bright streets, and the silence turns to shouts and laughter. I bought an almond pastry and a bag of brittle sweets, called *broas dos santos,* "saints' cakes," from a woman in black who stood against the sunlit white church. People were in their finest clothes, ready for terror or for gaiety, dressed for anything; they swarmed around the old woman like waves of life around a reminder of death. She sold her sweets quickly, her face a myriad web of upturned wrinkles, smiling with everything except her eyes. The pastries she sold were rich and the saints' cakes turned to a sweet soft powder on the tongue.

I got in my car and drove south from Lisbon with the powdered-sugar taste of the sweets in my mouth and a memory of the rolling, spreading pastel city and its river in my mind. Ahead of me, as if in the windshield, I saw the black, hard glitter and the fierce, unsmiling glow of the woman's eyes.

The road southward to Baixo Alentejo (which means "the low province beyond the Tagus") is lined in spring with cork trees that are peeled for their bark, revealing a bright orange color that gradually mellows to rust red. The coloring remains until the trees have grown new "skins," to be peeled for their cork again in seven years. The cork forests with their rust-red trunks and green tops are like landmarks in an animated cartoon, interspersed with fields of grass and blood-red dots of poppies. Beyond them fields of rice give way to rolling hillsides clotted with dark red houses that are covered with honeysuckle and separated by forests of green-smelling pine. Soon the road touches the sea again, and you drive on with the open ocean on your right and the twisting hills rising on your left as far as you can see. Stop at Setúbal, one of Portugal's most important industrial centers and fishing ports. Here you may buy a box of orange cakes, bittersweet to very sweet, chewy and smelling of orange oil from the peel. Walk through the Setúbal marketplace as you eat them, past stalls of ripe pineapples from the Azores and long bulging bananas from the Cape Verde Islands off Africa; you will see whole stalls of shredded kale next to other stalls of cows' feet for making stew. In the fish stands you will pass layers of many kinds of fresh fish heads, sold to those who can't afford the bodies but manage to make a fine thick fish stew with what they can buy. Fresh fruits glisten in the sun, and outside the market a man with a wheelbarrow stops to sprinkle a load of carrots with a bright-red watering can. Once back in your car and driving slowly out of town, you ride past palm trees and houses spilling with purple bougainvillea and trellises heavy with orange and red and white flowers. If you follow the road leading inland, a paved path that turns to a dusty sheen, it will

Continued on page 192

189

In a tranquil Iberian setting a workman sets out chrysanthemums beneath orange trees in Vila Viçosa, Portugal.

Bits of ham, sausage and tomatoes lend color and flavor to clams *na cataplana (Recipe Index)* from the province of Algarve.

take you through oak forests and wheat fields to the huge farm lands of the Baixo Alentejo where some very good food is cooked and served.

There are two dishes I especially like here in Baixo Alentejo; both are best when eaten at a country farm or roadside inn. Stop at a gleaming white-washed farm kitchen and beg a bowl of *sopa à alentejana (Recipe Index)*, a marvelous soup made with bread. This is a land of wheat, as you can see from the waving fields that surround the long white farmhouse. Alentejan bread is rich and dusty and is used in or with all cooking. You have already had a taste of the dry bready soups called *açordas;* this one is even thicker with bread, pork, garlic and egg—like a porridge of meats, related to the Spanish *migas* or bread-crumb dishes, but containing more sustenance in food. It is the finest compromise between a dry soup and a wet soup, not unlike Spanish garlic soup, but with an added zesty taste that changes it into another dish. The added flavor is, of course, chopped fresh coriander, which seems to melt into this dark broth and transform its taste. Even the smell of the steam changes to a rich herb-filled cloud. Once you have tasted *sopa à alentejana,* you will know it's worth growing your own coriander for this taste.

You can follow the soup with the second of the province's great dishes, *porco com amêijoas à alentejana*, Alentejan pork *(Recipe Index)*, which combines pork and clams. The Alentejan Portuguese have gone the Castilian Spanish one better in inventing a dish containing not one but two basic ingredients that are proscribed by Jewish and Moorish dietary laws. Like Madrid's *cocido*, this pork-and-shellfish combination probably began as a means of proving the diner's Christian zeal. The result today is a strange juxtaposition of flavors made by these remarkable Portuguese cooks, who can, apparently, combine anything in their kitchens and come out ahead. Alentejan acorn-and-truffle-fed young pig is sweet and tender, marinated in wine with bay leaf, garlic, paprika, salt and pepper. It is combined with pimientos, onions, tomatoes and the region's fresh, small tangy clams, then sprinkled with coriander and served with slices of lemon to be squeezed on it as you eat. This is a seductive dish that might well have converted more people to Christianity than did the Inquisition.

Below Baixo Alentejo lies the southernmost province of Portugal, called Algarve. Like Spain's Andalusia, Algarve is Portugal's land of the Moors. It is a lush garden province bordered on one whole side by the sea and swept each year by a froth of white flowers that rolls down the land to meet the water. The legend behind the flowers tells of a Moorish prince who married a Scandinavian princess and brought her here to live. During the first warm winter she began to waste away from homesickness for her native snowy land; there is no recognizable winter in Algarve and the eyes of the princess ached for the white of snow. She felt that she would suffocate. To save her, the Moorish prince planted Algarve solid with almond trees; every January the thick white almond blooms blanket the earth, shimmering like snow under a warm winter sky.

Figs also grow in profusion here and the fruit is dried and molded together in many different shapes, from small fig fish to great fig turkeys with almond beaks and raisin eyes. Algarve figs are fine when stuffed with toasted almonds and with cinnamon and sugar. They are not too sweet and they crunch wonderfully; the dry, almost smoky taste is very good with the delicately sweet almonds or alone with a glass of the dessert wine made on the Madeira Islands, 600 miles southwest of Lisbon.

In May Algarve changes from white to varied greens, as the leaves of almond, fig and silver olive trees move in the first hot breath before summer. The hordes of winter visitors leave now, only to be superseded by summer tourists flocking onto the dazzling white beaches. They appear nearly naked under the sun while the native Algarve fishermen seek shelter from the vicious light in the shade of trees, boats and houses, as do their wives, who wear black kerchiefs and carry umbrellas during the day when they must leave their dark, cool homes.

Fishing in Algarve is a way of life. Bass, mullet, hake, sole, and lobster, clams and other shellfish are brought in alive from the nets to be steamed in a *cataplana*, an Algarve cooking utensil that makes the simplest dish a pleasant surprise. The *cataplana* is a metal container with a heavy lid. It is shaped something like a clam, and in it almost any food at all seems to improve and intensify in flavor, from shellfish and fish to lamb or kid. To prepare the *cataplana* dish I like most—*amêijoas na cataplana (Recipe Index)*—the Algarvans heat a little oil until it is searingly hot and add onions, hot dried red pepper and paprika. Then they put in garlic and *linguiça* or *chouriço* sausage, tomatoes and chopped parsley, and finally they drop in handfuls of freshly dug clams and slam down the lid. The *cataplana* stays closed until it is flipped open at the table and the steam rises from it as from an earth fissure under the sea, heavy with the smells of fresh vegetables and herbs sifted through iodine odors and the fresh smell of newly opened shellfish. The taste combination is as good as the smell, full with the best flavor of the sea joined here by the freshest vegetables in the earth.

From Algarve it is not far to the Spanish border and the end of a circuitous tour of Portugal. The road goes east along the coast through pink and white towns with Moorish minaret chimneys, past green fields that slope up to clustered globules of red *medronho*, or arbutus berries, and down again to white sand and the blue rushing sea. A small coastal town called Olhão is a good place to stop along the way. Every summer in Algarve fishermen take off for the tuna run, battling the huge fish with clubs and torn nets, sometimes jumping into the water and wrestling them with their bare hands in a bloody siege called the "bullfight of the sea." Tuna steaks at any of several small port restaurants here are fine, cooked with garlic and chopped mint and the golden nutty Algarve wine called Afonso III. As usual in Portugal, the flavor combination will make you think you have never tasted the main ingredient before—in this case tuna. Eat it with the smells of the warped wood pier and watch the fishermen empty sacks of mussels, tiny clams and glistening sea snails into baskets and white hand nets.

Then drive back to the main coastal road and continue east. The sun is just behind you, against your shoulders. By evening you should reach the last town, Vila Real de Santo Antonio, by the Guadiana River, which marks the southern Spanish frontier. Have a glass or two or Afonso III with some olives, and then walk through the steamy fish smells of the dock-worker taverns. Sit at an outdoor table for some fish-and-shellfish curry, full of the day's finest ocean and river catches, tinged with the tastes of lemon juice and wine, turmeric and pungent green chopped coriander. There is no curry in the world quite like this one, and no coastal dish in all of Portugal that quite matches its full-faceted, exotic flavor.

The pungence fills your head and you eat slowly as you watch the shadows slice over the flat, flowing river water that shines like syrup in the last molten light of the sun. The smells of cooking begin to dim. From somewhere under the darkening water in front of you, a translucent, parasol-shaped sea creature called the Portuguese man-of-war flutters obliquely and delicately to the surface of the river for a taste of day-end air. Dragging its long stinging cluster of elegant, beaded tentacles up to the surface, it then sinks back down into them with seductive grace, like a courtesan curtsying deep into her jeweled skirts. Another fragile man-of-war, the only living thing in sight, appears farther across the mouth of the evening river, and two more float up where the dying sun touches the quiet water sliding slowly between the lands of Spain and Portugal to the open sea. Then the river is quiet and dark, as overhead the different grays of the passing clouds join the two countries in one light: deep ash gray and another gray as dark as slate flare up together in burning coral like a blending of two furnace flames, or like a great last lake of fire over the hushed earth of Iberia.

194

CHAPTER **IX** RECIPES

Escabeche

FISH PICKLED WITH CARROTS, ONIONS AND BAY LEAVES

In a heavy 10- to 12-inch skillet, heat ⅓ cup of the olive oil over moderate heat until a light haze forms above it. Add the fish steaks and cook them for 4 or 5 minutes on each side, turning them with a large spatula. When they are a golden brown, transfer them to paper towels to drain and cool.

In a clean 10- to 12-inch skillet, heat the remaining ¾ cup of oil over moderate heat until a light haze forms above it. Add the onion rings and, stirring frequently, cook for 5 minutes or until they are soft and transparent but not brown. Stir in the carrots, vinegar, bay leaf, garlic, salt and red and black pepper and cook for 5 minutes longer, stirring occasionally. Taste for seasoning.

Remove the skin and any bones from the fish. Spread a cup or so of the hot marinade evenly in a glass or enamel dish about 6 inches in diameter and 4 inches deep. Arrange half the fish on top, cover it with a cup of marinade, add the remaining fish and spread the remaining marinade over it.

Cover tightly with foil or plastic wrap and marinate in the refrigerator for at least 2 days. Serve the *escabeche* from the dish in which it has marinated.

To serve 4 to 6 as a main course or 6 to 8 as a first course

⅓ cup plus ¾ cup olive oil
2 pounds halibut steaks, cut about ¾ inch thick
2 large onions, peeled, cut into ⅛-inch slices and separated into rings
4 medium-sized carrots, scraped and coarsely grated
1 cup white wine vinegar
2 large bay leaves, crumbled
2 teaspoons finely chopped garlic
2 teaspoons salt
¼ teaspoon crushed dried hot red pepper
¼ teaspoon freshly ground black pepper

Bacalhau à Gomes de Sá

SALT COD WITH POTATOES, ONIONS AND BLACK OLIVES

Starting a day ahead, place the cod in a glass, enamel or stainless-steel bowl. Cover it with cold water and soak for at least 12 hours, changing the water three or four times.

Preheat the oven to 200°. With a pastry brush, coat the bottom and sides of a casserole 8 inches in diameter and 4 inches deep with 1 tablespoon of olive oil. Drop the potatoes into a pot with enough lightly salted boiling water to cover them completely. Boil briskly until they are tender but not falling apart. Drain, peel and cut the potatoes into ¼-inch slices. Set aside.

Drain the cod, rinse under cold running water, place it in a saucepan and add enough fresh water to cover the fish by 1 inch. Bring to a boil over high heat. (Taste the water. If it seems excessively salty, drain, cover with fresh water, and bring to a boil again.) Reduce the heat to low and simmer uncovered for about 20 minutes, or until the fish flakes easily when prodded gently with a fork. Drain thoroughly. With a small knife, remove and discard any skin and bones and separate the fish into coarse flakes. Set aside.

In a heavy 10- to 12-inch skillet, heat ½ cup of the oil over moderate heat until a light haze forms above it. Add the onion rings. Stirring frequently, cook for 5 minutes, or until they are soft and transparent but not brown. Stir in the garlic and remove the skillet from the heat.

To assemble, spread half the potatoes in the casserole, cover them with half the cod and then half the onions. Repeat the layers with the rest of the potatoes, cod and onions and pour the remaining ½ cup of oil over the top. Bake in the middle of the oven for 20 minutes, or until the top is lightly brown. Garnish the top with the olives and egg slices and sprinkle with parsley. Serve the *bacalhau* from the casserole accompanied by cruets of oil and vinegar, and a pepper mill, or a dish of freshly ground black pepper.

To serve 4 to 6

1½ pounds dried salt cod
1 tablespoon plus 1 cup olive oil
6 medium-sized potatoes
4 medium-sized onions, cut crosswise into ⅛-inch slices separated into rings
½ teaspoon finely chopped garlic
18 to 20 pitted black olives
5 hard-cooked eggs, cut crosswise into ¼-inch slices
2 tablespoons finely chopped parsley

1 cup dry white wine
¼ cup white wine vinegar
1½ teaspoons finely chopped garlic
1 medium-sized bay leaf, crumbled
4 whole cloves
1 teaspoon savory, crumbled
1 teaspoon marjoram, crumbled
1 teaspoon salt
½ teaspoon freshly ground black
    pepper
2 pounds lean boneless pork, sliced
    ½ inch thick and cut into strips
    1½ inches long and ½ inch wide
5 tablespoons lard
3 slices white bread, preferably
    homemade type, trimmed of crusts
    and cut diagonally into 4 triangles
1 orange, cut into 8 wedges

To serve 8

1 cup dried chick-peas (garbanzos)
3 pounds beef rump or round
A 1-pound smoked ham hock
Salt
4 quarts water
1 large onion, peeled and quartered
½ pound linguiça or substitute ½
    pound *chorizo* or other garlic-
    seasoned smoked pork sausage
A 1½-to 2-pound chicken, cut into
    6 to 8 serving pieces
4 medium-sized sweet potatoes,
    peeled and halved
4 medium-sized boiling potatoes,
    peeled and halved
3 medium-sized white turnips, peeled
    and cut lengthwise into quarters
4 medium-sized carrots, scraped and
    cut lengthwise into halves
1 medium-sized white cabbage, cut
    in half lengthwise, cored and
    sliced into 8 wedges
4 cups coarsely chopped turnip
    greens
1 cup raw medium or long grain
    regular-milled rice or imported
    short grain rice
Freshly ground black pepper
2 tablespoons finely chopped parsley

Carne de Vinho e Alhos
PORK BRAISED IN WHITE WINE WITH HERBS

In a large bowl, combine the wine, vinegar, garlic, bay leaf, cloves, savory, marjoram, salt and pepper. Drop in the pork strips and turn them about until they are well moistened. Marinate for at least 4 hours at room temperature or 8 hours in the refrigerator, turning the meat over from time to time.

Remove the pork from the marinade and pat it completely dry with paper towels. Reserve the marinade. In a heavy 10- to 12-inch skillet, melt 1 tablespoon of the lard over moderate heat until it splutters. Add the pork and brown it well, turning the strips with tongs and regulating the heat so they color quickly and evenly without burning. Pour off all but a thin film of fat from the skillet and add ½ cup of the marinade. Bring to a boil over high heat, meanwhile scraping in any brown particles clinging to the bottom and sides of the pan. Reduce the heat to low, cover tightly and simmer for 30 minutes, or until the meat is tender and shows no resistance when pierced with the point of a small, sharp knife.

Meanwhile, in another 10- to 12-inch skillet, heat the remaining 4 tablespoons of lard over moderate heat until it splutters. Add the bread triangles and brown them well on both sides. Then drain on paper towels.

To serve, discard the cloves and then transfer the pork and its sauce to a heated platter. Garnish the platter with the bread and the orange wedges.

Cozido à Portuguêsa
BOILED MEATS, CHICKEN AND VEGETABLES

Starting a day ahead, wash the chick-peas in a sieve under cold running water, then place them in a pan or bowl and add enough cold water to cover them by 2 inches. Soak at room temperature for at least 12 hours.

In a heavy 8- to 10-quart casserole, combine the beef, ham hock and 1 teaspoon of salt. Pour in enough water to cover the meat by 2 inches, and bring to a boil over high heat, meanwhile skimming off the foam and scum as they rise to the surface. Reduce the heat to low, add the onion, partially cover the pan, and simmer for 2 hours. Drain the chick-peas and add them. Simmer partially covered for 1 hour longer. The meats should always be covered with the liquid. Replenish it when necessary with boiling water.

Meanwhile, place the sausages in a small skillet and prick them in two or three places with the point of a knife. Add enough cold water to cover them completely and bring to a boil over high heat. Then reduce the heat to low and simmer uncovered for 5 minutes. Drain on paper towels.

With a ladle, transfer 2 cups of the meat and chick-pea broth to a heavy 1- to 1½-quart saucepan and set it aside. Add the sausages, chicken, sweet potatoes, white potatoes, turnips and carrots to the casserole, cover and simmer for 40 minutes. Add the cabbage and turnip greens and cook 20 to 30 minutes longer, or until the meat and all the vegetables are tender.

Meanwhile bring the reserved 2 cups of broth to a boil over high heat. Stirring constantly, pour in the rice, add 1 teaspoon of salt and reduce the heat to low. Cover tightly and cook for 20 minutes, or until the rice has absorbed all the broth. Add more salt and pepper to taste.

To serve, transfer the chicken and meat to a carving board. With a small, sharp knife, remove the skin and bones of the chicken and trim any pieces of meat from the ham hock. Cut the beef and sausages into ¼-inch-thick slices. Arrange the meats and vegetables on a heated platter and moisten them with a few spoonfuls of the cooking liquid. Sprinkle with parsley and serve accompanied by the rice. (Serve the cooking broth as a first course or reserve it for use in such soups as *sopa da panela, Recipe Index*.)

Massa Sovada
PORTUGUESE SWEET BREAD

In a small bowl, sprinkle the yeast and a pinch of sugar over the lukewarm water. Let the mixture stand for 2 or 3 minutes, then stir to dissolve the yeast completely. Set the bowl in a warm, draft-free place, such as an unlighted oven, for 5 to 8 minutes, or until the mixture doubles in volume.

In a deep mixing bowl, combine the 1 cup of sugar, 4 cups of the flour and the salt. Make a well in the center, pour in the yeast and milk, and drop in the eggs. Gently stir together with a large spoon, then beat vigorously until all the ingredients are well combined. Beat in ¼ pound of butter, then add up to 2 cups more flour, beating it in ¼ cup at a time, and using as much as necessary to form a dough that can be gathered into a soft ball. If the dough becomes difficult to stir, work in the flour with your fingers.

Place the dough on a lightly floured surface, and knead it, pressing down and pushing it forward several times with the heel of your hand. Fold it back on itself and repeat for about 15 minutes until it is smooth and elastic.

Shape the dough into a ball and place it in a large, lightly buttered bowl. Dust the top with flour, drape with a towel and set aside in the warm, draft-free place for 45 minutes to an hour until the dough doubles in bulk.

With a pastry brush, coat the bottom and sides of two 9-inch pie plates with 2 tablespoons of softened butter. Punch the dough down with a single blow of your fist, then transfer it to a lightly floured surface and let it rest for 10 minutes. Divide the dough in two and pat the halves into flattened round loaves about 8 inches across. Place them in the pie plates and let them rise in a warm place for about 40 minutes.

Preheat the oven to 350°. With a pastry brush, coat the top of both loaves with beaten egg. Bake in the middle of the oven for about 1 hour, or until the loaves are golden brown and crusty. Cool on cake racks.

NOTE: The same dough is often shaped into snail-like loaves *(caracois)* or braids *(trança à tricana)*. To make the *caracois*, divide the dough into two equal parts and roll each part into a long rope about 1½ inches in diameter. One at a time, loop a rope in ever-smaller concentric circles inside a 9-inch-round pie plate to fill the pan completely. Let the loaves rise for 40 minutes, brush with beaten egg and set a few raisins in the center before baking.

For the *trança à tricana*, gently incorporate ¼ cup of dried currants into the dough after the first kneading. Let the dough rise for an hour. Then punch it down, let it rest 10 minutes and divide the dough in two. Roll each half into three 14-inch-long ropes. Lay three ropes side by side and gently interweave them into a thick braid, turning the ends under slightly to smooth and seal them. Make the second braid similarly, then carefully place the loaves on buttered baking sheets and let them rise for 40 minutes. Brush the braids with beaten egg and sprinkle them with ½ cup of sugar (preferably coarsely granulated decorating sugar) before baking them.

To make two 9-inch round loaves

2 packages or cakes of active dry or compressed yeast
A pinch plus 1 cup sugar
¼ cup lukewarm water (110° to 115°)
5 to 6 cups all-purpose flour
1 teaspoon salt
1 cup lukewarm milk (110° to 115°)
3 eggs
¼ pound (1 stick) unsalted butter, cut into small bits
2 tablespoons softened butter
1 egg, lightly beaten

To serve 4 as a main course, 6 as a
first course

½ pound *linguiça* sausage or
  substitute *chorizo* or other garlic-
  seasoned smoked pork sausage
½ cup olive oil
4 medium-sized onions, thinly sliced
1 teaspoon paprika
¼ teaspoon crushed hot dried red
  pepper
Freshly ground black pepper
¼ pound *presunto* ham, finely
  chopped, or substitute prosciutto
  or other lean smoked ham
2 medium-sized tomatoes, peeled,
  seeded and coarsely chopped (*see
  huevos a la flamenca, page 16*)
½ cup finely chopped parsley
½ cup dry white wine
1 tablespoon finely chopped garlic
2 small bay leaves, crumbled
36 small hard-shelled clams, washed
  and thoroughly scrubbed

To serve 4

1½ cups dry white wine
1 tablespoon paprika
2½ teaspoons salt
Freshly ground black pepper
2 garlic cloves, cut in half
1 small bay leaf
2 pounds lean boneless pork, cut
  into 1-inch cubes
3 tablespoons lard
2 medium-sized onions, thinly sliced
1 large sweet red pepper, seeded,
  deribbed and cut lengthwise into
  ½-inch strips, or ⅓ cup canned
  pimientos, cut into ½-inch strips
2 teaspoons finely chopped garlic
2 medium-sized tomatoes, peeled,
  seeded and finely chopped (*see
  huevos a la flamenca, page 16*)
⅛ teaspoon crushed dried hot red
  pepper
2 dozen small hard-shelled clams,
  washed and thoroughly scrubbed
¼ cup finely chopped fresh coriander
  (*cilantro*)
1 lemon, cut into 6 or 8 wedges

Amêijoas na Cataplana
STEAMED CLAMS WITH SAUSAGES, HAM, TOMATOES AND SPICES

With a small, sharp knife, remove the casings of the sausages. Crumble the meat coarsely and drop it into a sieve. Plunge the sieve into a pan of boiling water and boil briskly for 1 minute. Then spread the sausage meat out on a double thickness of paper towels to drain.

In a heavy 12-inch skillet or similar-sized casserole, heat the olive oil over moderate heat until a light haze forms above it. Add the onions and, stirring frequently, cook for 5 minutes, or until they are soft and transparent but not brown. Add the paprika, red pepper and a liberal grinding of black pepper and cook for a minute or two. Then add the sausage meat, ham, tomatoes, parsley, wine, garlic and bay leaves, raise the heat and bring to a boil. Stirring constantly, cook briskly until most of the liquid in the pan evaporates.

Arrange the clams hinged side down over the meat and tomato mixture, cover the skillet tightly and cook over moderate heat for about 10 minutes, or until all the clams open. Discard any that remain closed. To serve, transfer the clams to heated soup plates and ladle the sauce over them.

NOTE: This dish takes its name from the Portuguese *cataplana*, a metal casserole shaped like a clam.

Carne de Porco com Amêijoas à Alentejana
MARINATED PORK WITH CLAMS, TOMATOES AND CORIANDER

In a large bowl, combine the wine, paprika, 1½ teaspoons of the salt and ¼ teaspoon black pepper and stir until thoroughly blended. Add the halved garlic cloves and bay leaf and then the cubed pork, turning the meat about in the marinade to coat the pieces evenly. Marinate for 3 hours at room temperature or in the refrigerator for 6 hours, turning the meat occasionally to keep it well moistened.

Drain the pork in a sieve set over a bowl and pat the cubes completely dry with paper towels. Discard the garlic and bay leaf, but reserve the marinade. In a heavy 10- to 12-inch skillet, melt 1 tablespoon of lard over high heat until it splutters. Add the pork cubes and turn them frequently, regulating the heat so they color quickly and evenly without burning. With a slotted spoon, transfer the pork to a bowl. Pour the reserved marinade into the skillet and bring to a boil over high heat, scraping in any brown particles clinging to the bottom and sides of the pan. Boil briskly, uncovered, until the marinade is reduced to 1 cup. Pour it over the pork and set aside.

In a heavy 6- to 8-quart casserole, melt the remaining 2 tablespoons of lard over moderate heat until it splutters. Add the onion and sweet red pepper (not the pimientos) and, stirring frequently, cook for 5 minutes or until the vegetables are soft but not brown. Add the chopped garlic and tomatoes, crushed hot red pepper, the remaining 1 teaspoon of salt and a few grindings of pepper. Simmer, stirring constantly, for 3 or 4 minutes. Spread the clams hinged side down over the tomato sauce, cover the casserole tightly, and cook over high heat for 10 minutes, or until the clams open. (Discard those that remain closed.) Stir in the reserved pork and its juices and the pimiento strips, if you are using them, and simmer for 5 minutes to heat them through. Sprinkle the top with coriander and garnish with the lemon wedges. Serve at once, directly from the casserole.

Iscas

MARINATED LIVER WITH RED WINE SAUCE

Combine the wine, vinegar, garlic, bay leaf, salt and a few grindings of pepper in a glass, enamel or stainless-steel bowl or baking dish. Add the liver, turning the slices about with a spoon until they are evenly coated. Marinate at room temperature for about 2 hours.

In a heavy 10- to 12-inch skillet, heat the olive oil over moderate heat until a light haze forms above it. Add the bacon and cook, stirring frequently, until golden brown and crisp. Drain on a double thickness of paper towels. Remove the liver slices from the marinade and pat them dry with paper towels. Reserve the marinade. Heat the bacon fat remaining in the skillet until it splutters. Add the liver and cook the slices about 2 minutes on each side, regulating the heat so they brown quickly and evenly without burning. Remove the liver to a heated platter. Quickly pour the reserved marinade into the skillet and boil it uncovered over high heat until it has reduced to about half, meanwhile scraping in any browned bits clinging to the bottom and sides of the pan. Taste for seasoning. Scatter the bacon pieces over the liver, pour the sauce over it and sprinkle with parsley. Serve at once, accompanied by Portuguese fried potatoes *(Recipe Index)*.

To serve 4

¾ cup dry red wine
2 tablespoons red wine vinegar
1 teaspoon finely chopped garlic
½ bay leaf, crumbled
½ teaspoon salt
Freshly ground black pepper
1 pound calf's or beef liver, cut
  into ⅛-inch-thick slices
3 tablespoons olive oil
3 bacon slices, coarsely chopped
2 tablespoons finely chopped parsley

Toucinho do Céu

"BACON FROM HEAVEN" ALMOND CAKE

Preheat the oven to 350°. With a pastry brush, coat the bottom and sides of an 8-inch springform cake pan with the butter. Then add 2 tablespoons of the sugar, tipping the pan from side to side to spread it evenly on the bottom and sides. Turn the pan over and rap it sharply to remove the excess.

Spread the almonds on a baking sheet and toast them in the middle of the oven for about 10 minutes or until they color lightly. Remove the nuts from the oven and increase the heat to 375°. Set ¼ cup of the nuts aside and pulverize the rest in a blender or with a nutgrinder or mortar and pestle.

In a heavy 1- to 1½-quart saucepan, bring 2 cups of the sugar and the water to a boil over moderate heat, stirring until the sugar dissolves. Add the pulverized almonds and, stirring constantly, cook for about 5 minutes or until the mixture comes to a boil and becomes translucent. So that it will cool more quickly, pour the syrup into a bowl or another pan and set it aside until it is lukewarm.

In a heavy 3- to 4-quart saucepan, beat the egg yolks with a whisk or a rotary or electric beater until they are thick and lemon colored. Still beating, pour in the lukewarm almond mixture in a thin stream and continue to beat until cool and thick. Add the almond extract, cinnamon and lemon peel and place the pan over the lowest possible heat. Cook, stirring constantly, for about 15 minutes, or until the mixture is thick enough to coat the spoon heavily. Do not allow it to boil or the eggs will curdle.

Pour the mixture into the pan and sprinkle the top evenly with the remaining 2 tablespoons of sugar. Bake in the middle of the oven for 15 to 20 minutes or until the cake is firm to the touch. Then remove it from the oven and let cool for 10 minutes before removing the cake from the pan. Serve warm, or at room temperature, sprinkled immediately before serving with a little more sugar and topped with the reserved toasted almonds.

To make an 8-inch round cake

2 tablespoons butter, softened
4 tablespoons plus 2 cups sugar
2½ cups whole blanched almonds
9 tablespoons water
8 egg yolks
1½ teaspoons almond extract
1 teaspoon ground cinnamon
1 teaspoon finely grated lemon peel

Ovos Moles

EGG YOLK ICING

To make about 1½ cups

1¼ cups sugar
⅓ cup cold water
10 egg yolks

Combine the sugar and water in a 1- to 1½-quart saucepan. Stirring constantly, cook over moderate heat until the sugar is completely dissolved. When the syrup begins to simmer and becomes translucent, remove the pan from the heat and cool to room temperature.

Meanwhile, in a heavy 2- to 3-quart saucepan, beat the egg yolks with a whisk or a rotary or electric beater until they are thick and light yellow. Beating constantly, pour in the syrup in a thin stream. Place the pan over the lowest possible heat and cook, stirring constantly with a large wooden spoon, for about 10 minutes, or until the mixture is smooth and thick enough to coat the spoon heavily. Do not let it come even close to boiling or it may curdle. Strain through a fine sieve set over a bowl and cool to room temperature. The icing will thicken further as it cools.

NOTE: In Portugal, *ovos moles* is not only used as an icing for cakes, but is served as a dessert in individual dessert dishes.

Bôlo de Amêndoa à Algarvia

ALMOND LAYER CAKE

To make an 11-by-4-inch layer cake

2 tablespoons softened butter
2 tablespoons flour
6 egg whites
A pinch of salt
6 egg yolks
¾ cup sugar
1¾ cups whole blanched almonds
1 teaspoon almond extract
Ovos moles (above)

Preheat the oven to 350°. Using a pastry brush coat the bottom and sides of an 11-by-17-inch jelly-roll pan with 1 tablespoon of softened butter. Line the pan with a 22-inch-long strip of wax paper allowing the extra paper to extend 2 inches over each end. Brush the remaining butter evenly over the paper, then sprinkle with 2 tablespoons of flour and tip the pan from side to side to spread the flour evenly. Now turn the pan over and rap it sharply on a table to remove the excess.

Place the almonds on a baking sheet and toast them in the middle of the oven for about 10 minutes, or until they color lightly. Set ¼ cup aside and pulverize the rest in a blender or with a nut grinder or mortar and pestle.

In a large mixing bowl, beat the egg whites and salt with a whisk or a rotary or electric beater until they form firm unwavering peaks on the beater when it is lifted from the bowl. In a separate bowl, beat the egg yolks and sugar with the same beater until the mixture thickens enough to fall back on itself in a slowly dissolving ribbon when the beater is lifted from the bowl. Then stir the pulverized almonds and the teaspoon of almond extract into the beaten egg yolks.

Mix about one fourth of the egg whites into the yolks and pour them over the remaining egg whites. With a rubber spatula, fold together, gently but thoroughly, using an over-and-under cutting motion rather than a stirring motion. Pour the batter into the pan, spread it into the corners with the spatula, and smooth the top.

Bake in the middle of the oven for 15 to 20 minutes, or until the cake is light gold and has begun to come away from the sides of the pan. Remove the cake from the oven and let it cool in the pan for 2 or 3 minutes. Then carefully turn it out on a fresh sheet of wax paper. Gently peel off the top layer of paper and let the cake cool to room temperature before frosting it.

To assemble the cake, trim the crusts from the edges with a large, sharp knife and slice the cake crosswise into four 11-by-4-inch rectangles. Place a rectangular layer of cake on a serving plate and, with a metal spatula or knife, spread it evenly with ¼ cup of the *ovos moles* icing. Set a second layer on top, spread with another ¼ cup of the icing and repeat the layers of cake and icing. Place the last layer of cake on top and spread the top and sides with the remaining *ovos moles*. Arrange the ¼ cup of whole almonds decoratively in two parallel rows along the length of the cake. Serve at once or let the cake rest at room temperature for 2 or 3 hours to absorb the icing.

Figos Recheados
DRIED FIGS STUFFED WITH ALMONDS AND CHOCOLATE

To make 12

¼ cup plus 12 whole blanched almonds
12 large dried figs
½ ounce (½ square) semisweet chocolate, finely grated

Preheat the oven to 350°. Place the almonds on a baking sheet and toast them in the middle of the oven for about 10 minutes, or until they color lightly. Set 12 of the almonds aside and pulverize the rest in a blender or in a nut grinder or with mortar and pestle.

With scissors or a small knife, cut the stems off the figs. Then with your finger or the handle of a small spoon, make a ½-inch depression in the stem end of each fig. Mix the pulverized almonds and chocolate and stuff about 1 teaspoon of the mixture into each fig. Pinch the openings together firmly. Arrange the figs stem side up on an ungreased baking sheet and bake in the middle of the oven for 5 minutes. Turn the figs over with tongs and bake for another 5 minutes.

Press a toasted almond gently but firmly into the opening of each fig and serve at once or cool to room temperature before serving. *Figos recheados* are traditionally served after dinner, accompanied by glasses of port.

Porto Pudim Flan
PORTUGUESE BAKED CARAMEL CUSTARD

To serve 12

1½ cups heavy cream
1½ cups milk
¾ cup sugar
6 egg yolks
2 teaspoons port

Preheat the oven to 350°. In a heavy 1- to 1½-quart saucepan warm the cream and milk over high heat until small bubbles appear around the edge of the pan. Set aside off the heat. In a small heavy saucepan or skillet, caramelize the sugar by stirring it over moderate heat, until it melts and turns a light golden brown. Immediately pour the hot cream and milk in a thin stream into the caramel, stirring constantly with a large spoon. Continue to stir until the caramel has thoroughly dissolved.

With a whisk, or a rotary or electric beater, beat the egg yolks until they are well blended. Then slowly pour in the cream mixture, stirring constantly with a spoon. Stir in the port and strain the mixture through a fine sieve into 12 4-ounce heatproof porcelain or glass individual molds or custard cups. Set the molds in a large roasting pan on the middle shelf of the oven and pour in enough boiling water to come halfway up the sides of the molds. Bake for 40 minutes or until a knife inserted in the center of the custard comes out clean. Cool to room temperature, then refrigerate for at least 3 hours, or until thoroughly chilled.

To unmold the custard, run a sharp knife around the inside edge of each mold and dip the bottom briefly in hot water. Then wipe the mold dry, place a chilled serving plate upside down over each mold and, grasping mold and plate firmly together, quickly invert them. Rap the plate on a table and the custard should slide out easily. In Portugal, the custard is sometimes garnished with a flower blossom.

Recipe Index: English

NOTE: An R preceding a page refers to the Recipe Booklet. Size, weight and material are specified for pans in the recipes because they affect cooking results. A pan should be just large enough to hold its contents comfortably. Heavy pans heat slowly and cook food at a constant rate. Aluminum and cast iron conduct heat well but may discolor foods containing egg yolks, wine, vinegar or lemon. Enamelware is a fairly poor conductor of heat. Many recipes therefore recommend stainless steel or enameled cast iron, which do not have these faults.

Recipe Index: Spanish and Portuguese

General Index
Numerals in italics indicate a photograph of the subject mentioned.

204

Credits and Acknowledgments

The sources for the illustrations in this book are shown below. Credits for the pictures from left to right are separated by commas, from top to bottom by dashes.

Photographs by Dmitri Kessel are on pages 21, 22, 23, 26, 27 (bottom), 34, 37, 38, 39, 44, 48, 62, 63, 67, 68, 73, 74, 75, 88 (left), 93, 102, 106, 107.
All other photographs by Brian Seed except:
Cover—Fred Eng. 4—Ken Heyman—Pierre Boulat, Leonard Wesney—Charles Phillips, Tom Moulin. 13—Map by Gloria du Bouchet. 15—Fred Eng. 16, 17—Arie deZanger. 35—From *Prehistoric Cave Paintings* by Max Raphael, the Bollingen Series IV, Pantheon Books, © 1945 by the Bollingen Series, Old Dominion Foundation, Washington, D.C. 42—Arie deZanger. 52—Vincent J. R. Kehoe, courtesy Spanish National Tourist Office. 57—Marvin Newman. 58, 59—Arie deZanger. 65—Arie deZanger. 72—Arie deZanger. 76—Arie deZanger. 101—Arie deZanger. 121—Drawing by Matt Greene. 123—Arie deZanger. 124—Fred Eng. 164, 169, 171—Fred Eng. 178—Dante Vacchi. 181, 192—Fred Eng.

For their help in the production of this book the editors wish to thank the following: *in New York City,* Antonio Alonso, Assistant Public Relations Director, Spanish National Tourist Office; Robert de Bragança Chanler; Country Floors, Inc.; Heyward Associates, Inc.; Fred Leighton Mexican Imports, Ltd.; Father Juan Maguanagoicoechea; Ralph Peck, Public Relations Director, Spanish National Tourist Office; Professor Gregory Rabassa of Queens College, N.Y.; The Rastro; Stern's Department Store; Treasures from Portugal; Ramiro Valadão, Director, Casa de Portugal; Joaquim G. de Vasconcellos, Information and Tourist Services, Casa de Portugal; Carmen Villanueva of the Spanish Consulate; *in Portugal,* Marie Joaquina Roquete, Lisbon; *in Spain,* Juan Agudo, Head Chef, Fenix Hotel, Madrid; Rafael Aguirre, Secretary General of the Office of Tourism, San Sebastian; Artxanda Restaurant, Bermeo; Asesino Restaurant, Santiago de Compostela; Rafael Abella Bermejo, Madrid; Cooperativa Sanchez Romero Carvajal, Jabugo; Avelina del Rio, Madrid; Milagros Balganon de Diaz-Canabate, Madrid; Felix Fernandez, Valentín restaurant, Madrid; Sabina Fernandez, Cabrales; Hotel Fuentebravia, Puerto de Santa Maria; Sociedad Gaztelupe, San Sebastian; Jose Antonio Lopez de Letona, Sub-director General of

Tourism, Madrid; Hauke B. Pattist, Oviedo; Eugenio Fontanedra Perez, Canduela; Jose Maria Pidal, President of the Office of Tourism, San Sebastian; Hostal de los Reyes Catolicos, Santiago de Compostela; Andres Rodriguez, La Argentina Restaurant, Madrid; Manuel Ferrand Rodriguez, Seville; Casa Vejo (bakery), Reinosa.

Sources consulted in the production of this book include: *The Classic Cooking of Spain* by Jeannette Aguilar; *Spain and Portugal* by Karl Baedeker; *Culinária Portuguésa* by António Maria de Oliveira Bello; *Spain* by Yves Bottineau; *The Face of Spain* by Gerald Brenan; *The Selective Traveller in Portugal* by Ann Bridge and Susan Lowndes; *Portugal* by Roy Campbell; *Santiago and the Rías Bajas* by J. Costa Clavell; *Image of Spain* by James Cleugh; *Your Guide to Portugal* by Douglas Clyne; *Your Holiday in Portugal* by Gordon Cooper; *The Home Book of Spanish Cookery* by Marina Pereyra de Aznar and Nina Froud; *Guia Gastronomica de España* by Luis Antonio de Vega; *Spain's Magic Coast* by Nina Epton; *Itinerarios por Las Cocinas y Las Bodegas de Castilla* by Julio Escobar; *Portugal, Madeira, Azores,* Hachette World Guides; *Spain,* Hachette World Guides; *A History of Spain* by Harold Livermore; *Tratado de Cocina* by Miss Culinaria; *Your Guide to the Costa Blanca,* by Christopher Moore; *Northern Spain,* A Blue Guide edited by L. Russell Muirhead; *Southern Spain,* A Blue Guide edited by L. Russell Muirhead; *The Spanish Cookbook* by Barbara Norman; *La Cocina Completa* (11th edition) by the Marquesa de Parabere; *This Is Spain* by Richard Pattee; *Guia del Buen Comer Español* by Dionisio Perez; *Rice, Spice and Bitter Oranges* by Lila Perl; *Tratado de Cocina* by Pilar Navarro Rubio; *Introducing Spain* by Cedric Salter; *A Taste of Portugal* by Shirley Sarvis; *Cocina Regional Española* by the Seccion Femenina of the Spanish Government; *Portugal and Madeira* by Sacheverell Sitwell; *Spain* by Sacheverell Sitwell; *Portugal's Other Kingdom, the Algarve* by Dan Stanislawski; *Cozinha Regional Portuguésa* by Maria O. C. Valente; *The Flavor of Spain* by Myra Waldo; *A Geography of Spain and Portugal* by Ruth Way; *The Cambridge Iruña Cookbook of Spanish and Basque Dishes* by Josefina Yanguas.

XXXX Printed in U.S.A.